Preparing for the road, with a full head of steam, No 777 *Sir Lamiel* waits to be the 0945 to Leicester North at Loughborough Central on Sunday 1 February 2015, during the GCR's 'Winter Steam Gala'. Now climb aboard and enjoy your journey.

GARRATTS AND GUITARS

Sixty trainspotting years
Volume 2: August 1985-2015

John Stretton

Silver Link Publishing Ltd

First published in 2017

British Library Cataloguing in Publication Data

A catalogue record for this book is available from the British Library.

ISBN 978 1 85274 470 9

Silver Link Publishing Ltd
The Trundle
Ringstead Road
Great Addington
Kettering
Northants NN14 4BW

Tel/Fax: 01536 330588
email: sales@nostalgiacollection.com
Website: www.nostalgiacollection.com

Printed and bound in the Czech Republic

Frontispiece: Ever since my first sight of these magnificent beasts, Garratts have always been among my all time favourites, hence the inclusion of this one picture outside this volumes time frame. On 16 January 1953 No 47983 heads south past Normanton, just north of Loughborough. *Bryan Jennings*

Right: Worthington Cup Final, 21 March 1999. City lost 0-1 in front of 77,892 at Wembley.

CONTENTS

Foreword by Chris Green   6
Acknowledgements   7
Introduction   8

Chapter 1   1985-1990   9
Chapter 2   1990-1995   56
Chapter 3   1995-2000   114
Chapter 4   2000-2005   165
Chapter 5   2005-2010   209
Chapter 6   2010-2015   254

Foreword by

Chris Green

John Stretton has given us a real treat as he reminds us how our lives have changed over the last 30 years. His welcome second volume continues his inspired idea of putting railway events into their social context. This makes for an unusual and memorable read.

He happens to have chosen the period when my own railway memories are at their strongest. I was still in ScotRail in 1985 and remember the new confidence of that period as the Scots took ownership of their newly branded railway and helped us roll back the Beeching era with the iconic reopening of the Bathgate-Edinburgh line, the opening of 15 other stations, and new trains and services across the network. I remember this as an era when motorways were half empty; laptops did not exist, and InterCity trains to London offered a full dining service with white table cloths.

In 1986 I moved on to lead the Network SouthEast revolution in London – and revolution it was! The City had just been deregulated and this was creating an explosion in demand for both office space and employment. Commuter numbers rose 25% and the railway was at the centre of the race to get Londoners to work. Both Thameslink and CrossRail were conceived in the late '80s, and most of the London termini were redeveloped to provide the extra office space as well as extra platforms.

Rail privatisation created a tide-mark in 1996, when everything changed again. An economic recession had slowed the economy and public investment in rail had virtually ceased. The Government was desperate to reboot the economy and the private train companies were encouraged to invest and expand. This was the period when train frequencies exploded across the country. I joined Virgin Trains and can remember our excitement at introducing 20-minute frequencies from London to Manchester and Birmingham.

I can also remember being told that there was no future in inter-city travel now that the electronic age had arrived with laptops, iPads and video-conferencing. And yet the truth has been just the reverse – Intercity travel has doubled since 1996 and passengers have simply asked for free Wifi on all trains. It did, however, change social habits, and meals have become trolley snacks so that passengers can continue working on their iPads.

Since 2000 we have been experiencing the greatest rail growth since the First World War. Rail travel more than doubled in those 15 years and this growth is set to continue. This growth mirrors all the social events described in the book: a growing population; a wealthier nation; more congested roads. We shall shortly see the opening of the two major new railways planned in the 1980s – Thameslink and Crossrail. And we already know that they are not the end of the story.

John Stretton's excellent dissertation reminds us of the amazing changes that have taken place in railway fortunes in just one generation – and how they are linked to the economic and social events that having being going on around us. The story continues unabated, and I for one cannot wait for his third volume in 2045!

Acknowledgements

I doubt that there will be a Volume 3 (!), so I would like here to thank all who have assisted in this edition. Especially, I would like to thank Paul Cleaver and Sue McCarthy for their companionship over the years and for proofreading this monster. They have pointed me in correct directions on more than one occasion! Others who are/have been important to me include: Chris Green (for his readiness to help and for the Foreword), Duane Eddy, Liz Simpson-Silva, Tim Maddocks, Julian Crow, Richard Dunn, the members of ATDRPG, Ian and Jack Boskett, my late wife Judi, and my two wonderful children Adam and Tammy. At the publishing end, Peter Townsend is always generous with his time and advice when he needed them more than me, and Will Adams keeps me on the straight and narrow. Thank you all.

Introduction

Those who bought Volume 1 will have noticed the change in my life and our railways as the years passed. Although still railway-centric in this second volume, my days of shed-bashing trips were increasingly numbered, as were the outings with other members of the 'Gang of Four', Paul Cleaver, Neil Beckley, John Eales and (occasionally) Paul Smart. Reasons were many and varied, not least as there were ever fewer depots to visit and fewer locos to spot, but my main reason was the change in the direction of my railway 'career'. As the years passed from privatisation, I was increasingly writing articles for publication, photographing for book projects and undertaking work in response to contracts and/or invitations from a wide variety of companies or organisations. This applied in non-railway spheres as well. In addition, changing work commitments and family life, with the children growing up and demanding more attention, together with moving to a new house, all contributed to tightening the screw. The desire, however, to capture as much as possible, especially through the camera lens, was as passionate as ever. And, from 2003, the adoption of digital greatly assisted.

I have literally thousands of images from these 30 years, with space here for fewer than 300. I therefore beg forgiveness if what you were hoping for is missing. I have tried to balance the importance of the views with aesthetics and variety. I hope you will enjoy the journey through these 30 years, which saw yet more world change. I hope, also, that my stories may stir some of your own memories. All the photographs are by me unless otherwise stated. Space has dictated what has been included and it has been an invidious task whittling down many of my own favourites. I have taken care to ensure as far as possible that all facts are correct, but if you do find any errors, please let me know via the publisher.

Chapter 1
1985-1990

Volume 1 ended with the appearance of Chris Green at the helm of ScotRail (see also the Foreword of this volume). Such was his success with the new corporate identity, aggressive marketing and, above all, a customer-led approach that 25% growth in revenue was rapidly achieved, leading to his promotion in November 1985 to take over BR's London and South East division. Such was the efficacy of his approach that a rebranding, as Network SouthEast, was launched within just seven months on 10 June 1986 – but more of that later.

The final outing of my first 30 years was 'The Cumbrian Coast Express', an LNER Society railtour on 26 August 1985, with wife Judi and children Adam and Tammy. We joined the train at 0710 at Hemel Hempstead for our journey to and from Carnforth, and scenic coach tour and cruise on Derwent Water. Hauled north by No 85002, the day started well, with me assiduously collecting numbers as we travelled, especially at Crewe, but on our return Adam, just short of his 10th birthday, was suddenly violently sick on the coach and then also on the train, each time it began to slow! Motive power south was No 47471 *Norman Tunna GC*, and diesel haulage was not as smooth as the outward electric. We tried to comfort him and to keep the distress to ourselves as much as possible, but it did not make for a happy, memorable day!

Adam recalls: 'I remember getting up very early, Dad excitedly introducing Tammy and me to pomegranates for breakfast, and us sort of both liking the taste, but being really surprised by the fruit! Then I remember a grey day on the lake, on a pleasure boat. I remember being attacked by wasps whilst drinking a Ribena carton and, in my flailing to get rid of the wasps, spraying the other passengers with juice, thus further enticing the jaspers! Mum did her nut as I recall. Then I can remember both their strained faces as I sat on the train on the way home, puking at every station, every time the train stopped – an experience that has associated pomegranates, Ribena and nausea for my whole life!' The Ribena rainbow was, indeed, a sight to see!

Thankfully the next trip in my second 30 years was a much more peaceful affair, when Adam and a fellow banker, Richard, accompanied me to the Old Oak Common Depot Open Day on 15 September. With bright, mostly sunny weather, we were treated to a wide variety of motive power with, in addition to routine fare, preserved Nos D1015 and D7018, Guinness-liveried *Lion* (ex-BR shunter No 08022), No 41001, the prototype HST power car, No 46229 *Duchess of Hamilton*, No 6000 *King George V*, and replica broad-gauge *Iron Duke*. Having covered the extensive acreage several times, after an early start we were glad to finally sit down on the 1531 tube train at Baker Street to take us back to Amersham. As identified in the Introduction, this was to be more the norm for my railway passion than had been the case of yore.

No 6000 *King George V* is a centre of attention at Old Oak Common Open Day on 15 September 1985.

Eleven days later, I was to visit a Bank department in Poole, so grabbed the opportunity of travelling there by train. After snapping stock at Waterloo, including units sitting in the western sidings that would later become the home of the Eurostar Terminal, I boarded my train formed of No 33110 hauling 4REP No 3012 and 4TCs Nos 411 and 423 (all three-car sets). Needless to say, I was glued to the window out and back, but most of what I saw was not new to me, the only exceptions being locos Nos 47433 at Waterloo, 33209 and 09010 (Woking), 33022 (St Denys), 47094 (Southampton) and 73141 (Woking on the way back).

Nos 5863 and 5709 stand at Waterloo on 26 September 1985, as empty coaching stock, in the area later occupied by the Eurostar Terminal.

On 5 October Judi left for the latest of her biannual breaks away from domestic duties, departing from Watford Junction as usual. With the opportunity of the kids being at school, I treated myself to a couple of trips – to Tring on the 9th and into London the following day. Friend Richard had told me of the branch line to Gospel Oak so, on the latter day, I journeyed to Liverpool Street from Amersham, via Marylebone and the Tube to Gospel Oak platform. Time there was short as I had to be back at home to meet the kids from school, but I savoured three passing freights (including copping No 47295), as well as the varied sights (and three cops) at Liverpool Street, including No 47487 in its new InterCity livery, the first '47' to be so treated.

'Growlers' Nos 37019 and 37038, still in 'Corporate Blue', pass Gospel Oak station on 10 October 1985 with a westbound container freight from Ripple Lane.

No 47487 waits to leave Liverpool Street on 10 October 1985 with the 1230 to Norwich. It was the first '47' to receive the new InterCity livery.

The final weeks of 1985 held only odd, inconsequential day trips for me, and on the railways little seemed to be happening. However, a harbinger of change was the setting sail from the USA of what would become Class 59 heavy freight locos, which would be transformative in many ways. They were dubbed by many the 'Quiet Americans', as they proved to be without the loud exhausts so prevalent on UK locos. New but not so brilliant were the 'Pacers', Classes 142 and 143, introduced this year. Elsewhere, 'Super Mario Bros' was released for Nintendo; Mexico City suffered a massive earthquake, 8.0 on the Richter scale, in the early morning of 19 September, killing at least 5,000 people; Garry Kasparov became the world's youngest ever World Chess champion; and, on 26 December, Leicester City had their highest attendance of the season, when 42,551 watched their home 3-1 win over Aston Villa. On the final day of the year, Ricky Nelson was killed in a Texas plane crash. Other deaths included Laura Ashley on 17 September (born 1925); Rock Hudson, Yul Brynner and Orson Welles in October (the last two on the same day); Phil Silvers (aka Sgt Bilko) on 1 November (born 1911); and writers Philip Larkin on 2

No 34092 *City of Wells* storms away from the High Wycombe stop on 16 November 1985 with one of the early Marylebone-Stratford-upon-Avon steam specials.

December and Robert Graves on 7 December. Births included footballers Luke Modric (9 September) and Wayne Rooney (24 October).

1986 began with the arrival of the first four abovementioned Class 59s, General Motors Type 5 locomotives that would soon be putting our indigenous engines to shame with the loads they could handle. Brought in by Foster Yeoman, operating out of Merehead Quarry, they were all named in June.

Musically, the year began with Duane Eddy flying into London on 23 January to record a wholly fresh version of long-term favourite *Peter Gunn* with The Art of Noise. Completed by the 28th, it was released on 10 March, as both 7- and 12-inch versions, and rapidly made it into the Top 10, establishing Duane as one of the very few artists to have had hits in four consecutive decades! Elsewhere, 28 January saw the *Challenger* disaster, when the Space Shuttle broke apart 73 seconds into its flight, disintegrating over the Atlantic Ocean off the coast of Cape Canaveral, Florida, and leading to the deaths of its seven crew members. The year was also to witness more devastation. On 26 April a catastrophic nuclear accident happened in the No 4 light water graphite moderated reactor at the Chernobyl Nuclear Power Plant near Pripyat, then part of the USSR.

My first expedition of 1986 was on 8 February when, with friend Mike from Chesham Bois church, I joined the Hertfordshire Rail Tours' railtour, delightfully titled 'The Derbyshire Dingle'! We boarded at High Wycombe after watching the train loco, No 50016 *Barham*, complete with headboard, gingerly make its way to the station through the snow-encrusted tracks, nearly an hour late at its first stop out of London! Mike was not a rail enthusiast and had never been on a railtour before, but came to keep me company and 'for the sheer fun of it'! Previously, trains to him had merely been a means to an end. The omens did not look good, with overcast skies, but the clouds dispersed as we travelled north and the day went without a hitch, with both *Barham* and sister loco No 50012 *Benbow* (from Derby) performing faultlessly. After visiting Buxton, the short hop to Manchester Piccadilly was a real delight for both those on board and the local spotters, who were then very unused to seeing a '50' in their neck of the woods. Sixty-seven locos were espied during the journey, of many types, and the small haul of just seven cops did not diminish the day's enjoyment.

Taking it carefully in the snow, No 50016 *Barham* approaches High Wycombe on 8 February 1986 with the LNER Society's 'Derbyshire Dingle' railtour, bound for Buxton and Manchester.

No 50016 *Barham* curves away from the Midland Main Line at Knighton South Junction on 8 February 1986 at the head of the 'Derbyshire Dingle' railtour. To the left is the recently opened Leicester sports stadium.

Three days after this my life was to take a turn. On 11 February I was summoned to Barclays Bank Local Head Office in Oxford for an interview with one of the Local Directors. While not having blotted my copy book — as far as I was aware — I was nevertheless nervous as to its import. Thus I was duly surprised when offered promotion, with a transfer to Faringdon Branch, at a grade above what I currently enjoyed. This was confirmed in writing on the 21st by Mr Goodenough, as Senior Director, and I was to start at my new branch on 19 March for five days of handover with my predecessor. This would necessitate a house move, the thought of which Judi did not particularly relish, but it would mean an uplift in salary and a slightly cheaper area in which to live. Not surprisingly, as I had driven from home to the appointment, I took the opportunity of visiting Oxford station afterwards for a short spell of therapy!

My next spotting/photographic opportunity came on 14 March, when I escaped for a visit to the local station at

The Barclays ten-pin team relax in the bar at Ilkeston before the matches on 11 March 1986. Your author is extreme left trying to steer clear of Sally with a fistful of darts!

Wokingham while there for a ten-pin bowling tournament. No locomotives to see, but a chance to photograph a mix of diesel and electric units.

For the Faringdon move, I was billeted in The Bell Hotel, next to the Bank, until our move of house, so took the freedom of being by myself to explore the nearby railway – Brunel's 'billiard table' through the Vale of the White Horse. One immediate implication of the move, however, was to find a facility for me to continue reviewing videos for *Railway Magazine*. Fortunately, one of the staff at my new branch had a machine at home and offered evenings when she and her husband were not watching anything else on TV! I also contributed in like medium for a new magazine – *Railway Photography & Video*.

On the Great Western Main Line at Longcot on 1 May 1986, No 37232 accelerates with an up mixed freight.

31 March saw the official closure of Swindon Works, with the loss of 1,000 jobs. I was too late for the pace of change once more – the story of my life! No 08616 was the last loco overhauled there, three months later.

Judi was off again to Plas Tan-y-Bwlch, in North Wales, on

16 May, with me still taking her to Watford Junction for her train – and photographing the new Class 313s on the local Euston runs – but she was back in time for my highlight of the year. On the 28th I was honoured to be invited by Jeremy English to accompany him in the cab of No 43042, an HST power car, as he videoed the journey from St Pancras to Sheffield for Railscene, including passing through my home town of Leicester! A previously unfulfilled ambition, it was both spectacular and unspectacular – the latter being the total lack

The southern approach to Leicester Midland station is seen from the cab of an HST forming the 1100 St Pancras-Sheffield service on 28 May 1986. The ex-Midland Railway signal box was due to be demolished not long after, when signalling in the 'Leicester Gap' was modernised.

of any sense of speed, even at 100mph!

The next excitement was the 10 June unveiling by Chris Green of 'Network SouthEast', when a gathering of 200 VIPs witnessed the birth of a 'new railway'. Comprising 930 stations and 2,350 route miles in and around London, bedecked with red, white and blue livery, the first locos in these striking new colours were Nos 50023 *Howe*, 50017 *Royal Oak* and 47573 *The London Standard*.

Away from the railway, 22 June saw England lose 1-2 to Argentina in the Quarter Final of the World Cup, at the Azteca, Mexico, the defeat helped by Diego Maradona's infamous 'Hand of God'! A month later Prince Andrew married Sarah Ferguson, on the same day that we travelled to south-west Wales for the family holiday at Field Studies Council centre at Orielton. Tammy, aged 7, was the youngest ever to have attended a course there, but she was a star! As she recalls: 'I remember being inspired by it all. Some 14 years later, while working for the Field Studies Council, I took part in a staff trip to Orielton, where I met Robin Crump. He had been our course leader all those years before; amazingly he remembered me and was delighted to see me and working for the FSC too!' We returned seven days later and prepared for the house move to Longcot, Oxfordshire, on 11 August. The move was an eye-opener, leaving a three-bed house (sold for £101,000) and moving to a five-bed version, for just £95,000! With financial help from the Bank, I have been ever grateful to them for this transfer. With all this upheaval, there was no time for other than local trips to the railway!

Disaster struck on 19 September when driver Eric Goode, 33, died in a head-on collision between Nos 86211 *City of Milton Keynes* and 86429 at Colwich, near Stafford. The locomotives became the first of their class to be withdrawn as result. High-profile deaths in the final quarter of 1986 were Cary Grant on 29 November (born 1904) and Harold Macmillan, Prime Minister between 1957 and 1963, on 29 December (born 1894). On happier notes, Kasper Schmeichel (Danish international footballer and Leicester City goalkeeper in the Premier League Champions team of 2015/16) was born on 5 November.

Elsewhere, Brush Engineering introduced its innovative Class 89 on 2 October, but it had a chequered career and was to remain solo. On 9 October *The Phantom of the Opera*, the longest-running Broadway show, opened in London; Mrs Thatcher opened the M25 motorway on 29 October; HST power cars Nos 43109 and 43118 created a new world diesel speed record of 144.7mph between Darlington and York on 19 November; and the British Gas Corporation was privatised as British Gas plc by the Thatcher Government on 8 December, when its shares were floated on the London stock market. Remember Sid?

18 October was the start of Judi's next trip to North Wales, only this time from Oxford, where I recorded the numbers of the various locos on view, but none were new to me. This was almost the case at Swindon, later in the day, but No 37430 (named *Cwmbrân* just five months earlier) did give me what was becoming a rare cop. The reverse journeys a week later, to meet Judi's return, were totally devoid of fresh visions. Fortunately, she was back in time for me to pack and depart from Swindon on 3 November, to make my way to Wimbledon to attend an Industrial Relations Course at Chester House, on the corner of the Common. Wimbledon's third oldest building, opened much earlier in the century, it was the Bank's first training centre for staff. I travelled via Didcot, Reading, Paddington, Waterloo and Clapham Junction. Interestingly, I copped three on the GW route – Nos 33053 (Southall), 56040

No 43139 leads the 1030 Paddington-Bristol express under the threatened Uffington road bridge on 2 November 1986, close to its 100th birthday.

(Ealing) and 31404 (Old Oak Common) – but only one on the Southern Region, an area not so well visited – No 33006 at Clapham. My return from the course, on the 7th, yielded just two further cops, Nos 33050 at Clapham Junction and 56002 at Acton.

From the end of November I was on yet another course, this time for managerial training, from the 30th until 5 December, at the Bank's residential college, Ashdown House in Sussex, a deconsecrated ex-convent. Interestingly, the building had been used in the filming of a television rendition of *Colditz*! It was later to become an upmarket hotel and country club. I enjoyed the palatial facilities, not least the Olympic-style swimming pool, after each day's training. I also appreciated the liberal availability of alcohol in the bar and took advantage of this, sometimes to the detriment of my general health! Travelling by rail from Swindon to Haywards Heath (where we were met by a Bank coach) and back, I garnered yet more numbers and cops, this time mostly on the southern end of the routes.

Other notable outings in December were Swindon to Bournemouth on the 7th and back on the 12th, and to Vic Berry's scrapyard in Leicester on the 28th during our Christmas holiday with parents in Birstall. The journey to this latter venue was in our new (to us) Peugeot 305 estate, bought for £2,095 during the month. On that day – the 28th – Leicester City were trounced 5-1 away at Everton, as they struggled to stay in the League's Division 1. Such was their 'appeal' during the 1986/87 season that many of their home games were attended by fewer than 10,000 and, on 8 October, their lowest ever League Cup gate saw just 5,884 witness their 4-2 victory over Swansea City! They were relegated to Division 2 and Alan Smith, though again top scorer, was to transfer to Arsenal.

1987 opened with the birth of Jamie Vardy, in Sheffield, on the 11th. Twenty-nine years later he was to be one of the most celebrated footballers, gaining a record of scoring goals in 11 consecutive matches in the Premiership during Leicester City's

Vic Berry's scrapyard, Leicester, on 28 December 1986, with cabs of '25s' and '45s', including No 25284.

League Champions' year. However, it was to prove a year of negative and even disastrous events, both nationally and for me (more of that later).

Between 11 and 14 January the southern half of the country was blanketed by a very heavy snowfall, affecting areas of East Anglia, South East England and London. The heaviest snowfall to fall in that part of the United Kingdom since the winter of 1981/82, more than 50cm (20 inches) fell widely, but the North Downs just east of Maidstone recorded 75cm (30 inches). Parts of West Cornwall also had heavy falls. On 20 January Terry Waite was kidnapped in Lebanon and held captive for four years.

February was not good on the railways either, with, on the 4th, No 47131 rolling down a bank after derailing at Dorrington, and just one day later Nos 31440 and 47089 colliding at Chinley. Later, on the 20th, No 50011 *Centurion* became the first 'Hoover' to be withdrawn, initially to be a test bed at Crewe. The *Herald of Free Enterprise* disaster occurred on 6 March 1987, after the Townsend Thoresen vessel left her berth at Zeebrugge, Belgium, with her bow doors open. She capsized soon after leaving the harbour and 193 people died.

Other than continuing local trips, my first outing of note was a visit to Bristol (Bath Road) depot with fellow bankers Paul Cleaver and Phil Reade on 20 January. I had met Paul during a Bank-organised visit to Swindon Works in the summer of 1983 and we had begun to pair up for trips to various locations. On this day Paul noted the relevant numbers – including his first sighting of No 56001 – as I toted my camera, and it was one of the few times when we managed to gain access to this tightly guarded facility. We had been on a visit to Bristol Cash Centre, with Phil driving, and perhaps it was being in our Bank suits that swayed the decision!

Next was a solo return to Vic Berry's Leicester scrapyard, on 1 March, where the locos being dealt with were exclusively Classes 25 and 45, totalling 20 examples. A trip across the city then followed to the old Leicester Midland engine shed, now housing just diesels. This was rewarded with cops of Nos 20207 and 56101. Home beckoned after a flying visit to Syston to witness HSTs on the Midland Main Line.

Into March and the Oxford District Ten-Pin Bowling team was off on another tour, this time a three-day jaunt to Manchester and Nottingham. Once again, I engineered an escape when not needed on lane, first to Manchester Victoria station on the 10th, where, in hindsight, I was able and fortunate to capture on film locos that would go to the great engine shed in the sky within short years, or even months in some cases. On view were Class 25s, 31s, 45s, 47s and a solitary No 56079. A short step to Piccadilly then brought me No 08915 as a cop.

Over the Pennines to Nottingham on the 11th gave me an opportunity to visit Toton depot – and record a grand total of 77 locos, including 24 cops, predominantly the relatively new Class 56s and 58s. Nottingham station was quickly visited on the 12th before the next game, where the fare was primarily Class 20s and 31s, a pleasing selection of these older types. This was a day of competitions, and I had been selected for the

One of last seven of the class to survive to the end, No 25191
approaches Manchester Victoria on 10 March 1987 with a short empty
engineer's train. It was switched off eight days later.

Men's Singles. I began with six strikes (!) and attracted a large
and loud gathering behind the lanes. This obviously had some
effect, as a three-spare followed, then it all went 'pear-shaped'! I
finished the first game with a career high of 249, but the second
and third games continued the decline and I was way off the
pace for any sort of award!

My reviews for *Railway Magazine* continued, with books
sharing space with videos and even Transacord vinyl LPs, and it
was gratifying that so much space was allocated in the magazine
for reviews. Elsewhere on the railways, Sectorisation was
introduced; in addition to Network SouthEast, the sectors were
Provincial Railways (later rebranded Regional Railways), Parcels,
Departmental, Freightliner and InterCity. Each vehicle was
allocated a four-letter code that indicated who owned it and its
intended use. Despite (or partly because of) this change, BR still
made huge losses on the year, not helped by a reduced subsidy
from the Government. The idea of privatisation was looking
increasingly politically attractive! On 3 April Gil Hunter's near
40-year career in the Bank ended and I was glad to be invited
to his farewell party at Nottingham Local Head Office on that

The imposing North signal box at Syston Junction, seen on 5 April 1987, was one of the boxes shortly to be closed and demolished with the closing of the 'Leicester Gap'.

Another escape from a ten-pin bowling tour enabled me to snap No 7348 leading a train into Portsmouth & Southsea Upper station on 23 April 1987.

day. Having served under him at the Charles Street, Leicester, branch, he was, without doubt, the best manager I ever worked for!

May was Judi's next 'sanity restoring' trip to North Wales, during which time I took a trip to Bristol, from Swindon, on the 20th. I claimed another six to add to my records and enjoyed the view of ten named Pullman cars on the 'Venice-Simplon Express', but why I recorded that I spent £2.28 on a meal at the station is lost in the mists of time! On the 31st we made another trek to Leicester, this time for my parents' wedding anniversary the day before, and I escaped to once more soak up the atmosphere at Vic Berry's scrapyard – where Class 26s and 27s had now appeared from Scotland, adding to the infamous pile of '25s' – then to the main-line depot and, finally, Thurmaston, where I was taken by surprise at my first view of a complete HST set in the new 'Raspberry Ripple' livery.

Less than a fortnight later, on 11 June, Mrs Thatcher won a third term in the General Election, despite a swing of 0.2% away from the Tories and 21 seats lost. Yet another trip to Vic Berry's site and the old MR engine shed was made on 5 July, the day after Dad's birthday, and purely local trips were the fare

During my birthday treat on 3 August 1987, No 5572 waits at Williton before returning to Minehead. A West Somerset Railway DMU stands to the left.

26

until our family holiday between 1 and 8 August, to Lynton and Lynmouth. A visit was made to the West Somerset Railway as a treat for my birthday, on the 3rd, graced by glorious weather for our Minehead/Williton round trip.

In addition to yet another Vic Berry visit on 16 August, this second year ended with the delights of seeing No 6201 *Princess*

No 58023, in new 'Railfreight' livery, stands 'on shed' outside the small workshop at Leicester depot (always known to me as '15C', its BR code) on 16 August 1987.

The somewhat experimental three-car DEMU No 210002 was a most unexpected sight at Newbury on 31 August 1987, on an unidentified duty.

Elizabeth at Kemble, on 22 August (at the head of a Pullman Rail special, hauled by the glamorous steam loco from Chester to Swindon via Newport) and the restored prototype No D200 at Worting Junction on the 31st on Traintours' 'The Desert Songster'. Truly testing its restoration credentials, it hauled this 1Z37-coded train throughout from Preston to Exeter St David's, except for the brief run between Kensington Olympia and Waterloo. It looked magnificent in its early BR green livery.

For me, September began with a bang on the 7th, with the release of a new Duane Eddy single – *Rockestra Theme* – composed by and featuring Paul McCartney on bass! A 12-inch extended version was released two weeks later and this was followed by the album from which it was taken on 12 October. Simply yet boldly titled just *Duane Eddy*, the album featured a host of famous musicians as well as the ex-Beatle, including George Harrison, James Burton, Jeff Lynne, Ry Cooder, Ann Dudley, Steve Cropper and ex-'Rebels' Jim Horn and Larry Knechtel. By December it was No 1 in the UK's Country Album charts! Elsewhere musically, reissues were popular and Michael Jackson's *Bad* album was the top seller. I ended

The infamous pile of loco bodies at Vic Berry's site on 26 September 1987. Nos 25285, 25042 and 25089 are part of the collection of nearly 40 locos!

September with a trip to Basingstoke Open Day on the 27th with Adam and Tammy as company. Sunny weather graced the long line of locos set out for appreciation, with marquees alongside, on the non-rail side of fencing, to give punters a chance to spend their readies!

Come the night of 15-16 October and the last three months of the year were beginning to echo the first three! The Great Storm of 1987 was a violent cyclone that occurred during that night, with hurricane-force winds causing casualties in many parts of the UK. This was followed three days later by Black Monday, the 19th, when stock markets around the world crashed, shedding huge values in a very short time. The crash began in Hong Kong and rapidly spread west to Europe.

A crash of a different kind hit me on Friday 4 December when I suffered a fractured femur as a result of an argument with a car – or, more accurately, the car's argument with me! Making my way home from work on my motorbike approaching 1800 on a dark but dry evening, I had just turned off the A420

A happy meeting, as 24-year-old No 47406 *Rail Riders* pauses at Oxford on 24 October 1987, next to Adam and Tammy who were both members of the Rail Riders Club.

Oxford to Swindon road onto a short stretch of straight country road when the headlights of an approaching car suddenly changed direction and headed straight for me! With no time for avoiding action and nowhere to go, despite there not being a distinct curb, the next thing I knew was coming to, lying in the gutter. My first thought was, 'At least I am still alive,' but I could not feel my right leg (it lay at near 90 degrees to my body), and my right thumb felt strange (it was dislocated). My bike and the car were behind me. My next thought was one of concern, as I had the keys to the Bank; I was due to attend the branch with workmen the following morning. Thankfully, one of the persons who stopped to help knew one of my deputies. I had to take a decision to trust him to deliver the keys to that person, as they should always have been in my care under normal circumstances. The car driver had, apparently, suddenly seen a person all in black walking on her side of the road. She had swerved to avoid him (but clipped him and flung him into the ditch) and had then hit me. The car and my bike were written off, but, thank the Lord, I was not.

I spent the next six weeks in Princess Margaret Hospital in Swindon, before being well enough to return home, but not before meeting Bobby Charlton! It was his custom to visit local hospitals when he called on a nearby football club and I was graced with a 20-minute chat as he sat on my hospital bed – a real delight to meet a true gentleman. It was a further period before I returned to work.

Several good things came out of this experience. One was that I had very recently taken out a personal accident insurance policy and had paid one premium of £10; the policy paid out £5,000, enabling me to be rid of the ageing motorbike and to buy a second car. An answer to my prayers to the Lord, but not in a way I would have chosen! Needless to say, there were no railway exploits thereafter until well into 1988.

Leicester City were struggling in their first season down in Division 2. With a new manager – David Pleat – they used a club record of 31 different players in the league through the season! Steve Walsh, in his second season at the club, was captain – he would be a major contributor to the club's future development until his departure to Everton, as Scout, just short of 30 years later!

As 1988 progressed, 3 March saw the launch of a new political party, the Liberal Democrats, created by a merger of the Liberal and Social Democratic parties. Paddy Ashdown assumed leadership from 16 July. Among deaths were Kenneth Williams on 15 April (born 1926) and Kim Philby on 11 May (born 1912). No 56062 derailed at Ardingly on 14 June, rolling down an embankment, and on 6 July there was a massive explosion aboard the Piper Alpha oil rig, leading to 150 workers losing their lives.

In late March/early April, to aid my post-op rest and recuperation – and to be a sort of early 40th birthday celebration for Judi (in May) – we accepted an invitation from Judi's aunt to spend Easter with her in Portugal, leaving on 29 March and returning 8 April. Though no longer on crutches, I still had to be careful about walking any distance, so the break was quite leisurely, but I still jumped (not literally!) at the

Not having the same appeal as when I visited Santo Tirso to see steam in 1970, on 31 March 1988 a DMU set (No 9 0945 0 09622-9 leading) pauses at the station as the 1638 Porto-Guimaraes local service.

chance of 'recreating' our 1970 honeymoon trek to Santo Tirso station. Sadly, the weather on 31 March was not as appealing and neither was the sight of a DMU in place of the steam we had seen 18 years earlier.

Back home, Adam and Tammy (then 11 and 9) were to enjoy a residential school trip (cost £130 for the two) to Yenworthy Lodge in Devon, which had been 'inspiring students with unique experiences in "The Great Outdoors" since 1969'. So, grabbing the opportunity of being without them, Judi and I left home on 28 May, in my recently acquired Talbot Horizon car, to spend seven days in the Brecon Beacons, staying in Llandovery. Apart from the obvious scenic splendours for two photographers, I was interested to see the railway operation. The local station was a temporary southern terminus for the Heart of Wales line from Craven Arms, due to the collapse, seven months earlier on 19 October 1987, of the rail bridge over the River Towy at Glanrhyd, a few miles south. A two-car Class 108 DMU fell into the river, although only travelling at the regulation speed for the bridge of just 10mph, with the front carriage being swept away in the floods and the driver and three passengers being drowned. A bus linked Llandovery with services to Cardiff, south of Glanrhyd, until the bridge was rebuilt. We stayed at a B&B run by a photographer and his wife. He volunteered to process my film while I was there, but, in hindsight, I wish I had not taken up the offer, as he obviously did not control the chemical temperatures properly and the slides came out with a greenish/yellow tinge!

June 1988 was a profitable month for me, with that month's issue of *Railway Magazine* unusually publishing four pages of reviews, of which 12 were penned by me! On the 10th I journeyed to Kew Gardens station, in Surrey, to visit the Public Record Office to undertake research on British Railways' loco shed allocations, for possible future publication opportunities. Around this, I enjoyed a rail day out from Swindon, travelling to Paddington, Willesden and Euston before the journey back to Swindon. I hurriedly scribbled 86 numbers into my notebook, but cops were few – Nos 31248 at Southall, 56038 at Acton,

90005 at Willesden, 86439 at Euston, 97654 at Reading and 56074 at Pangbourne. Three days later I drove to Salisbury, where I enjoyed photographing the various station movements but, sadly, without cops, winding up the day by calling in, for my first visit, to Pewsey station in Wiltshire.

On 7 August I made another trip to Leicester, with visits to the engine shed and Vic Berry's yard – where I witnessed the expanding semi-pyramidic pile of bogieless loco bodies. My third year closed with receipt of a letter from Brush Electrical Machines, politely declining my request to visit the Works to see and record the construction of the proposed new-build Class 60s. Happily, I had had previous dealings with the writer and we later came to 'work something out' and ongoing access was granted

Another view of '15C' as elderly Nos 20040 and 20078 stand outside the workshop on 7 August 1988. Resting between duties for Petfoods at Melton Mowbray, both were withdrawn in the early 1990s.

My first railway outing in September was on the 14th, with another day trip to London from Swindon. I visited Paddington, Euston and Willesden, before retracing my steps to Paddington for the journey home behind No 47584 as the 1807 to Swindon. I recorded 78 locos but, sadly, just three cops! – Nos 47647 at Reading, 90009 at Willesden and 37294 at Didcot.

The next outing was on 9 October, when, with companions Paul Cleaver, Neil Beckley and John Eales, we undertook a day-long 'Midlands Tour' by car, meeting up in Oxford. Bescot Open Day was our first port of call, where we were blessed with 52 locos on show, of varying types (and conditions!) including a healthy selection of preserved vehicles. We all employed our cameras liberally, despite the dull conditions, and were just in time to witness the naming of No 31430 *Sister Dora*, celebrating a 19th-century nurse who developed a special bond with railwaymen in Walsall. From the West Midlands, we travelled north-east to Nottinghamshire and Toton depot, where 68 engines were present, mostly Class 20s, 56s and 58s – 13 were new to me. Moving south to Leicestershire, I was pleased to introduce the others to the delights of Vic Berry's scrapyard – complete with wellies, which I had warned them to take after recent rainy weather! As well as the expanding pile of loco bodies awaiting their appointment with the cutter's torch, we were intrigued to see No 31275, the first '31' to be repainted

Despite being closed as a functioning station for many years, the delightful 'double mushroom' design at Faringdon was still intact on 20 September 1988, in use as a general goods merchant.

into 'Railfreight Coal's two-tone grey by Vic, in an attempt to win a contract from BR by showing the company's skills in that direction.

In the late 1980s Vic Berry attempted to diversify from purely scrap work. No 31275 stands in his yard on 9 October 1988, the first to be repainted into 'Railfreight Coal' sector colours.

Our tour then turned to thoughts of home, via Leicester shed and a brief call at Saltley, Birmingham. A total of 205 locos were seen on the day and it would not be the last time that members of this 'Gang of Four' would boldly go… This day out was to be my last of any note in 1988, apart from a further visit to Vic Berry's scrapyard at the end of October and a brief visit to Coventry station on 11 December.

Elsewhere, deaths were announced of Roy Kinnear on 20 September (born 1934), Jackie Milburn on 9 October (born 1924), Son House, one of the vintage blues legends whom I saw live at St Pancras Town Hall in the late 1960s, on 19 October (born 1902), and Charles Hawtrey on 27 October (born 1914).

On 28 October locos Nos 31202 and 31226 ran away

Bread-and-butter work: one of the two '31s' involved in the Cricklewood runaway incident, No 31202, has certainly seen better days when photographed in Vic Berry's yard on 30 October 1988.

and off the end of a siding at Cricklewood, ending up on the North Circular Road, one on top of the other! Needing to rapidly clear the mess from the road and being capable of swift response, the contract was given to Vic Berry's company and the locos transported to his Leicester site.

Another string to Vic Berry's bow on 30 October 1988 was the cosmetic restoration of No D212 *Aureol*.

Tammy had been enjoying piano lessons with an excellent teacher in our home village of Longcot, and was desirous of having an appropriate piece of furniture added to our home. She finally had her wish fulfilled on 6 December, when a carefully chosen piano was delivered from Duck, Son & Pinker, Swindon piano manufacturers and retailers. We were £2,000 lighter!

That was also the day that Roy Orbison died (born 1936), and the month was to see other disasters. On 12 December there was a crash at Clapham Junction, when the 0614 Bournemouth-Waterloo ran into the back of the 0718 Basingstoke-Waterloo commuter service, at the height of the morning peak. An empty coaching stock train then hit the debris, leading to 35 being killed. Four days later Edwina Currie was forced to resign over the politically damaging 'salmonella in eggs' controversy, and on the 21st Pan Am Flight 103 was blown up over Lockerbie, believed to be by Libyans, causing 270 fatalities. On happier notes, the year ended with 8% passenger growth over the 12 months, with the highest number of passenger miles recorded for 27 years – 20.6 billion. Leicester City recorded their biggest win of the 1988/89 season on 31 December – 4-0 at home to Blackburn Rovers – and Cliff Richard's *Mistletoe & Wine* was the Christmas No 1 and the year's top-selling single.

Ancient and modern: No 47628 *Sir Daniel Gooch* swings round the curve on the northern approach to High Wycombe on 7 December 1988 as a railman climbs the signal post to refresh the oil lamps of the semaphore signals.

1989 began with another family trip to Leicester, on New Year's Day, ready for Mum's birthday on the 3rd. On 13 January I wrote a letter to Brian Morrison asking how to become a professional railway photographer, as this seemed like a good idea at the time and I very much respected his talent, his work and his standing among the railway enthusiast fraternity. His swift response began, 'For starters, one needs a good supplementary income, as there are no fortunes to be made, believe me.' How right he was!

On 16 January Mrs Thatcher named No 89001 *Avocet*, a somewhat strange choice as, despite hailing from Grantham, she very rarely had anything to do with the railway and hardly ever travelled on it. As the month ended, I sent out my 'trawl' letters to photographers for material for my upcoming book on Leicestershire's railways. January also witnessed the deaths of two notable personalities: Beatrice Lillie on 20 January (born 1894) and Salvador Dali on 23 January (born 1904).

February was another eventful month, with Rupert Murdoch launching Sky TV on the 5th and the viaduct over the River Ness, in Inverness, being washed away in floods on the 7th, leading to the Dingwall line suffering dislocation. Vic Berry sent formal written authority to me on the 8th, confirming instructions to Security at his yard to allow me access. On the 14th Ayatollah Ruhollah Khomeini issued a death threat fatwa against Salman Rushdie for *The Satanic Verses*, published by late 1988; and on 20 February No 45106 was withdrawn from Tinsley depot, the last of its class and the result of fire damage on the 3rd.

I spent three of the first four days of March staying at Mum's hotel! This enabled me to repeat visits to Leicester shed on the 2nd, Brush on the 3rd (to photograph No 60001, the very first of the new class, which was named *Steadfast* at Brush on 30 June, but not finally accepted by BR until 1991!), then to Leamington, to visit Alec Ford. A few years my senior, he had employed a 35mm camera since the late 1940s and the quality of his images was way beyond my standard. He had promised to show me some material he had for my Leicestershire book and he was generous with the loan of prints, as well as the gift of an A3-size photograph of a Birmingham train leaving the city of Leicester. I have treasured that ever since. The following day I was back at Vic Berry's yard, this time with my permit in hand! 3 March had also seen the first Class 91 introduced onto the ECML, No 91001 on the 1736 King's Cross to Peterborough. These new locos would rapidly replace the HSTs that had been the mainstay of services on the route for more than a decade. Over recent months my outings were local and literally for just a few minutes, but I was still reviewing for *Railway Magazine* and in the March 1989 issue I had no fewer than ten gracing its pages!

While I was at Vic Berry's on 4 March there was a major crash at Purley, leaving five dead and 88 injured, as the 1217 Littlehampton-Victoria train ran into the back of the 1250 Horsham-Victoria train. The driver of the Littlehampton train was found guilty of a SPAD (Signal Passed At Danger) offence and was imprisoned for his misdemeanour. Two days later, on 6 March, two died at Bellgrove when Nos 303005 and 303071 collided head-on. Later in the month, on 24 March, the *Exxon Valdez* supertanker ran aground in Prince William Sound, Alaska, spilling millions of gallons of crude oil into the water and causing one of the worst environmental disasters ever. Not a good month!

13 March saw our first match as the Thames Valley District Ten-Pin Bowling team, on another tour, this time to the Manchester area, playing against Liverpool, Manchester and Radbroke Hall, then to RAF Wyton for our annual 'varsity' match against Cambridge. I managed an escape on the 14th to visit and photograph at Manchester Victoria and Piccadilly stations. Time was limited, due to the need to be back for the next match, but I was able to capture No M65457 at the former, which would become the 1144 service to Bury, not many months before this route was totally transformed. A surprise at Piccadilly was the sight of No 82106 at the buffer stops, one of the new Driving Van Trailers (DVT) that would shortly be introduced in the area. Sadly, my bowling prowess

was not so pronounced on this trip, although others had star moments!

3 April was the date of the 10th Duane Eddy Circle Convention, which took the opportunity of also celebrating (to quote from the publicity) 'Duane's 30th Anniversary as the World's No 1 Guitar Star'. Eight days later, the Government confirmed the reprieve from closure of the Settle-Carlisle railway line, thanks in no small part to MPs Paul Channon and Michael Portillo. On 17 April the Vale of Rheidol Railway was sold by BR to two officials of the Brecon Mountain Railway.

Over the next four months there were three tragic events: 95 football fans were crushed on 15 April at Hillsborough, Sheffield, during the game between Liverpool and Nottingham Forest; on 4 June the world was rocked by the Chinese authorities' over-savage crackdown of Tiananmen Square protests, with hundreds killed by army tanks; and on 20 August 51 people died when the *Marchioness* pleasure boat collided with a barge on the River Thames, adjacent to Southwark Bridge. Also during that period the deaths occurred of Daphne du Maurier, on 19 April (born 1907), Lucille Ball seven days later (born 1911), Mel Blanc (the voice of Bugs Bunny) on 10 July (born 1908), and Lawrence Olivier on 11 July (born 1907). Births included Gareth Bale on 16 July and Daniel Radcliffe seven days later.

On 18 April I broke out of my 'routine' lineside jaunts to travel to Theale, just west of Reading, ostensibly to witness one or more of the oil trains emanating from the local terminal, but also to record motive power on a line not previously frequented. Three pairs of double-headers were noted – Nos 33002 with 33053, 33057 with 33110, and 37215 with 37221 – together with two '56s' and No 59001 *Yeoman Endeavour*, the pioneer 'Quiet American' heavy freight loco mentioned previously. Colour film was used for their portraits, but the dull conditions sadly did not lead to much satisfaction at the end result!

Since the birth of our children in the late 1970s, my moves for the Bank – and the advent of punk! – our concert-going days had largely ended, but on 8 May we journeyed to the Apollo Theatre, Oxford, to see performances by Clannad, one of Judi's favourite artists of the time. Later in the month I drove to Sundon on the Midland Main Line to capture what I could, in a brief visit, of Hertfordshire Railtours' 'InterCity Diesel Day' celebrations on the 21st. Locos used included Nos 20145, 20228, 33021, 33022, 37058, 37066, 47347, 56017 and 58050, on a series of special trains run between London St Pancras and Leicester.

In the past it was steam excursions that drew the crowds, but on 21 May 1989 the Hertfordshire Railtours' 'InterCity Diesel Day' swung the pendulum. At Sundon No 37058 speeds north with one of the St Pancras-Leicester rosters.

A highlight of the summer came on 1 June when I joined cousin David, his wife Pam and their two children for a trip on the 'Midland Borderer' to Carlisle. Driving up from Longcot, I stayed overnight with them before we travelled to Langley Mill station to make our connection with the special, which had started from Leicester behind No 97561 (ex-47561). Named *Midland Counties Railway 150 1839-1989* just nine days earlier, it had been repainted in a special livery to celebrate the earlier railway. This gave way to Stanier 8F No 48151 at Hellifield before a steam run to Carlisle. After detraining at that destination, David, Pam and kids went into the city, while I made my way south to visit Upperby engine shed, where I was to see the 8F, with its support coach, being serviced ready for the return journey. It would hand back to No 97561 at Skipton on this return trip. A very pleasant day, not least with cops of Nos 97252 'Ethel 3', 20220 and 08910 at Upperby. Taking the opportunity of being in the Midlands, I paid yet more visits to Vic Berry and Leicester shed on the following day, calling in at Hinckley station for photographs on the way, just in time to see a double-headed oil train.

In highly unusual but evocative colours, No 97561 (ex-47561) *Midland Counties Railway 150 1839-1989*, named just nine days earlier, stands at Hellifield for steam loco No 48151 to take over on the Leicester-Carlisle special on 1 June 1989. The diesel was renumbered 47973 six weeks later.

Having earlier had glimpses of the workshop at '15C', we now move inside to see No 08697 receiving attention on 2 June 1989.

The next month, on 8 July, Judi and I enjoyed a ride on London Transport's 'Chesham Branch Centenary Shuttles', using electric loco No 12 *Sarah Siddons* and Metropolitan Railway steam loco 0-4-4T No 1, with support vehicle and a 4VEP in NSE livery. We journeyed from Chesham to Watford (Metropolitan – slated for closure) and returned with 'Met 1' on the country end of the rake. Due to the number of people in confined spaces at each end of the route and the misogynistic attitude of some males towards Judi and other ladies toting cameras, photography did prove difficult!

Our family holiday that year was to comprise a week at Plas Tan-y-Bwlch (a Council-run study centre near Maentwrog, in North Wales). Judi and Adam were to study local topography, flora and fauna, while Tammy and I joined a course to study the narrow-gauge railways of North Wales. We drove north on 29 July, with the courses starting the following day. The first day for us was concentrated on the Ffestiniog Railway, visiting both ends of the 13-mile line and many other places in between. On the 31st we went by rail from Penrhyndeudraeth (aboard No 150143) to Aberystwyth, with a reversal at Machynlleth. Joining the terminus for the Vale of Rheidol Railway, adjacent to the main-line facility, the treat was the climb up the line to Devil's Bridge terminus behind No 8 *Llywelyn*. Our return to Penrhyn was on No 150126.

The real treat for Tammy and me was on 1 August, when we were treated to a ride on the Snowdon Mountain Railway and access to the engine shed in Llanberis. One major attraction of the course was being given privileged access to areas normally off limits. A ride on the Llanberis Lake Railway afterwards, literally along the edge of the lake, was the icing on the cake that day. The 2nd was spent in the classroom, with relevant facts and figures about the places being visited. We ventured out again on my birthday, 3 August, to the Talyllyn Railway, again with rides and shed/works visits. On the final day, the 4th, attention was firmly fixed on the Welsh Highland Railway, both the past and the 'hoped-for' future. Seeing what had been and what remained, including the old trackbed, bare of rails at the foot of Snowdon (on the other side of the mountain from

One of the many delights of Tammy's and my holiday at Plas Tan-y-Bwlch, in North Wales, was being given access to the shed and yard at the Snowdon Mountain Railway. No 3 *Wyddfa* is between duties at Llanberis on 1 August 1989. A truly rare view.

Another beneficial part of the Welsh holiday was walking the trackbed of the erstwhile Welsh Highland Railway. Here our group approaches the tunnels in the Aberglaslyn Pass on 4 August.

Llanberis) was truly fascinating and it powered my interest in the rebuilding efforts that would occupy the next two decades. Overall, a fascinating and highly enjoyable and rewarding holiday (and one to be repeated in 1991, when there would be developments for Tammy!).

Just a week after being in North Wales I was back in Leicestershire to enjoy the delights of the Brush Engineering Open Day on the 12th. As well as the first half-dozen of the new Class 60s on show, in various stages of undress and the opportunities for close-up photographs, enthusiasts were treated to the sight of Nos 89001 *Avocet* and 47152. After that, of course, were the de rigueur trips to Leicester shed and Vic Berry's before travelling back home.

My first 'non-routine' trip in September was on the 17th when I drove south to Kemble, to see Nos 20227 and 20188 double-heading the later part of Pathfinder Tours' 'Gloucester Open Day Shuttles', which they had originally brought from

At the Brush Open Day on 12 August 1989 No 60003 (to be *Christopher Wren*), on the left, shares the display with No 60006 (to be *Great Gable*). It was to be more than two years before the locos were accepted into service by BR.

How the mighty are fallen! Once on front-line duties on both the West Coast and Great Western main lines, No 50012 *Benbow* now has a broken back in Vic Berry's yard on 12 August 1989, just seven months after withdrawal from Laira depot.

Birmingham New Street. Predominantly freight locos, they had recently celebrated their 21st birthday and were a welcome sight at the head of a rake of coaches. Next was 24 October, the day after Judi left for another week in North Wales, when I again took the opportunity of the children being at school to undertake a day trip by rail, this time from Swindon to Cardiff. Lots of numbers were collected en route and at Cardiff Central station, together with photographs – both colour and b&w, as I was now toting two Canon AE1-P cameras on many occasions. Sadly there were only three cops: Nos 37884 at Newport, 47427 at Cardiff and 37142 on the return trip through Newport. The '47' was withdrawn as 'Unserviceable' at Crewe Diesel Depot just three months later. I had driven to the car park in Swindon in my new car, which I had bought earlier in the month for just £1,300.

Elsewhere, on 17 October an earthquake measuring 6.9 on the Richter Scale in Northern California, near Santa Cruz on the San Andreas Fault, shook San Francisco and claimed 63 lives. On a happier note, on 10 November East German leaders opened the Berlin Wall, allowing freedom for residents on both sides to cross the border. Demolition started seven months later.

18 November was to prove an eventful day for me, as my *Leicestershire Railway Memories* book was published and celebrated by a special train on the Great Central Railway, from Loughborough Central to Rothley and return, hauled by the unique preserved No 506 (ex-62660) *Butler-Henderson*. Among the guests in attendance, in addition to Neville Mays of Brush and the publisher, were cousin David and contributing photographers Alec Ford, Barry Hilton, Chris Banks, Chris Milner, Colin Marsden, Tom Heavyside and Geoff King. The launch went well but, with minimal advertising, sales were only modest.

On 11 December I paid another visit to Brush and recorded Nos 60003 and 60007-15 in varying stages of construction. On that same day No 60005 *Skiddaw* became the first of the class on a revenue-earning turn. There had

A celebration for the publication of my second book took place at Loughborough Central on 18 November 1989. No 62660 *Butler-Henderson* poses with me and photographers whose work was used in the book. They are Alec Ford, Barry Hilton, Chris Banks, David Richards, Chris Milner, Colin Marsden, Neville Mays, Tom Heavyside, unidentified, and Geoff King.

been some faults in the early builds, unacceptable to BR, and it took until February 1993 before all of the first 16 had been accepted!

The 17th was also a special day. Another fan of Duane Eddy won an auction on the 'Children in Need' appeal to be invited to BBC Wiltshire Sound, in Swindon, to contribute to DJ Alan Burston's *Cruising* programme, showcasing the man and his music. Living in Faringdon, just 4 miles from me, he asked me to take part. We compared notes and compiled a total of 17 different tracks, predominantly rarer tracks or those associated with Duane. It was so well received on the night by the DJ that he abandoned his earlier plans and we had the whole show! Would that I had a tape of that!

To round off the year, Black Box's *Ride On Time* was the top-selling single and Jason Donovan's *Ten Good Reasons* was top album. Leicester City were hovering mid-table in Division 2, with a win on 30 December, 1-0 at home against West Ham United. Sadly, in what was their worst 'goals against' tally for 25 years, they conceded more goals than any other team in the League, apart from Hartlepool! It didn't help as Mike Newell, their top scorer in the previous season, had been sold to Everton – a repeat of the departure of Gary Lineker in 1985.

In many ways, 1990 was a positive year: no passengers were killed, the first time this had been the case for some time; progress was being made on construction of the Channel Tunnel; there were more station reopenings; the ECML electrification reached Newcastle; Nelson Mandela was released from prison (on 11 February); on 15 March Mikhail Gorbachev was elected first executive president of the Soviet Union, with more Cold War thawing; and destruction of the Berlin Wall started on 13 June. Sadly, there were deaths too, including Terry-Thomas on 8 January (born 1911); Ava Gardner on 25 January (born 1922); Del Shannon on 8 February (born 1934), who took his own life; both Sammy Davis Junior (born 1925) and Jim Henson, 'Muppets' creator (born 1936) on 16 May; and Ric Grech on 17 March (born 1946). This last-named was bass player with the Leicester group Family and many other high-profile bands. I had become acquainted with him in later years, as I interviewed him regarding his plans for a new line-up, then spent some time with this new group. It was not successful in the end and he died of renal failure due to alcoholism. It was a sad day, as I had seen him fighting to put his life straight.

The February issue of *Railway Magazine* published an article of mine, under the grand title 'Always Chasing "Cops"'. It was a look at my early days of trainspotting and ended with a plug for my two recent books – *30 Years of Trainspotting* and *Leicestershire Railway Memories*. That issue also contained 11 of my reviews, a mixture of books and VHS videos. 10 February saw me making yet another visit to Leicester depot and to Vic Berry's. Not surprisingly, many of the locos on display had changed since the previous visit and now included a handful of the Class 47

'Generators', the first 20 of the class built – Nos 47419, 47404, 47410 and 47415. Also there was No 08297 (ex-D3367), withdrawn from Doncaster on 16 August 1988, and bearing the strange appellation 'TS002'.

7 March saw me on another outing from Swindon to London and back, with photographs taken at Paddington, Euston, Barons Court Underground station, King's Cross and St Pancras. While I enjoyed pointing the camera at the various locations, there was nothing of major interest, although the variety compared to my normal fare at Barons Court was welcome. Around 100 numbers were collected on the journeys but, again, relatively few cops – just Nos 31317 and 47236 at Reading and 47830 at Paddington – before a higher return at Euston (Nos 90031, 90004, 90032, 90027, 90022 and 90014), King's Cross (Nos 43198 and 43105), and St Pancras (Nos 43154, 43059 and 43153). Five days later I was off with Bank colleagues on another ten-pin bowling tour on the 12th to the 16th, competing against the same opponents as 12 months before. Happily, we were more successful this year overall, with many of our team members excelling, and I was certainly in

Another escape from ten-pin bowling gave me the opportunity for my only visit to New Brighton, where No 508129 stands as empty stock on 12 March 1990.

better form on day one, rolling a 524 series. Again, I escaped for moments to be behind the camera! At the end of the month, issue 118 of *Rail* – dated 22 March-4 April – saw publication of my article on Vic Berry and his scrapyard.

They might well have been April Fool stunts, but on 1 April Mrs Thatcher introduced the Poll Tax, amid widespread protests – a decision she would regret – and the longest prison riots in British history began at Strangeways, Manchester, lasting until finally quelled on the 25th! Happily, there were no riots (except as wildly appreciative ones) as Duane Eddy began a UK tour at Gloucester Leisure Centre on 7 April. Accompanied by 'Rebelette' Kathy Louvin, Duane twanged his way through 18 numbers, including *Blueberry Hill*, *Trambone*, *Boss Guitar* and *Detour*, not normally part of his live performances. He even had his son Chris on drums. As a family, we thoroughly enjoyed the evening and chatting to him afterwards as he came out to meet his fans. After a slow start, the end of April saw a rise in the number of reviews of my two recent books, both in railway magazines and local newspapers, even as far away as *Derbyshire Life & Countryside*!

Following my return to 'full-time' railway interest, just short of a decade earlier, I was now used to my 'little but often' approach, to both photographs and number-crunching, but I did make specific trips on occasions, in addition to renewed visits to Brush and Vic Berry. One such was to Appleford on 7 April

I have been fortunate to meet Duane Eddy on several occasions. Captured by the wife of a friend, after Duane's show at Gloucester, Adam, Tammy and Judi seem to be sharing a joke with the great man on 7 April 1990.

Above: Keeping abreast of developments on the railways pays dividends, and I was in position at Appleford on 7 April 1990 to see No 71000 *Duke of Gloucester* on its first outing since restoration, roaring into the station at the head of 'The Red Dragon' railtour.

to witness the first outing of the newly restored No 71000 *Duke of Gloucester*. Another was on 5 May, to take Adam and Tammy to the Great Western Society site at Didcot, where they enjoyed being 'up close and personal' with the preserved locomotives. Tammy then joined me on 19 May to see more preserved locos inside the old Swindon Works, there on display while repairs were being undertaken at the National Railway Museum in York, their normal home. Something approaching a shed-bashing weekend took place on 30/31 May, as the 'Gang of Three' (Paul, John and myself) undertook our 'Midland & Humberside Tour'. Although I had arranged access to the various ports of call in advance, we were to meet some restrictions.

The first was arriving at Vic Berry's yard, when we were supplied with safety helmets and requested to wear them throughout our visit, the first time I had encountered this need at the yard. Items of note were CIE No 225 (a new arrival from Ireland), sister loco No 212 on fire, as it was being cut up, and an Underground carriage newly repainted, as Vic attempted to vary his workload. On arrival at Brush I was the only one allowed to use a camera, but we all captured the long line of stored Class 20s at Stanton Gate, alongside the main line in Nottinghamshire. There were some quite tall weeds here, into which all three of us were peeing when I said, 'Do you remember when we were kids and had competitions to see who could get their wee to go the highest? Now we are happy to just miss our shoes!' It was late in the afternoon when we arrived at Immingham, but we were welcomed and guided round the depot and the foreman even volunteered to 'put in a good word' with his equivalent at nearby Frodingham, our next destination; otherwise, he said, we had no chance. He must have done a good job, for we were even given a ride around the shed yard in the cab of No 37058!

Left: While refurbishments were under way at the NRM, some of the National Collection were brought south to occupy part of what was Swindon Works. On 19 May 1990 I have my portrait taken with Brush-built Bo-Bo No 1, aka BR No 26500.

Staying overnight in Louth, we began day two at the small junction station at Ulceby, which was very busy with freight, as was Brocklesbury, a couple of miles away. Closed but accessible, the signal box, squat on the platform, gave a fine backdrop to

These Stanton Gate 'choppers' on 30 May 1990 include, left to right, Nos20179, 20217, 20065, 20193, 20224, 20100, 20086, 20147, 20097, 20005 and 20158. I copped No 20224.

Not only were we not refused entry to Frodingham depot on 30 May 1990, but we were also given a ride around the shed yard in the cab of No 37058. Here we approach the entrance to the shed building.

some of the photographs. From there it was to Conisbrough, to act as a park-and-ride for our visit to Doncaster station. The variety of motive power here was very satisfying, which is more than can be said for the subdued volume of traffic at Rugby, where we broke our journey home. In total, however, the two days were voted 'a hit' by all three.

22 July was the next excursion, to Chorleywood and Chalfont & Latimer stations, to witness preserved Nos 80080 and 9466 on that year's 'Steam on the Met' shuttles. The month also saw the last Class 50 haulage on the ex-GWR Birmingham-Paddington route, the class I had snapped so readily some years earlier when working at Flackwell Heath.

Our family holiday this year was between 11 and 18 August, enjoying the delights of a 40-foot narrow boat – Anglo-Welsh's *Whixall* – negotiating the Cheshire Ring. Their first holiday on board, Adam and Tammy took to the experience like ducks to

Highly unusual bedfellows at Vic Berry's on 5 August 1990 were, left, ex-WCML electric No 85019 sharing the yard with 5ft 3in-gauge CIE No 208 from Ireland. The arrival of both rare types to the area stirred much interest among Leicester enthusiasts.

water and were unfazed by the instructions given to us at the outset to descend the flight of locks approaching Manchester as early as possible in the day, before the vandals woke up! It was a little disconcerting that the lock gates were locked on this stretch (for which we had keys), something we had never seen before! We survived the ordeal – and avoided the supporting pillars as we drove the boat *underneath* Manchester – and thus ended this chapter of events.

Chapter 2
1990-1995

The new football season began on 25 August, with Leicester City in the 2nd Division winning 3-2 against Bristol Rovers at home. Sadly, they then suffered seven straight defeats! They struggled all season and finally had to avoid defeat in their last game on 11 May 1991 to escape relegation to Division 3. They beat Oxford United 1-0 at home and were safe.

Another struggle was also ongoing at the end of August. Codenamed 'Desert Shield', the Gulf War against Saddam Hussain's invasion and annexation of Kuwait, begun on 2 August, was well under way.

Over the years, the number of photographs taken on my trips to the railway had steadily increased, as I was now better off financially and carrying two cameras on many occasions, with colour and b&w film. This was evidenced on 16 September with a 'South Wales Tour' by the 'Gang of Four'. An early start saw our first stop at Bristol Bath Road shed at 0700! It was still quite dark, and we arrived as shifts changed. No 47202 was an interesting sight early on, with both cab ends smashed! Into Wales, a snap visit to Pantyffynon recorded Nos 08995 *Kidwelly* (in Railfreight Coal livery) and 08994 *Gwendraeth*, two of the trio of '08s' with cut-down cabs for working on the nearby height-restricted Gwendraeth Valley branch from Celtic Energy's Cwmmawr coal plant. The third – No 08993 *Ashburnham* – was noted at Landore, our next depot call. The rest of the day took in Swansea station, Maliphant Sidings and Margam and Cardiff Canton depots. At the latter we were fortunate to have the cooperation of the depot Foreman in moving 'pioneer' No 37350 (ex-D6700) from the confines of the shed into the yard for us to take our photographs. The trip ended with brief looks at the railway at Barry and Radyr. A full day, with approaching 150 locos noted and a late return home.

Seven days later, I was again in Leicestershire for more photographs at Brush, Vic Berry's yard and Leicester depot. A further seven days saw me return to Swindon Works to photograph the preserved locos in their temporary home. Before my next railway outing there was an important event of much wider significance. On 3 October the world witnessed the reunification of Germany.

We were delighted to see and photograph these '08s' at Pantyffynon on 16 September 1990. With cut-down cabs, to enable access to the nearby freight branch, Nos 08995 *Kidwelly* (in Railfreight Coal livery) and 08994 *Gwendraeth* await their next call.

Thanks to the generosity of the shed supervisor at Cardiff Canton on that day, No 37350/D6700 was hauled from within the shed and into the light for us to capture this portrait of the prototype 'Growler' in original 1960 green colour.

My ports of call were becoming more widespread and frequent than of recent times, with a trip on 9 October close to my old Buckinghamshire stamping ground, at Princes Risborough, Monks Risborough, Wendover and Aylesbury, where I was delighted to see one of the oldest '08s' still on front-line duties – the February 1953-vintage No 08011 (ex-13018/D3018). Named *Haversham*, after an ancient village near Milton Keynes called 'Hæfærsham' (meaning Haefer's homestead) in the 1086 Domesday Book, it was withdrawn just two months later but, happily, preserved on the Chinnor & Princes Risborough Railway.

Another '08' that I was very pleased to see before its withdrawal was No 08011 *Haversham*, in smart livery between duties at Aylesbury on 9 October 1990. The former D3018 from July 1958, it was withdrawn in 1991 but, thankfully, preserved.

I was at Theale on the 17th and Didcot and Reading on 5 November. Elsewhere, Judi was driving back home from her week in North Wales on 13 October (unlucky for some) when she fell asleep at the wheel near Dymock, on the B4215, heading towards Newent. A hot sunny afternoon did not help, but she was fortunate to enjoy a gap in oncoming traffic as she veered to her right and ploughed through a garden fence. She awoke to the sounds of wood striking the windscreen and came to a halt alongside a tall conifer. She was unhurt, though her pride was dented, as she rang me at work from the phone of the householder whose fence she had demolished. Apparently, she was not the first to breach the fence here, despite it being a straight stretch of road! She and the car were then brought home by ETA (the Environmental Transport Association, our car recovery service). Then began the formalities of finding and funding a replacement vehicle.

This is what happens when you pick an argument with a fence and tree! Incredibly, Judi was able to drive this onto a low-loader after she fell asleep at the wheel. The Peugeot 305 Estate awaits collection at Longcot on 14 October 1990.

On the 30th there was a breakthrough of a different kind, when, without ceremony, a Channel Tunnel service tunnel broke into the daylight. A more formal break was made in front of the world's media on 1 December. On 22 November, Mrs Thatcher had resigned as Prime Minister after not winning an outright victory against Michael Heseltine, who had stood against her in a leadership contest. John Major took over. The following day, the staff of Barclays Bank, Faringdon, and I entered into the spirit of 'Children in Need', dressing up as inmates of 'Cell Block F' (for Faringdon), complete with shirts liberally adorned with arrows, with me as gaoler. Some seemed to think I was typecast! Including a tour of the town in costume, we raised £436 for the charity on the day.

27 November was my final railway jaunt of the year, to Leicestershire again, to Brush – where the new builds had reached from Nos 60035 (complete and named *Florence Nightingale*) to 60054, to be named *Charles Babbage* four months later. Vic Berry's yard was again explored, revealing ex-WCML electric No 85025, three Class 33s and a similar number of ex-Isle of Wight coaches. Unusually, Coventry station was visited on the way home, giving me a cop of No 86213 *Lancashire Witch* together with photographs of Nos 321432 and 321406, units new to me.

The Righteous Brothers' *Unchained Melody* was the year's bestselling single, with Sinead O'Connor's *Nothing Compares 2U* close behind. Although struggling with other results, Leicester City's biggest win of the season was 5-4 at home versus Newcastle United on 1 December. Later, unusually, the team did not play on the last days of the month, appearing on Christmas Eve and Boxing Day instead – 0-0 at home to Watford and 1-2 away to Millwall respectively. Once again, their top goal scorer of the previous season had been sold, this time Gary McAllister to Leeds United of the 1st Division.

1 January 1991 saw the family back in Birstall, again to be with Mum on her birthday on the 3rd, and I made my usual trips, but this time including both Loughborough stations. Nothing special, but it was pleasing to see 'Merchant Navy' No 35005 *Canadian Pacific* outside the Central engine shed. This was the last outing of note until 24 February, when I made a slight detour from my journey by road to Bournemouth for another course, to visit Westbury's engine shed. Few locos were present, but they did offer pleasing photographic opportunities, not least No 60008 *Moel Fammau* viewed through the single-road shed building.

My next venture was on 13 March, by rail from Didcot to Cannon Street, Waterloo, King's Cross, St Pancras and Euston. This was my one and only visit to Cannon Street and I was particularly impressed with the station architecture. Ninety locos were in the book, but cops were few – Nos 91029 at King's Cross, 90002 at Euston and 47334 at Didcot. Two days later – 'Red Nose Day' – the staff at Faringdon were suitably bedecked in Bahamas-type beach wear, including dark glasses, grass skirts (not the men!) and a picnic table in the banking hall complete with parasol. This time £320 was raised.

The annual ten-pin tour this year was from 18 to 21 March, with our driver this time a young girl from the branch of one of our team members. She was confident and drove as such, much to the occasional disquiet of the rest of us in the car, not least on the M6. It was drizzling rain as we sped north in the fast lane when we were suddenly confronted with a desk sitting in that lane – looking for all the world like the Monty Python desk without John Cleese! Without hesitation, braking or looking over her shoulder, she swung the steering wheel to the left, then back again, and we rounded the desk. Fortunately, there was no one in the middle lane at that time and we all offered a prayer of thanks as we reopened our eyes, glad to be unscathed! I managed to escape on the 19th to visit Manchester Victoria and Piccadilly stations, then Longsight depot, and on the 21st to photograph variety at Milton Keynes station.

From 9 to 11 April I was on another course, with the Bank's sanction but one of a different sort. I travelled daily to Kidlington, north of Oxford, to attend a First Aid Course run by the local Red Cross. It proved harder and more challenging than I expected and there were even a couple of male participants who abandoned it part way through. I took the opportunity of the lunch breaks and/or journeys home to go to the railway at either Kidlington or Handborough with my cameras.

The first 'Gang of Three' trip of 1991 saw me join Paul and John on our 'Northern Tour' visiting, progressively, Nottinghamshire, Yorkshire and Leicestershire. Day One – 13 April – began with 5 minutes at Banbury before moving on to Toton depot, with permission for a 1400 start, and we were even graced with a guide, who was changed mid-way for no apparent reason. The menu was a mixture of old and new, with Class 60s, 56s and 58s cheek-by-jowl with a plethora of ancient Class 20s. We knew the latter would not be around for much longer and were delighted at being able to photograph so many. Inside the shed building, No 58049 was adorned with a sticker saying 'Switch off all lighting on leaving loco unless required for safety reasons'. This was the only time I ever saw such an instruction. I was content with seven cops, and such was the volume on show that we overran the 1700 exit deadline by quite a few minutes!

The Toton depot permit for 1400 on 13 April 1991, for three persons.

No 60032 *William Booth* is surrounded by older loco types inside Toton on 13 April. The loco lost its name 19 years later, but at least, at the time of writing, it had not been graced with one of the silly names that keep appearing.

Our second visit to Stanton Gate produced just seven Class 20s in store together with No 58028 passing with a freight on the main line. Mirfield station was next. The area was a shadow of its former self and I tried hard to visualise where the old engine sheds had been that I had visited nearly three decades earlier. It was dark after checking into our B&B near Haworth, but we still ventured onto Keighley station, to consume fish and chips purchased en route. Our leisure was disrupted somewhat, however, by the arrival of a crowd of noisily exuberant footfall fans detraining from an incoming service at 2100. We still had not finished and went to Skipton station, where John set up to take a 27-second still shot for posterity, then on to Colne.

We had an 0630 breakfast on the 14th before the drive to Neville Hill depot. Although we had permission, the 'jobsworth' on duty thought otherwise and it took some perseverance (and threats to report him to higher authority) before he relented. Happily, our guide was much more accommodating and happy to take us where we wanted to go and for us to spend as long as we needed. A highlight was the sight of No 158907, literally brand new from BREL Derby in its Metro red and white livery. Holbeck was another depot not enhanced by the passage of time, with just a dozen locos and the odd unit on show and nothing of note. Knottingley was a relatively new depot and was largely a concentration of Class 56s for work on coal and other more general freight turns. The sun continued to shine brightly

The railway constantly turns up pleasant surprises when you least expect them. One such was this vision at Neville Hill of No 158907, brand new, in a new livery and not yet in service, on 14 April 1991.

and clean locos offered pleasing views. Just Paul and I toured the shed, while John set up his video on the adjacent hillside to capture a truly panoramic scene.

Tinsley was another case of a 'jobsworth', but eventually our permission was accepted and more than 50 locos were recorded and photographed, the clear majority being Class 47s. Many had names, some unofficial, applied by the depot. Worksop was next, and again suffered from antipathy; this time we were only allowed to view locos from the staff car park! And so to Leicestershire, for Brush Works – and 14 locos between No 60039 and No 60058 – Leicester shed and, finally, a view of the burned-out piles in Vic Berry's yard. These had been destroyed by a massive fire at the yard on 10 March – with an attendant asbestos scare as acrid smoke drifted over the city of Leicester – and we had to view on this occasion from the walkway on the ex-Great Central trackbed alongside the site. Another eventful and satisfying weekend, graced with glorious weather for a change.

The remains of the pile of coaches at Vic Berry's yard on 14 April 1991, after the disastrous fire that all but ended his business on this site. The temperature at the fire's height can only be guessed at.

64

Portrait of my new car, a Peugeot 205 at Longcot on 3 May 1991. It was later written off by Adam!

It is recognised that memory is selective and I know mine is not perfect, but why I was in hospital in Swindon between 26 and 30 April totally escapes me!

Monday 13 May was to be a special day for me and it was with pent-up anticipation that, as a family, we drove to Birstall the previous day to stay overnight with Mum and Dad. I took the opportunity of escaping for an hour or so on the 12th to view the latest position with the fire carcases in Vic Berry's yard, as well as brief visits to the usual suspects in the town and county. I copped just one all day, No 60059, being the latest in construction at Brush. The Monday evening was to be the special event when, with Judi and the kids, I took my seat at Leicester's De Montfort Hall to enjoy the Everly Brothers in concert with special guest Duane Eddy, mid-way through their month-long UK tour. The only time I would see the Brothers live, I felt I could now die happy at the close of the concert, having witnessed Duane singing with them on *Shake, Rattle & Roll*! Truly a night to remember.

DE MONTFORT HALL
THE EVERLY BROTHERS   £ 15.00
with DUANE EDDY   .
Mon 13 May 91 at 20.00
P-W STALLS   R   16

My Leicester De Montfort Hall ticket for the Everly Brothers/Duane Eddy concert on 13 May 1991.

A week later I embarked on the first of four consecutive day trips of spotting and photography. The first was another trip to London by rail, revisiting previous haunts but adding, this time, a brief sojourn at Kensington High Street station. Cops were few: Nos 43162 at Paddington on the outward route, 91023 and 08709 at King's Cross, 43107 at St Pancras, 90003 at Euston, and 47146 at Reading. On Tuesday the 21st, in my new Peugeot 205, I went to Didcot and Reading, but had no cops at all. The following day rang the changes, with a visit to Bicester Town and North stations, followed by Heyford and Handborough. The 23rd saw me back at Theale once more. Apart from photographs, all these three days were barren of new visions for me.

It was more than a month before I again ventured away from 'home' when, on 30 June, I made another excursion to Leicestershire to visit Brush – where the newest of the Class 60s was No 60073 – and the private Great Central Railway at Loughborough. For the first time in several years I did not investigate Vic Berry's yard. It was not the last time I was at the site but, with the aftermath of the fire, there was precious little new to record. The site was eventually cleared, with new housing taking its place.

My next 'real' outing was with a substitute 'Gang of Four' – with Paul Smart replacing Neil – on our 'Southern Electric Tour' over the weekend of 6 and 7 July. We began at Chart Leacon Train and Rolling Stock Maintenance Depot on Saturday the 6th. Being inside a third-rail depot and yard, with the rails being 'live', was a new experience for us and we treated the area with great caution. Our respect was proved when our guide paused to point out to us the dangers of being too close to the live rail and promptly received a 'bang' himself. Happily, he survived! The nearby stabling point, station and Old Wheel Works and yard were next. Inevitably, the vast majority of stock seen was EMUs, but variety was presented by a number of Class 08s and 09s, 33s and a small handful of 47s. In fading light Wye station was visited, where we were serenaded by birdsong as we stood on the station footbridge, waiting for the next arrival. Two four-car 4CEPs, Nos 1526 and 1577, arrived and provided some entertainment, arcing on the live rail as they left and passed over the level crossing. Now in the dark we rolled up at Canterbury East, noting 4VEP No 3167 before parking nearby to partake of our ritual evening meal of fish and chips.

Our permit for Ramsgate depot was for the early afternoon on the Sunday, but this would have meant some unnecessary travelling and mileage, so we decided to try our luck before breakfast. Though unexpected so early, we were granted permission and with the day promising to be another very hot one, we were glad to tour the large area in relative coolness. The rest of the day was still a full one, despite our reorganisation. After delighting in the 'holy grail' of the interior of Ramsgate signal box, our day comprised Canterbury West, with its elevated signal box; Faversham and Sittingbourne stations; Gillingham depot – where the live rail had been isolated for us; and Slade Green depot, with elderly No 5001 standing proudly in its restored BR green livery. This would eventually return to the main line on 28 August 1992. Selhurst Level 5 depot contained eight Class 73s and No 09003, and nearby Tennison Road had Nos 73103 and 73006 – technically withdrawn but to be reinstated two weeks after our visit – standing close to Nos 08854, 09010, 09007 and 09014. Sir Arthur Conan Doyle lived at No 12 Tennison Road from 1891 to 1894, and a blue plaque adorns the property to commemorate this. My only haul from the two days were Nos 73211, 73119 and 73208 inside Selhurst.

On 5 July Leicester North station, the southern terminus of the expanding Great Central Railway, was formally opened by Michael Heseltine, who presented a cheque for £110,000 to the railway from 'Paymaster General'. I visited the station on the 17th, during a three-day stay with Mum, to capture No 6990 *Witherslack Hall* arriving. The month also witnessed the end of the Speedlink freight service and the first Class 155 being split to form single-car Class 153s. Partly due to an intermittent problem with couplings, 35 of the 42 sets were to be so amended.

The family holiday this year was a re-run of two years earlier, with a stay at Plas Tan-y-Bwlch. Judi and Adam studied

Eager to please, Michael Heseltine MP climbs the rostrum at Leicester North to present a cheque for £110,000 to the GCR on 5 July 1991. *Peter Thwaites, MJS collection*

Nature and Tammy and I explored the Land of Little Trains. We drove north from Longcot on 27 July and I was to receive a bonus of an unexpected railway photograph at Leominster. Stopped at the level crossing on the outskirts of the town, we were the lead vehicle. With my driver's window open, I heard a steam whistle, so leapt out with my camera and was just in time to photograph No 70000 *Britannia* on its first run out from a recent restoration, at the head of the appropriately named 'The Britannia Phoenix' special.

Pure happenchance saw me by the line at Leominster to see No 70000 *Britannia* on the 'Britannia Phoenix' railtour, on its return to the main line on 27 July 1991.

The first day of the holiday proper, the 28th, incorporated a look at the abandoned line from Blaenau Ffestiniog to Trawsfynedd together with the private Bala Lake Railway. In the bright sunshine of this very hot day, locos at the latter looked most attractive. The Ffestiniog Railway was the destination on the 29th, including a visit to Boston Lodge Works, then by rail to Llandudno Junction and Llandudno on the 30th. The highlight of the break at the Junction station was to see preserved No 30777 *Sir Lamiel* arrive with 'The North Wales Coast

Express'. A return visit to the Snowdon Mountain and Llanberis Lake railways was made on the 31st, followed by the Welsh Highland Railway in Porthmadog on 1 August and the Talyllyn and Fairbourne railways on the 2nd, our last day. We drove to Leicester on my birthday, the 3rd, to finish the holiday spending three days with Grandma for the kids. Not surprisingly, I took the opportunity for another excursion to Brush, where the new build had now reached No 60076.

August saw the closure of the Bury-Manchester heavy rail line, to allow it to be converted for use by Metrolink trams. Nos M65451 and M77172, the last of the old motive power still operating, were preserved for posterity. My final photographs of the month were taken on the 29th, at Lower Basildon, on my way to a National Union of Bank Employees meeting in Pangbourne. The month ended with Leicester City securing two wins and a draw in the new season. They were to battle for promotion, just missing out, ending fourth.

September began in our household with Adam travelling to Germany for a school exchange. While he didn't learn much of the language, he did enjoy himself, even when standing very close to the East German border and seeing the Communist watch towers! Elsewhere, on the railway, I enjoyed viewing and snapping No 6024 *King Edward I* on a (sadly unidentified) special out of Swindon on the 9th, followed by a trip by rail to Shepperton via Waterloo the next day, for a meeting with Handel Kardas, then Editor of *Railway World*. We discussed various ideas, but none came to fruition. This was followed by another Trade Union course, this time in Bournemouth, from the 18th to the 20th. I broke my journeys at Westbury and Salisbury both ways and took the opportunity to photograph at all three locations. The following day, the 21st, 150 years of the Brighton Main Line was celebrated with VSOE rolling stock hauled by No 73101 *The Brighton Evening Argus*, especially painted in Pullman colours.

Apart from a three-day sojourn in Leicestershire between 23 and 25 October, where Brush new builds had reached No 60093, a visit to the railway site at Old Dalby, and a further

The sadly short-lived Charterail wagons service is seen in action at Melton Mowbray on 23 October 1991. To the left, No 08511 waits to shunt more into the reception sidings.

A photographers' night shoot at GWS, Didcot, highlights No 6024 *King Edward I* on 26 October 1991.

course, at Teddington, between 20 and 22 November, there were no more outings for me before the end of the year other than those local to Longcot. However, November was important to me on a totally different front. Part of my daily duties as Office Manager at Barclays, Faringdon, was to examine incoming cheques over £1,000, after the cashier had checked them for irregularities. One day I spotted fraudulent alterations on a cheque drawn by one of our larger industrial customers. The cashier had passed it, but I could not criticise him, as the alteration of payee's name and the amount from £7,000 to £70,000, was very expertly done and it was purely by gut instinct that I 'smelled a rat'. After checking with the customer by telephone, the cheque was returned unpaid and the situation reported to our Regional Office. In December I received a letter of congratulation from the Bank, together with a payment of £100 as a reward. This was very gratefully received!

At the close of 1991 Bryan Adams's *(Everything I do) I Do It For You* was streets ahead of the competition as the best-selling single, after a record 16 weeks at No 1! Leicester City finished the year with two home matches and two wins – 2-1 versus Brighton & Hove Albion on 26 December and 2-0 against Southend United just two days later.

1992 was the year that the Government outlined plans for rail privatisation, always assuming they won the General Election! They wanted to eliminate BR – which later announced losses of £145 million for 1991 – and create an open-access railway. But how to do it? An early indication of what was to unfold was the ending of BR's London Midland Region, which ceased to exist on 5 February. Around the same date, the February issue of *Railway Magazine* appeared with, inside, my article *Holiday with a Difference*, telling the story of my holiday with Tammy at Plas Tan-y-Bwlch some six months earlier.

It was to be 23 February before I ventured away from local and/or well-trodden paths. Paul and I headed south from Oxfordshire for a day's drive to Winchester, Eastleigh, Fratton and Newbury. Winchester was of distinctly limited interest as regards locos, with us seeing only No 47806, but the variety of units, even in the very short time we were there, was satisfying photographically. By contrast, Eastleigh was roughly 50/50 locos and units with Class 20s, 33s, 47s, 08s, two 60s and a solitary 56 providing welcome variety – and me copping No 33009. It was also good to witness the relatively diminutive No 08847 hauling D. C. Tours/Network SouthEast's 'Solent & Wessex Wanderer (No 7/Train G)' from the station to the Works, as part of the

Waterloo-Bournemouth and back railtour. The visit to Fratton was not my first but was the only time I managed to investigate the shed, although it was only home to units. A single unit, elderly No L407, was all we saw at Newbury apart from two rakes of HSTs, in what was a flying visit on our way home.

On 1 March there was another photographic foray to Swindon Museum, to place on film the iconic 'King' No 6000 *King George V* (built 1927) and 'Star' *Lode Star* (from 1907), before the next rally by the 'Gang of Three' (without Neil for some reason) on the 16th. Our 'Humberside Revisited' tour's first port of call was Melton Mowbray station, where we were delighted to have a second look at the Charterail service in action in the adjacent sidings. A road-rail intermodal service, established in 1990 to serve potential customers post-Speedlink and using 'piggyback' wagons from Tiphook, it was here for shipments to and from Petfoods, a large local employer. Sadly, the system went into liquidation only months after our visit, claiming that high locomotive haulage rates had made the enterprise unsustainable. So, in hindsight, we were very fortunate to be in the right place at the right time.

It is a truism that it is who you know rather than what you know that can bring success. This certainly applied to our 16 March visit to RFS Kilnhurst, arranged through one of my old banking colleagues. Being the company's banker he pulled a few strings and gained us access to the site, normally out of bounds to visitors. The lure was seeing a cluster of Class 20s being prepared for Channel Tunnel tracklaying work, including the prototype, BR No 20001. Twenty-four in total were to be treated and renumbered, with five on loan from preservation groups, and it was gratifying to be given this privileged access, with no photographic restrictions. A very brief look at Rotherham Central then saw us using Conisbrough station as a 'park and ride' for Doncaster, where we soaked up the atmosphere for a while before gaining entry to the nearby Works complex. Sadly, John was not allowed to use his video camera 'inside', but Paul and I were sanctioned for stills!

The Works contained a wide variety of locos and units,

Privileged access to RFS Kilnhurst let us see work on Class 20s for Channel Tunnel work. No 20056 is in the later stages of conversion on 16 March 1992.

diesel and electric, and I even managed three cops – Nos 37154, 56117 and 37194. Forty-two locos were recorded and many photographed before we transferred to the Doncaster Carr engine shed. The menu here was another 39 locos with, again, a wide variety including Class 08s, 37s, 47s, 56s, 31s, No 91011 *Terence Cuneo* and even a woebegone No 46010. In addition to the '91', cops for me here were three '08s' and Nos 56101 and 37003. Back at the station I copped Nos 91022, 91024 and 91028 *Guide Dog*. Night was closing in by the time we reached Barnetby – to see Nos 37048 and 47010 – and even darker at the diminutive Habrough station, but this did not stop me taking a time-delay shot of No 144002 working the 2100 Cleethorpes-Barton-on-Humber local, courtesy of my tripod.

Our next morning's trip began at Immingham depot, our main goal of the morning. Reluctant to enter the shed, after the refusal to allow him to video at Doncaster and the fact that

The proliferation of semaphores at Barnetby were a Mecca for railway photographers. Dutch-liveried No 37066 rumbles past a selection to the east of the station on 17 March 1992.

we did not have an official permit, John decided to forego the visit. With his sanction, Paul and I continued and were granted permission and even given a guide. Although the Brush '60s' were by now staking their claim, the 59 locos on show still contained much variety of older types, including prototype '47' No D1500, alias 47401. The sole remaining example of the original 20 built by Brush in 1962/63, it was a celebrity locally and had been named *Star of the East* on 1 May 1991 (replacing its earlier *North Eastern* identity). Sadly, it was withdrawn less than three months after our visit, but did go on to enjoy preservation at MRC, Butterley.

Reuniting with John, it was back to Barnetby station via the small 1848-vintage Stallingborough station, where a couple of local trains were photographed. Then we motored to an equally sparse facility at Healing (opened in 1881), to see No 144011 non-stop to Cleethorpes. Next was Great Coates, yet another wayside station built in 1848 by the Great Grimsby & Sheffield

Junction Railway, where we again saw and photographed No 144002, this time in daylight! After Barnetby, where John stayed to film, Paul and I journeyed to Frodingham depot, then on to the nearby Scunthorpe CHP (coal handling plant). Here there were two lines of stored locos, including several of those first 20 Class 47s, but we had been warned that it was a 'no-go' area. To avoid detection, in order to reach the locos we climbed inside a large overhead pipe that straddled the running lines – it was certainly the most unusual mode of entry to a railway yard that I had ever used!

The long drive home was broken by another visit to Toton depot, where 77 locos awaited us, including many of the stored '20s' that we had seen previously. A brief inspection of Rugby station from a nearby car park noted several Class 86s and 87s on main-line express duties during a busy time, before we left satisfied with a productive and enjoyable two days 'up north'.

The following day I was back with the ten-pin team on another tour, this time to the Midlands from 18 to 20 March, bowling in Wolverhampton and staying overnight just off the M54. With me driving this time, I could make my usual escapes from the lanes to the lineside at Wolverhampton on the 19th, where I copped No 86216 *Meteor*, and to Oxley depot and Bushbury on the 20th. Sadly, there were no fresh gains for me that day. A brief visit to Oxford on 11 April enabled me to capture the dual-organised RAIL/Network SouthEast 'The Carlisle Fifty Farewell' railtour, double-headed by Nos 50007 *Sir Edward Elgar* in green and D400 in blue. Originating at Waterloo, it literally travelled the length of the country, via the WCML, to Carlisle and back.

Later in the month, on the 19th, a day trip back to Leicestershire enabled me to photograph No 60098, named the previous month *Charles Francis Brush* after the factory's originator, then to view the remains of Vic Berry's yard, now cleared of stock and rails, ready for redevelopment. The same day saw the death of Frankie Howard OBE (born 1917) and the following day the demise of Benny Hill (born 1924).

On 25 May the family travelled south to the Swanage

Railway, to take up an invitation from Vic Mitchell of Middleton Press to participate in the celebrations of the company's 100th book. Tammy and I joined the special train, running behind preserved 'T9' No 120 with an appropriate 'MP1' disc headcode, from Swanage to Harman's Cross and back, while Adam and Judi took time to tour the town and seaside. The month ended with me on a day trip to Paddington from Swindon. Forty-eight numbers were logged but nothing new for me, apart from a handful of photographs at the terminus.

The Manchester Victoria-Bury Metrolink replacement of the heavy rail route finally opened on 6 May; seven days later Leicester City triumphed with their biggest win of season, 5-0 against Cambridge United in the second leg of the Division 2 play-offs; and on 25 May they lost 0-1 versus Blackburn Rovers away, in front of 68,147, the highest attendance for a City match that season. Thus they ended fourth and failed to go up, as mentioned above. On 17 May I went to Amersham and Chalfont & Latimer to see this year's 'Steam on the Met' offerings. As well as the opportunity to snap some London Underground units, there was the presence of steam locos Nos 44932 and 69621, together with the Met electric No 12 *Sarah Siddons*. Two days later it was to Hungerford, to see what was there and to be rewarded by No 59001 on freight.

How things have changed! By 2015 these Great Bedwyn trackwalkers, seen on 19 May 1992, would have had motorised equipment and would have been in full orange PPE gear.

By this time Paul and I had begun a series of weekend trips, many to the South East to visit various locations with a view to me submitting photographs to Middleton Press for upcoming books; they had supplied me with forthcoming titles. On 27 June we travelled first to Stewarts Lane depot, where I copped six out of the 29 locos present, including No 60094 *Tryfan*, which somehow I had missed during my Brush visits. At Hither Green we initially struggled to obtain permission but perseverance paid off, and in the depot yard we were blessed by the sight of No 73101 *The Royal Alex*, resplendent in its Pullman Livery. Ashford had the prototype electric No E5001 in the depot, and the day ended with brief visits to Chatham and Whitstable, where I photographed a ghost train!

The main line's own ghost train! 4VEP No 3421 whistles into Whitstable in the late evening of 27 June 1992.

The next morning started at Ramsgate, where Robert, the depot manager, demonstrated the manual method of cleaning unit windscreens. Then to Margate, with the noise of the funfair nearby, Swanley, Tennison Road, Selhurst – Levels 5 and 4 – and Three Bridges. Locos were relatively sparse, mostly '73s', '08s' and '09s', but Nos 33033 at Swanley and 47600 at Three Bridges were captured for posterity.

Our family holiday this year was from 25 July to 1 August, based at a farmhouse in Tregaron in mid-West Wales. Once on the Carmarthen-Aberystwyth railway line, there was virtually no sign of this except for a short stretch of the old trackbed, which, of course, I examined. We liked the area and accommodation so much that we returned exactly one year later for another week's stay. The only opportunity to boost my railway blood was a trip to Aberystwyth on the 31st, to sample and savour the delights of the Vale of Rheidol Railway, climbing the steep gradient to Devil's Bridge. We then crossed to the East Midlands to visit Mum and Dad for my birthday on 3 August, and to again visit my old haunts at Thurmaston. By the end of August Leicester City had played five, won three and drawn one, a good start to their campaign to escape from the 2nd Division.

10 September saw the introduction of a new small 10p coin, not to everyone's liking. Just nine days later, on a visit to Oxford, I took the opportunity to spend some time at the station and nearby depot site and sidings, with Nos 47535 *University of Leicester* and 47558 *Mayflower* on shed and 60026 *William Caxton* and 37886 passing on freights on the main line.

The next outing for Paul and me was on 3 October, initially back to the North East. Starting early, Paul's driving was such that we arrived in Darlington, a couple of hundred miles distant, in what seemed to be an incredibly quick time. It was raining heavily when we arrived at Darlington station but by the time we had moved on to Thornaby depot it had dried up, although the clouds still threatened. This relatively new depot provided a wide variety among its 52 locos on view inside and out, and appropriate photographic opportunities were readily snapped up. Heaton, via Ferryhill, provided more, before we crossed the country to visit Carlisle. Upperby shed was first, where No 46229 *Duchess of Hamilton* was stabled but not in steam, and the weather did not lead to award-winning photographs. Moving to the station, we had more rain but at least canopies gave us shelter as the evening wore on and the puddled platforms led to some interesting reflections, aided by the station lights.

The next day we began our long journey home at Carnforth, where we noted the plaque to the filming of the superb film *Brief Encounter* at the station. Wigan (Springs Branch) shed provided variety but, sadly, the numbers recorded were not huge. Longsight shed, in Manchester, was next and housed an interesting mix of diesel and electric traction. Many older units were noted alongside 19 locos, including equally elderly Nos 31423 and 31102. Allerton depot housed Nos 47353 and 31413 alongside 15 Class 08s! Numbers dwindled as we reached Speke Junction shed, and even fewer at Norton Junction, the final venue for the day. But it was a satisfying trip, having captured five cops at Thornaby, three at Heaton and two at Carlisle on day one, and two at Wigan, two at Longsight, one at Allerton and two at Speke on day two; I also secured both colour and b&w images in my two cameras. We continued our 'holiday', after an overnight rest, by travelling by rail from Didcot to Bethnal Green station, by way of Paddington, St Pancras, King's Cross, Willesden (Low and High Level) and Stratford. We spent concentrated time at our destination, with me capturing on film as much as I could from my one and only visit to the site. Having finally decided to begin our return journey, we watched No 305528 pull into the platform. We had intended to ride the short distance to Liverpool Street 'on the cushions', but the minute the train stopped the driver hailed us and offered a ride to the terminus in the cab. He had seen us

No 43121 is about to be swallowed by Gasworks Tunnel at King's Cross as it trails a down express out of the station on 5 October 1992.

during the afternoon more than once and decided we deserved some reward! We gratefully accepted.

Apart from a brief visit to Wellingborough station on 15 October, when apart from 12 HST power cars all that was on show was Nos 56078 and 47307, the next excursion was a 'Gang of Three' foray to the east on the last day of the month. Again by rail from Didcot, through Paddington to King's Cross — where I copped the first three locos seen, Nos 91031 *Sir Henry Royce*, 91017 and 90021 — we then had an out-and-back trip to Cambridge, for a quick photo shoot (to the displeasure of one of the railway staff!), before crossing London to Fenchurch Street and a journey to Shoeburyness, my first investigation of this outpost. Thanks to an understanding depot supervisor, we had the run of the yards and were glad to snap several of the units that would soon be replaced with newer types. I took the opportunity for a few 'arty' shots. Thence to Southend Victoria, from where we finally headed back to the Metropolis and Euston before Paddington and home. After the encouraging start at King's Cross, all I copped for the rest of the day was No 90019 *Penny Black*, on our return to King's Cross, No 08594 as we passed Hitchin, and No 08496 on our arrival at Cambridge. With the banter and camaraderie of the three of us, it was another very enjoyable day.

Except for a specific excursion to Peterborough — to clear my HST power cars by seeing and copping No 43115 on a northbound ECML express — there was to be nothing of note in my railway calendar for the rest of the year. Elsewhere, however, momentous things were happening. On 19 November BR announced 5,000 job losses as a direct result of the national recession, and one day later there was a fire at Windsor Castle. At 1115, in the Queen's Private Chapel, a curtain was ignited by a spotlight pressed up against it during ongoing works in the chapel. The damage was extensive, with the final cost amounting to £36.5 million. Just four days after that the Queen would make the oft-remembered quote during her Guildhall speech that 1992 had been an 'annus horribilis'. It was a year when all three of her eldest children's marriages were to end!

As the year closed, *I Will Always Love You* by Witney Houston was the top-selling single (from the film *The Bodyguard*) and film of year was *Silence of the Lambs*, winning five Oscars.

1 January 1993 saw the creation of the European single market. Elsewhere, it was the year that saw the opening of the Robin Hood Line (Nottingham-Newstead initially) and the Ivanhoe Line (Leicester-Loughborough). Both were scheduled for extensions, but only the former was successfully completed to Mansfield, even including the demolition of some newly built houses on the way! The Ivanhoe Line was planned to be circular, from Loughborough to Derby and Burton-on-Trent before returning to Leicester, but politics and financial constraints proved its death knell. There would be further plans for the route, but nothing came of them. Further north, Manchester Airport station opened on a short branch from the Styal line, south of Piccadilly. Meanwhile, rail privatisation planning was continuing. On 16 January came Leicester City's biggest win of the 1992-93 season, 5-2 at home against Watford as they battled for promotion from Division 2; on 12 February two-year old James Bulger was murdered by two 10-year-olds, Robert Thompson and Jon Venables; and in March the Channel Tunnel Rail Link was announced.

The Gang was out again on 30 January, with another rail adventure but this time from Oxford. Via Paddington and Liverpool Street stations, our Eldorado this day was to be Stratford depot, a location that defied so many would-be visitors. With permit in hand, we were shown around the large acreage, enabling us to record the 50 locos on site. In steam days it would have been six times that number! The variety was again wide, including No 56049, a type almost unknown there but present to provide driver training for future use on local freights. Then it was back to Liverpool Street, Enfield Town, Enfield Chase, Hornsey, King's Cross, London Bridge – where capturing the number of trains proved taxing – and Euston, before the return home.

On 9 February there was another ten-pin bowling match, this time only against one other district, and I managed a brief time away to visit Tolworth station and the small goods depot, which housed a BR Class 04 diesel loco. Not overly busy at the best of times, it became part of a National Rail Freight Depot and was still in operation into the 21st century. I was back in time to accompany Judi to Oxford Playhouse in the evening to see Loudon Wainwright III.

Ex-BR shunters were often sold to industrial sites. At Tolworth on 9 February 1993 an unidentified '04' (thought to be either D2246 or D2310) waits its next duty.

The following day I drove to Reading, and my plan was to first approach the rear of the depot. As I arrived a railman was leaving and, incredibly, after I explained why I was there, he gave me the combination for the entrance gate, with the advice to take care not to be spotted by the supervisor! My first visit to Reading West station was next, for photographs, before making my way down the Basingstoke branch to Mortimer and Bramley. I wanted to capture on film the ageing DEMU units and was fortunate with the weather, which helped to capture pleasing images of Nos 205031, 205032, 205029 and

207001, the last at Basingstoke. To complete a trio of road trips, on 11 February the itinerary was Fenny Compton (due to lose its signal box), Bescot (where I captured 46 locos and photographed the remains of the old steam engine shed), Oxley, Bushbury, Leamington Spa and a very brief glimpse of Banbury on the way home. Interesting views, but not a single cop all day!

24 February was a sad day for many football fans who remembered the 1966 World Cup. England captain Bobby Moore died of bowel and liver cancer, aged just 51. Another sad death, not so widely known but mourned by your author, was that of Steve Douglas, from heart failure at just 52 (born 1938). In 1958/59 he was one of Duane Eddy's Rebels backing group, playing his saxophone to great effect, not least on the huge hit *Peter Gunn*. I had the pleasure of meeting and interviewing him in 1979, as part of the preparations for my biography of Duane, and I found him an unassuming but very likeable gentleman.

Our next three-day railway adventure began on 15 March, when visits were made to Crewe (both electric and diesel depots), Heaton and Blyth on day one. At Crewe 107 locos were recorded, and although only eight of these were new to me, they were, to my mind, of pleasing quality. The 16th presented Immingham, Barnetby, Frodingham, Scunthorpe CHP and Tinsley. Cops were again few, but I was very pleased to see No 60050 *Roseberry Topping* at Immingham, as somehow this had escaped me during my many visits to Brush. Only Lincoln was involved on day three, the 17th, where locos were few among the units in employment, but I was gratified to be able to discover and examine the old steam engine shed to the south of the station – altogether another very satisfying outing. 27 March saw Paul and me travelling to Selhurst Level 5 depot, following an invitation from depot supervisor Tony Francis, to witness the re-emergence of No E6003, resplendent in original BR livery and prepared to receive *Sir Herbert Walker* nameplates. By rail from Oxford, we collected many numbers en route and at subsequent locations Clapham Junction, Strawberry Hill, London Bridge, King's Cross, St Pancras and Euston. At London Bridge we witnessed two of the three participating units in

'Spirit of the Past': No 5001 pauses in the platform at London Bridge on Saturday 27 March 1993 on the third leg of SEG3's 'Spirits of…' tour.

Elsewhere in London Bridge, 465009 and 465008 are the 'Spirit of the Future' as they terminate the 2nd leg of SEG3's 'Spirits of...' tour on Saturday 27 March 1993.

Newly refurbished and turned out in original BR green livery at Selhurst Level 5, Depot Manager Tony Francis bravely holds the nameplate for No E6003 *Sir Herbert Walker* on Saturday 27 March 1993.

SEG Railtours' trains — Nos 465008 and 465009 as 'Spirit of the Future' and No 5001 as 'Spirit of the Past'. This last, in Southern Railway green, was especially returned to the main line for this celebration.

April was an eventful month. The 3rd produced a truly unique event, to become known as 'the race that never was'. Aintree's Grand National suffered a false start, but seven horses went on to complete the course — the 'winner' in a second-best course time! The authorities decided against re-running the race and the bookies paid out about £75 million in bet refunds! Earlier in the year I had made a proposal to the Bank for a procedural improvement in a system, for which I was awarded £75 in recognition this month. On the 22nd 18-year-old Stephen Lawrence was murdered in a racially motivated attack, and it was to be nearly 20 years before any conviction was achieved. The 30th saw another event to personally affect me, when Cashmore's scrapyard in Great Bridge, Birmingham, closed its gates. I had enjoyed my visits there in the 1960s. I was still having five or six reviews in each month's *Railway Magazine*, but there were to be none between April and August, and fewer thereafter, due to a slowdown in my receipt of product and the magazine cutting back on available slots.

Personally, May began on the 2nd, with a trek to North Wales to take part, as a volunteer, in the Ffestiniog Railway's three-day 'Hunslet Hundred Gala'. With a mix of visiting locomotives, my volunteering efforts, fine weather and lots of good company, the days were immensely pleasurable and literally sped by.

On 6 May I made another brief investigation of the Reading-Basingstoke branch, with further visits to Mortimer and Bramley, seeing the same units as earlier plus No 207010. The 12th was the date for the 200th issue of *Rail* magazine, now firmly settled into its fortnightly frequency; and a day later Robert Adley, railway author and Tory MP, born in 1935, died from a heart attack. He had been Chairman of the Commons Transport Select Committee and, personally, strongly against rail privatisation. He published nine railway books before his untimely death and it was through some of these that I was

The one photograph where I would not alter anything. All components have met to create this portrait of *Merddin Emrys* approaching Dduallt on 2 May 1993 with the 1400 Blaenau Ffestiniog-Porthmadog service during the FR's 'Hunslet Hundred Gala'.

prompted to approach his publisher with a book of my own. It was agreed, and *Steam on Shed* appeared in 1984. I shall be forever grateful to Mr Adley for his inspiration.

For the last days of the month I was back in and around Amersham, to enjoy the delights of this year's 'Steam on the Met' celebrations, with No 46441 being a most unusual visitor, captured on film by me on the 30th on the climb into Chalfont & Latimer station. The following day, 31 May, was also unusual, as Leicester City were to be shown live on TV in a Division 2 play-off against Swindon Town. Adam and I supported City while Tammy was for the Town as we settled in front of the box. When Town went 3-0 up, Tammy was ecstatic, but very much subdued later when City drew level. Swindon were to prove 4-3 victors but, for the second year running in the play-offs, City were defeated by a disputed penalty kick. Blessed with a 73,802 attendance, it was undoubtedly one of the best matches I have watched live.

On 5 June Adam went with me to Cheltenham Spa station, to photograph (with him using one of my cameras) the very rare sight of a triple-heading of Class 50s. Nos 50033 *Glorious*, D400 and 50007 *Sir Edward Elgar*, at the head of a rake of coaches painted in Pilkington Glass colours, were truly a sight for sore eyes on Pathfinder Tours' 'The Bishops Triple', from Minehead to York. 18 June was exciting and full of anticipation for both Tammy and me. She was off to Germany, on a school exchange (cost £55 to the school and £18 for her passport), with £120 travellers' cheques and £20.75 in currency in her pocket). She was 'blown away' with the sights, sounds and even tastes of this foreign land (not least Hubba Bubba bubble gum!) and her first experience of horse-riding, and she did not stop talking about it for days after her return on the 28th. For my part, three days 'far up north' beckoned.

The 'Gang of Three' had felt for some time that a trip north of the border would be desirable, so on the 18th we set out, Paul at the wheel and joined by 'guest' Paul Smart, initially visiting Bescot, then Crewe. We parked on the downhill road adjacent to the parcel bay at Crewe station. Having been round the diesel depot, we were challenged when returning to the car and accused of trespassing. Even my eloquent negotiating skills did little to pacify this rather intransigent 'gentleman'. Paul was concerned at the time as he took details of his car, but thankfully nothing came of it. From a collection of 81 locos I copped just five, all Class 90s.

A brief comfort stop was made at Lancaster station before we sped up the M6 to Carlisle. After trawling the 11 on shed at Upperby, including Nos 60532 *Blue Peter* and 46203 *Princess Margaret Rose* flying the flag for steam, it was another dash north to Motherwell. After some discussion we finally secured access to the depot, where I copped just two from 32 – Nos 08753 and 37424 *Isle of Mull*. Striking north-east, we continued our journey and ended the day on Perth station for a brief glimpse before the obligatory fish and chips, then to our B&B.

The morning of the 19th saw us back at Perth, as Paul had forgotten his camera the previous evening, to capture No 37428 *David Lloyd George* in the early morning sunshine, waiting in the platform to form the 0705 to Edinburgh. Again travelling northwards, we called in at Pitlochry and Aviemore on our way to Inverness. More negotiating enabled us to tour the depot, to see 15 Class 37s and an equal number of Class 26s, 10 of which were in store, awaiting disposal.

An early breakfast on 19 June 1993 allowed us to be at Perth in time to capture No 37428 *David Lloyd George* preparing to leave with the 0705 train to Edinburgh.

With thoughts turning homeward, we journeyed south to Berwick-upon-Tweed via a brief call at Carrbridge, seeing No 37428 again. After another overnight stay – at the Old Vic Guesthouse in Berwick – Blyth was our next target, where the depot was all '56s' except for No 37424, which had beaten us to the depot after we had seen it at Motherwell the previous day. We were now becoming used to Heaton, with its usual mix of diesel and electric, Knottingley and Toton, where we hoovered up 101 locos. The ambience of this last location had changed since our last visit, with the predominance now being Class 56s, 58s and 60s. There were still many '20s' around, but virtually all now in store and side-lined. We had a brief look at Leicester depot, which housed predominantly Class 60s, which was no surprise, but it was pleasing to cop No 56127 and see old favourites Nos 08697 and 08473 still in work.

Away from the railway, there was some considerable excitement on 23 June when world news was full of American John Bobbitt awaking to find that his wife Lorena had cut off

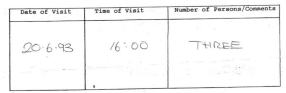

Dear Sir(s),

AUTHORITY FOR ACCESS TO TOTON TRACTION MAINTENANCE DEPOT

This letter of authority is issued to the conditions shown and will be taken as the official receipt for the permit fees payable.

This letter must be presented to the Visits Supervisor at Toton Depot at the time of arrival.

Note   Your attention is drawn to items 4 and 7 (2) of the conditions for issue of this permit, overleaf.

Date of Visit	Time of Visit	Number of Persons/Comments
20.6.93	16:00	THREE

I trust your visit to the depot will be enjoyable.

Toton depot permit, 20 June 1993.

his penis, at its base! She had driven off with it and thrown it into a field! Thinking better of it, she then phoned 911 and, happily, the police responded and finally found it. It was rushed to the hospital and reattached during a 9½-hour operation. Slightly less exciting, a week later we had to make use of a pest controller to hunt out and dispose of a rats' nest in one of the wooden compost bins in our garden, setting us back £30.

As mentioned earlier, we had a repeat holiday in Tregaron, from 24 July to 1 August. The B&B served up sumptuous and appetising meals and I felt the cost of £182 for the week for four of us was real value for money. Unless the landlady grew most of her own vegetables, she could not have made a profit! We had just two days on railways, with a trip to and ride on the Gwili Railway on the 25th and a trip north to the Ffestiniog on the 30th. Tammy was in her element on the FR, but Adam, now nearing 17, was becoming bored with trains, but fortunately for us he suffered in silence.

On 15 August Paul and I had another day out, photographing for Middleton wants, this time around the Home Counties, visiting Strawberry Hill again, Streatham Hill, West Norwood, Sydenham Hill, Gipsy Hill, Crystal Palace, Birkbeck, South Croydon, Sanderstead and Purley Oaks. Despite often only having moments at locations, the new vistas were satisfying.

The 1993-94 football season saw the introduction of the Premier Division, so Leicester City were in Division 1, although not promoted earlier in the year! They began this new season well, with two wins from the three matches in August, the biggest being 4-0 at home against Millwall on the 28th.

On 8 September there was something new for me, taking a break from work but still in my work suit to visit BBC Radio Berkshire, in Reading. There I was to participate in a programme on Duane Eddy, the invitation being a welcome spin-off from the earlier Swindon Radio programme. I called in to Didcot on the way home, camera in hand. Eight days later provided another escape from work, going north to Tinsley Depot to interview Bill Foster, the site's supervisor, for an article for *Rail* magazine, published the following year.

Afterwards I made my one and only visit to a rather careworn Woodhouse station nearby, then called in at Toton and Loughborough on the way home. Just one cop from the whole day – No 37420 *The Scottish Hosteller* – from the 81 locos seen! On the 19th Paul and I had another excursion, beginning at Nuneaton. Rugby followed, then Northampton, Bedford and our ultimate destination at Bletchley, where we were blessed with bright sunshine, the run of the depot and first sight of the new Class 323 electric units. Again, there was only one new capture – No 08628 at Northampton. 21 October witnessed Leicester City's biggest win of the season, 6-1 away against Rochdale in the Coca-Cola Cup 2nd Round, 1st leg.

Our next weekend away began on 9 October with Paul again behind the wheel. Eastleigh was first, in pouring rain, to see ex-Southern Railway 'S15' No 828 at the head of the first of the Eastleigh-Salisbury shuttles organised by Network SouthEast (Salisbury Area) over the weekend. Happily, the weather improved to the extent that arrival at Bristol, to explore Bath Road depot, was in bright sunshine. From 44 locos

This won't hurt! A fitter attacks No 43163's 'molar' at St Philips Marsh on 9 October 1993, presumably with a high-speed drill!

on view I again copped just one, No 47814, before the very short drive to St Philips Marsh, which produced Nos 47509, 47508 and 47432, all recently withdrawn and in store, together with one more cop for me, HST power car No 43167. The day ended at Landore, on the outskirts of Swansea, where we were surprised to be greeted by 2-6-4T steam locos Nos 80079 and 80080, a long way away from their normal homes. Whether from a railtour or for attention, we were not able to ascertain.

The following day started again in the Swansea area before we headed west to Margam depot and the adjacent Gwent Demolition scrapyard, where we snapped some ageing DMUs before they were reduced to scrap metal. Cardiff Canton was next, both the loco shed and the Regional Railways facility on a higher level. The latter provided an interesting mix of liveries on the DMUs present.

Another variety to my outings came on 21 October, when I visited the 1843-vintage Brunel-built Swindon Works, with permission, in preparation for a magazine article. Closed nearly a decade earlier, the buildings were devoid of previous activity but the views of skeletons of the past within the walls were an enjoyable challenge to this photographer.

This was followed at the end of the month by a visit to Didcot for the Great Western Society's 'Photographers' Evening' on the 30th. With the usual spotlights illuminating the locos on show, I again purposely employed colour and b&w

Stripped of machinery in preparation for conversion to shop units, the innards of Swindon Works' 1873 Erecting Shop and Boiler Shop are laid bare on 21 October 1993.

cameras and tripod to capture some truly evocative steam-powered vistas.

On 5 November the Railways Bill, heralding rail privatisation, received Royal Assent. The sell-off had begun of BR assets! The same month saw my fourth book published. My first since 1990, it was also the first with Silver Link Publishing Ltd, a new publisher for me. The result was *Closely Observed Trains*, a quality hardback book portraying some of the changes on BR in the 1980s. It was gratifying to receive complimentary reviews in various publications over the next six months and it cemented a relationship with the publisher that has lasted to the book that you are now reading.

Away from home territory, there was just one trip this month, to Crewe on 20 November, investigating both electric and diesel depots, but for some reason that I now cannot recall I did not take any photographs. It would have been most unusual for me not to have my cameras with me. I do, however, remember sitting outside the electric depot listening to the lunchtime *Archers* repeat, to hear of the death of Mark Hebden, Shula's husband!

Another death was on 4 December, with the demise of acclaimed but quirky musician Frank Zappa (born 1940). Aged just 52, he died with his wife and family beside him. He remains a major influence and honours include an induction into the 1995 Rock 'n' Roll Hall of Fame and a 1997 Grammy Lifetime Achievement Award. 10 December saw the first Class 92 loco emerge from Brush. A total of 46 were ordered and constructed, 16 for Channel Tunnel work, but it would take two years before they were accepted onto the main line. Meatloaf monopolised the bestselling records of 1993, with the single *I'd Do Anything For Love (But I Won't Do That)* and the bestselling album *Bat out of Hell II*. Leicester City were doing well in the Division 1 table and ended the year with a 4-4 draw at home against Watford.

The end of my railway year came at Loughborough Central on 28 December, during the family's trip back to Birstall to spend New Year with Mum and Dad. I captured locos in the snow, including No 45231 entering the station from the south and No 4498 *Sir Nigel Gresley* making a spirited exit from Loughborough with the 1300 train to Leicester North during the Great Central's Christmas Gala.

Loughborough Central is left behind by No 4498 *Sir Nigel Gresley* on 28 December 1993, as it leaves with the 1300 service to Leicester North during the GCR Christmas Gala.

The January 1994 issue of *Railway Magazine* featured my article 'Echoes of Glory', looking at Swindon Works 150 years on from Brunel's 1843 creation and what remained of the buildings, etc, nine years on from closure. Swindon also featured in my first railway concentration of the year, going to Uffington and the embankment to the west of Acorn Bridge, alongside the A420, the eastern approach to the town. I photographed Nos 37077 and 37264 topping-and-tailing a materials and stone train at Uffington, bound for the Swindon landslip, then moved to the embankment site to record Nos 47121 and 47366 at either end of the engineering train on site.

19 January saw Duane Eddy inducted into the Rock 'n' Roll Hall of Fame in the USA, and on the 30th I made further

'double-ended' trips, this time to snap No 6024 *King Edward I* at Baulking, to the east of Swindon on the Gloucester line as it leaves Swindon station, and to photograph it again as it departed with the 'Red Dragon' Didcot-Cardiff railtour. Another out-and-back day's journey from Didcot to Reading on 7 February garnered more satisfying shots, not least that of No 59001 *Yeoman Endeavour* towards the end of the visit.

Three days of varied interest began on 12 February, when 100 people walked through the Channel Tunnel for charity. HM The Queen would officially open it on 6 May. On the 13th, at 1100, Wantage Camera Club was given a guided tour of Swindon Works for photos, courtesy of Tarmac Swindon Ltd. The members now had access to the 'graveyard' that I had seen in preparation for my article.

Valentine's Day saw my 'Great Escape', as I took early retirement from Barclays Bank – the reverse of a 'Valentine's Day massacre'! My final monthly payment, of £1,402.69 including holiday pay, was received on the 23rd; my first pay, on 23 October 1961 to the end of that month, had been £8.38! I gave £6,000 from my redundancy payment and pension commutation to each of the kids to help them through university. Looking for ongoing employment, I visited the local Post Office Sorting Office in Faringdon. I was told by the Office Manager, who happened to be one of the Bank's customers, that there were no vacancies, but I could stand in for a short period for a girl who was absent with ME. I agreed and finally left exactly ten years later!

Now that I was free, apart from my postman's duties, Paul and I travelled to Crewe on the 16 February, receiving a guided tour of the electric depot. Out of the 24 locos present – largely Class 90s and 86s – I pocketed three cops, Nos 90136, 90126 *Crewe Electric Depot Quality Approved* and 90140. There were 66 on the diesel depot, with '47s' and '31s' proliferating, but none new to me, and 28 on the old Works site, now under the management of ABB (ASEA Brown Boveri), a Swedish/Swiss multinational company. Again, Class 47s were in the majority, and no cops. Happily, photographic opportunities compensated for lack of new numbers. Seven days later I made my way to the Rover Plant in Swindon, accepting an invitation to record the naming of No 47323 *Rover Group Quality Assured*. The dull day did not lead to stunning photographs and the name did nothing to lift my spirits!

Earlier in the year, as my parting shot, I had put another proposal to the Bank for a procedural system improvement. Surprisingly, it too was accepted and I received a £100 reward in March! On 16 March Paul and I made another long trip, this time south, to Exeter St David's, the Dawlish sea wall and Laira depot. By now the Class 50s had ceased normal front-line duties, but one at least was to see further work and it was interesting to see a young lady painstakingly painting the large numbers on No 50033 *Glorious*. Judi undertook a journey to Paddington on 31 March by rail and, taking her camera with her, snapped No 43164 at the buffers on the last day of British Rail.

I April finally heralded Rail Privatisation, with the creation of three rolling stock leasing companies and plans for 25

At Laira depot on 16 March 1994, Denise carefully applies the large numbers to No 50033 *Glorious*.

different franchises, seven initially and a further 18 to follow. It was also the birth of Railtrack. On the 5th I received a financial surprise, with the refund of the Bank's pre-retirement seminar travel costs for both Judi and myself. The 10th saw another trip with Paul, this time to London and Stewarts Lane depot, via brief calls at St Pancras and King's Cross station. While not welcomed with open arms at the depot, we were given freedom to roam and, in glorious weather, the shutters were busy. There were three cops for me – Nos 33040, 73106 and 33211 – and it was interesting to see Nos 60001 *Steadfast* and 60099 *Ben More Assynt*, the first and (very nearly) the last of the class. Sadly, it was disappointing to see the Class 33s in store. With my contributions to Middleton Press in mind, we rounded off the day with brief excursions to Eynsford, Shoreham, Otford and Bat & Ball.

On 22 April I made another visit to a Rover Plant, this time at Longbridge, to interview and photograph in preparation for another magazine article. No 47033 was on site with a

On 22 April 1994 No 47033 begins its journey away from Longbridge Rover with a rake of Cargowaggons to Washwood Heath. Note the old Midland Railway signal box still in use. Sadly, within a few years the site was closed and all had gone.

load ready for the main line, and it was pleasing to see the old Midland Railway signal box still in use in the Works complex. Little did I realise that the whole site would be closed and demolished within a decade!

On 2 May came another visit to Eastleigh with Paul, then to Little Bedwyn to capture Nos 20131 and 20118 on Hertfordshire Railtours' 'The Big E' Paddington-Exeter St David's working. I was at Rover in Swindon on the 9th for the above-mentioned article, and Paul and I were again out and about on the 15th, to East Grinstead, Tonbridge, Three Bridges and '5-minute' visits for Middleton at 11 other locations, before finally ending up at Selhurst (Tennison Road). Being on the former Southern Railway system, most motive power was electric units but there were the occasional locos to add variety.

On 19 May the first freight train ran through the Channel Tunnel; on the 23rd I completed a triple by visiting Rover's Cowley Oxford plant; and the 27th celebrated the opening of the new Ivanhoe route from Leicester to Loughborough, with new stations opening at Syston, Sileby and Barrow-upon-Soar. The first and third were on totally new sites, but I visited all three and both stations in Loughborough on the following day. On the 29th I made what was a nostalgic journey to Peterborough and March, thinking back to the sights there during my steam-days visits. 30 May recorded Leicester City's highest gate of the 1993/94 season, 73,671, against Derby County in the play-off final at Wembley, winning and gaining promotion to the Premiership. On the 31st I was back at Brush, delighted to see the construction of Nos 92006 to 92024 inclusive, then to Tinsley, where I copped just one – No 47361 *Wilton Endeavour* – out of 46 locos present and photographed the unique No 18000, squeezed between walkways inside the shed.

This post-Bank period was becoming truly frenetic, as Paul and I made our way north for another weekend away. Heaton was our first call and I felt sheer delight at the sight of the second loco on shed. I had long wanted to see – and preferably

With its bulk obvious in comparison with No 47375 *Tinsley Traction Depot/Quality Approved*, preserved No 18000 just manages to squeeze between the walkways at Tinsley on 31 May 1994.

photograph – No 08888. The number fascinated me (I don't know why!) and the loco had been absent on all previous visits to the depot. So it was in the camera before anything could prevent me! Two decades later it was preserved on the K&ESR. By comparison, the rest of the day paled into insignificance, but cops of Nos 56131 and 37059 were gratefully received at Thornaby. A break was taken at Thirsk before moving on to Neville Hill and Knottingley depots, the latter presenting me with No 08776, not seen before. We closed the day with time spent at Doncaster, where several of the Class 20s refurbished by and previously seen at RFS were noted. After the overnight stay, 5 June began with a return to Immingham. Despite the repeat visit, I still copped four from 73 – Nos 37707, 56126, 56120 and 56098. Tinsley followed, then Toton, where we were still allowed access despite our permit being for 1600 the previous day! No 31252 was a cop here out of 77, and we ended the day briefly at Derby station.

Our family summer holiday this year was to Corris, in mid-Wales, from 23 to 30 June. The quaint village and countryside had real attraction, but so did the then moribund Corris Railway line. Now 17, Adam had his own ideas and stayed away, but Tammy came with us and she made friends with the daughter of our hosts. Trips were made to the Ffestiniog Railway on the 26th, the Talyllyn on the 29th and Machynlleth on the 30th.

Early in July I was one of the first group of mature students (!) to receive accreditation in Oxfordshire's 'Next Step' course, aimed at helping recent 'out of work' individuals make the 'next step'.

6 July saw the USA release of the film *Forrest Gump*, which included Duane Eddy's *Rebel Rouser* during the chase sequence and on the soundtrack album. Duane and wife Deed went to see the film, unaware of this. Very surprised at hearing it, he then spent some time trying to identify which version had been used! Another of Duane's tracks, *The Trembler*, was featured in the film *Natural Born Killers*, released on 26 August. Duane's *Shazam* was also in the film, but not included on the soundtrack album.

Our Gang's next outing was to Doncaster Works Open Day, on the 10th, when among the delights was the sight of some locos in brand-new freight liveries. Eleven days later Tony Blair became the youngest ever leader of Labour Party, elected in place of John Smith, who had died on 12 May.

Another highlight of the year was an invitation to Peter Best's 40th birthday, on the NYMR on Saturday 23 July. Judi and I had an horrendous journey north, in sweltering heat and traffic chaos on the M42, M6 and other roads as we travelled up on an unusually busy Friday. We were glad to reach our B&B in Sleights for two nights. The train was due to leave Grosmont at 1350, behind USA 'S160' No 2253, Peter's own locomotive, but this failed minutes before departure. Replacement by No 34027 *Taw Valley*, from the nearby engine shed, took a while to organise and the train was late leaving. I had been offered a cab ride up the gradient to Goathland, where I was to rejoin Judi in the coach behind for lunch. Unfortunately, due to the delay, the train was non-stop to Pickering, so I was on the footplate for the whole length of the line. This was fine by me, except that everyone had enjoyed their lunch before Pickering and I then had to be provided with food from what was left!

The final trip of the summer for The Gang was to another Open Day, at Basford Hall yard, Crewe. There was huge variety to see, in perfect weather conditions, and the organisers had taken great care to have the exhibits arranged with photographers in mind, leading to the day being a great success. After the event, we visited the diesel depot and the nearby station for more photographs. At the latter, we were in time to see Nos 33208 and 33116 on Hertfordshire Railtours' 'The Cheshire Cat & Cheshire Kitten' outing from Euston. Our way home was via Buxton and Peak Forest, where it was interesting to view the layout of the area and the locomotives lined up awaiting their turn.

A rare sight on the line beyond Blaenau Ffestiniog: on 27 August 1994 No 31190 brings up the rear of the return Pathfinder Tours' 'Trawsfynydd Trekker II' to Llandudno Junction, with No 31327 on the other end. The tour had originated in York.

27 August was Tammy's 16th birthday. She was volunteering on the FR, and Mum and Dad were asked to join in her birthday celebrations, which we did from 26 to 29 August. The weather was kind and we enjoyed ourselves on the railway, but Tammy's party was not an unmitigated success as she found out something of what it feels like to drink too much! Leicester City's first appearance in the Premiership did not start well, losing three and drawing one from their first four games in August!

The next three months saw several of my articles published. The September-dated *Traction* No 2 had 'God's Wonderful Diesels', an article on Swindon Works in the non-steam era. This included my shot of two 'Westerns' outside the famous A Shop but, sadly, the slide was lost by the magazine and never came back to me! Within days, *Rail* No 235 published 'Crewe is now International', an interview with Dave Spillets, Director and Fleet Manager at Crewe IED about the depot and his role within it. This was followed in October by *Rail* No 236 and an article on Tinsley depot, near Sheffield, and this hectic period continued in November with 'Rail Rovers', an article on Rover Group's use of rail, for *Railway Magazine*.

The death of Dai Woodham was announced on 12 September, a truly sad day for all steam lovers, as he had been 'saviour' of 212 steam locos at Barry, buying them from BR for scrap but then not cutting them until preservationists had raised funds to rescue them. Without him we would not have the preservation movement that is the joy of the 21st century. Another sad death came just nine days later, that of O. S. Nock, a much-celebrated railway author (born 1905).

It was 1 October before Paul and I sallied forth for more 'new' locations and photographs. Brighton was first, with a visit to the station and access to the nearby depot. Six other spots were investigated, exclusively populated by EMUs and one DEMU – No 207102 – before arriving at Dover West Docks. My first visit there, I was keen to see the 1919-vintage station, with its impressive listed architecture and wonderful diamond crossing on the approach to the platforms. Sadly, it had closed just six days before our visit and, although there were trains in two of the platforms, there seemed to be no way that we could reach them. A distance photograph had to suffice. Thankfully, stabled nearby and easily accessible were Nos 47367, with its unofficial *Kenny Cockbird* name, 47270 *Swift*, 47396 and 47395. Our last destination of the day was Broadstairs before our overnight stay in Ramsgate. The next day was another exhausting one, with an early start at Ramsgate station, then on to Minster, Sturry, Canterbury West and East, Wye, Ashford, Gillingham and, finally, Slade Green. All was electric, apart from Nos 47245 *The Institute of Export* and 47365 *Diamond Jubilee* at Ashford and all station stops apart from Ashford and Gillingham depots.

I had long wanted to see this layout at Dover West Docks station, but, by the time I finally arrived on 1 October 1994 the station had closed just seven days earlier! No 1533 stands on the left, with No 3521, both empty stock until needed at Dover Priory.

On 10 October I made the long journey from home to Beckenham, to visit renowned railway photographer R. C. 'Dick' Riley and see what images he had to offer for a forthcoming book. He was very accommodating and a true gentleman.

It was the last time I would see him. A trip to the Junction station briefly afterwards gave me some more of my own images for possible future use. A week later I stayed with Mum and Dad in Birstall, enjoying the sights of No 60007 *Sir Nigel Gresley* and others at Loughborough Central on the 16th. I hopped over to Peterborough on the 17th, where the locos were predominantly Class 31s, then back to Loughborough, to check on the construction progress of the Class 92s (with Nos 92018-33 on view). I then went to Crewe, to witness, by invitation, the formal opening of the wheel lathe facility at the IED. More '92s' were there together with other electrics, including No E27000 in a glorious restored BR green livery. A week later, I drove to Cardiff Canton on the 24th, for an interview with foreman Mike Bates at the Transrail depot and Tony Leaves at the Regional Railways facility on a higher level, in preparation for a magazine article. I was there again on 15 November, going to Margam and the adjacent Gwent Demolition site afterwards, this time with Paul. As was now becoming the norm, I was without cops from 66 locos seen.

Elsewhere, on 9 November the jury was sworn in for the O. J. Simpson trial, for the murder of his ex-wife Nicole and her friend Ron Goldman on 12 June, and on the 19th the first National Lottery draw was made. On the 24th Paul and I had another outing, partly for me to capture images for Middleton, to Bath Spa and locations on the branch to Trowbridge and Westbury. While we employed our cameras along the way, the only locos encountered were Nos 59003 *Yeoman Highlander*, 59104 *Village of Great Elm*, 59001 *Yeoman Endeavour* and 59004 *Yeoman Challenger*. This was to be our last trip of the year.

Wet Wet Wet had the bestselling single, with *Love is All Around*, after it featured in the film *Four Weddings and a Funeral*, and Leicester City closed the year with three matches in five days (unheard of two decades later!), including the highest attendance for the club that season, when 43,789 witnessed a 1-1 draw with Manchester United at Old Trafford. The season was not going well for City, whereas United ended as Premier League runners-up.

I've heard of spare tyres, but…! No 09107 stands at Cardiff Canton Transrail depot on 15 November 1994, with the wheel lathe in the background. Converted from No 08845, the loco was withdrawn in September 2011.

1995 opened with the shock news that Fred West had killed himself on 1 January while in prison, on a charge of multiple murders with his wife Rose. Also dramatic was the earthquake on 17 January in Kobe, Japan, measuring 7.2 on the Richter Scale and leaving nearly 3,000 dead. The same day I took delivery of my second Peugeot 205; costing £2,400, it was a replacement for the one that Adam had written off just before Christmas. Driving home from a night out in Swindon, with his girlfriend in the front and his sister and her boyfriend in the back, he fell asleep at the wheel and ran straight into a 'Keep Left' sign on a roundabout! Happily, none of them was badly injured, apart from Adam's pride and his concern at what I might say. I was not amused!

My first railway outing was back in Leicestershire, on 3 February to Brush (where the Class 92s had reached No 92037), Loughborough Midland and Central stations, and Leicester depot. The following day I began lineside at

Cossington, then moved to Syston. I took the opportunity to photograph the remaining buildings of the old station and reminiscing about my school trips to and from there. The new version was on the opposite side of the tracks, situated on what had been the goods lines. Further nostalgia was to be had at the railway bridge at Thurmaston, but this was limited by new fencing and the growth of bushes along the embankment leading to a far less open feel than of yore. They say you should never go back! Leicester station was on the agenda on my way home, with more nostalgic thoughts and appreciation of how so much had changed, with a car park on the site of the western station sidings.

The original station in Leicester for the Midland Railway was in Campbell Street. Despite being replaced by London Road station, seen in the background, the old entrance gates still stand on 4 February 1995, around 150 years old.

The remains of Syston's station are seen on the same day. From September 1954 to July 1956 I caught my train to school in Loughborough from the platform since lost under the bushes.

20 February was the first outing with Paul in 1995, with locations again dictated by Middleton needs. Using it as a sort of 'park and ride', we twice visited Knockholt, where an amazing coincidence occurred. I was standing on the station footbridge to photograph 4CIGs Nos 1806 and 1879 arriving while Paul remained on the platform, and we both photographed them, without planning, *at precisely the same second* – 09:40:46! Others locations were Hither Green, Orpington and six others before we ended up at Epsom. Again it was all electric, apart from four locos at Hither Green – Nos 73114, recently named *Stewarts Lane Traction Maintenance Depot*, 33046 *Merlin*, 58034 *Bassetlaw* and 73104 *Quadrant*. I took photographs of vandalism at South Merton station and subsequently wrote a letter to *Rail* magazine, with illustration, saying how even Paul and I had felt intimidated at this unstaffed location, so what must lone females or the elderly feel?

Three days later we were out again, by rail this time from Didcot. Via Paddington, Euston and Willesden Junction High

One of the delights of visiting Kensington Olympia on 23 February 1995 was seeing the Eurostar sets passing through. No 3103 is operating as a North Pole-Waterloo empty coaching stock working.

Level we finally arrived at Kensington Olympia. A station that witnessed inter-regional workings, as well as more local duties, we hoped for excitement. We were satisfied with the frequency of trains and their inherent interest, but the delight came in the shape of Nos 3103 and 3104, my first close view of a Eurostar set. I was impressed with its sheer length. Others were seen on the day, not least at North Pole depot, north of Paddington. Going via Clapham Junction on our way back, I took photographs of a derelict platform and its signal box. Other than the Eurostar power cars, my only cop was No 90001 *BBC Midlands Today* at Euston. The month ended with a visit to the GWS at Didcot on the 26th, to see and photograph Nos 60009 *Union of South Africa* and 70000 *Britannia*.

On 1 March I drove Adam to Southampton University for an interview. On the way we detoured to Wootton Bassett to witness No 6024 *King Edward I* on a railtour. The bridge we chose, just north of the old station site, was decidedly cramped with enthusiasts and, with time pressing, we were just about to leave when the train hove into view. I barely managed to squeeze among the throng to capture my record of the event!

On our way to Southampton on 1 March 1995, Adam and I paused at Wootton Bassett to see No 6024 *King Edward I* on an FSS Railtours Swansea-Paddington-Didcot special.

Rarely photographed at Swindon Rover, No 08460 shunts ex-Longbridge Cargowaggons on 12 March 1995. New in August 1958 as No D3575, it carried that old number on the cab side.

My new Peugeot 205 seen in Longcot on 13 March 1995, bought in January for £2,400 to replace the one written off by Adam.

Another day trip, with Paul and Neil, took place on 15 March, to Southampton Central station and Eastleigh. Photographs were the draw for the former, whereas locos at the latter were in greater number. No 60009 was again seen, but this time the diesel with that identity, named *Carnedd Dafydd*.

The April issue of *Railway Magazine* featured 'If Anyone Can Canton Can', Part 1 of my article on Cardiff Canton shed (Part 2 followed in the September issue), and the May *Traction* magazine published my article on Vic Berry's scrapyard. 2 April was another 'Middleton' day for Paul and me in the outskirts of

London, beginning at Strawberry Hill – where we were graced with a cab investigation on new No 465197 – and Chessington North, before eight more stops en route to Wimbledon and Surbiton, where we saw No 37377. Again, everything else had been electric units and photographs were the real satisfaction. One thing I had learned since the end of steam in 1968 was that it is harder to achieve a really satisfying photograph of modern traction. Basically, one must choose the location and composition with care, then place the train within that set-up – not always easy or successful.

A change affecting us all came on 16 April, with 'National Phone Day', when 01 numbers were introduced to our telephone system.

6 May saw the renumbering of Nos 47834 *Firefly* and 47835 *Windsor Castle* to 47798 and 47799, and their renaming to *Prince William* and *Prince Henry* respectively, being repainted into a claret and grey livery for Royal Train duties. The same day was the first of the May Day Bank Holiday, traditionally a three-day Gala extravaganza on the Ffestiniog Railway. As usual, Judi, Tammy and I were in North Wales. Celebrating 50 years since the end of the Second World War, there were guest locos from France, and *Mountaineer* was in a grey First World War livery, with the number 1265 and sans name. With mostly near perfect weather conditions, I covered much ground over the whole railway, either by rail or on foot, and was satisfied with the results, not least capturing the 'foreign invaders'! On the 17th I was back at Brush, for the naming of No 47146 *Loughborough Grammar School*. It rained, not only a nuisance for the masters and young boys standing for their portraits, but also less than ideal for me, both photographically and for the fact that I had attended Loughborough *College* School. There was always 'friendly rivalry' between the two, and I still felt it!

Paul and I were back together on 21 May, beginning at Bristol. After a brief spell on Temple Meads platforms, we again obtained access to Bath Road depot, blissfully unaware that it was under threat. It all seemed so important and permanent. Thirty locos were present, with Class 47s and 08s the majority and nothing new for me. After St Philips Marsh, we were off to Cardiff Canton, both depots, which boasted 48 locos and, magically, a cop of No 37408 *Loch Rannoch*. It was also good to see aged Nos 20087 and 20165 on shed. Further west, Margam brought us 23 locos, Barry hosted just three, together with two HST sets passing, the Newport sidings adjacent to the station had seven, and finally Didcot gave us 27, including ten HST power cars. Just one cop all day, but the sun shone brightly for our cameras.

With my next book being a 'Past & Present' look at the Ffestiniog and Welsh Highland Railways, I was back in the Principality on 4 June, armed with a collection of 'past' photographs. Staying at a B&B in Penrhyndeudraeth run by Paul and Hilary Davies, I was out and about accompanied by Paul. It seems I was fated to have a 'Pauline' companion! We both had a great time seeking out the various locations and identifying the 'footsteps' of the original photographers. I stayed until the 10th and for the most part the weather played ball … and I even captured a nuclear flask train at Blaenau Ffestiniog behind Nos 31134 and 31319. The July issue of *Railway Magazine* contained my review, with photos, of the May Bank Holiday FR Gala.

Another scene not frequently photographed: at the Trawsfynydd terminal for nuclear flasks the latest consist waits for its journey north on 10 June 1995. The last train ran to/from here on 10 August.

22 July was again something different, when the GWS at Didcot put on a 24-hour steaming event. I was there at 2345 capturing shots of locos positioned and some in steam, lit by spotlights. A little awkward with the tripod and some guesswork as to shutter settings, I was pleased to practise something out of the ordinary. Nos 1466, 6106 and 70000 *Britannia* stood proudly in the main yard outside the shed building.

Between 31 July and 5 August we were back to Corris for the annual holiday, with Adam this time. The sun beat down for much of the time and during one walk towards Aberllefeni and a rest by the river, we attempted to shield our heads from the midges by turning fern fronds into caps! Back home, on the 15th I drove to Ford's motor plant in Bridgend for more data for my upcoming magazine article.

Back in the 1st Division, after relegation in May, Leicester City began the new season moderately well, with two wins and a draw in the first four matches in August.

Visited for an article for *Railway Magazine*, the Swansea Ford plant is seen on 15 August 1995 as No 09105 shunts empties into the loading bay.

Chapter 3
1995-2000

The September 1995 issue of *Railway Magazine* published my short piece on the progress of restoring No 4277, an ex-GWR 'Heavy Freight' 2-8-0T, by enthusiast Peter Best. As that edition hit the news-stands I was again in North Wales, taking more present-day photographs for my forthcoming book on the FR and WHR. Future publication was also echoed in my visit to Ford's Plant in Dagenham on the 12th, where I was pleased to see two ex-BR '03s', in bright blue Ford livery.

The first truly spotting trip was on the 17th, at Old Oak Common depot and on to Willesden, Acton, Gunnersbury, Kew Gardens, Richmond, Kensington Olympia, Hayes &

Another visit to a Ford plant for a *Railway Magazine* article saw me at Dagenham on 12 September 1995. Nos 2 (D2280) and 4 (D2051) were on duty, both ex-BR shunters.

Harlington and Didcot. The mix of diesel, electric and London Underground stock was captured on film, compensating for the total lack of cops. The most unusual sight was a train of mixed on-track plant behind a Unimog 1650 in the down main platform at Hayes & Harlington during an engineer's possession of the line.

On the 19th I was back at the FR for more 'past and present' work, travelling home on the following day via a stop for photographs at Leominster station. The 23rd saw me at the GWS shed, Didcot, to witness the naming of No 47524 *Res Gestae*. The first Rail Express Systems locomotive so adorned, the intention was to name others with titles beginning with 'Res.', but the plan was not long sustained! The operator was later subsumed within EWS, and No 47524 was withdrawn from Crewe Diesel Depot less than a year later, on 6 July 1996, but then reinstated on 1 August! Elsewhere, the Robin Hood Line from Nottingham opened on the 24th, with two Class 58s first along the line to check clearances. Four days later, Bristol Bath Road depot ceased operation when operator Great Western Trains transferred all work to St Philip's Marsh depot. Once such an important engine shed, it seemed strange to see it disappear.

After 18 months of excitement and travels post-Barclays, the latter part of 1995 and into 1996 showed a slowing down in trips. My habits had changed before – after the 1968 end of steam and my return to railways in 1981 – and they were transmogrifying again. Not only was the focus now on photography rather than 'number crunching', but I was also attracted to the work on the main lines under engineering possession, and this aspect would assume greater attention over coming years. Moreover, the assumption of my new career as a postman in Faringdon was also playing its part. Up at 0400 to start work at 0500 and not home until around 1000, I was somewhat exhausted after walking/cycling for around 4 miles, delivering to more than 350 houses. With the morning hours being eaten up, it left less time to contemplate long-distance outings.

October saw me back in Leicestershire on the 11th with a one-day trip to Brush and Rothley station on the GCR. Showing versatility, the former was in the process of creating brand-new shunting locomotives for Hong Kong's railways and refurbishing some of the Channel Tunnel Class 20s that I had seen at RFS and, in the process, generating a new sub-class. Nos 20304 (ex-20120) and 20305 (ex-20095) were mid-rebuild in the Works, while earlier conversion No 20302 (ex-20084) was out on the Great Central undergoing testing. Thereafter, I was only to venture once beyond local Oxfordshire lines until Christmas, when Paul and I had a brief day trip to Westbury and Frome, where we witnessed the unusual sight of No 158842 overshooting the platform and having to reverse into the station!

After my stint distributing the Christmas post and collecting tips (cash and gifts from grateful customers), the family returned 'home' to spend the festivities with Mum and

Pounding out of Loughborough Central, with the sharp frost clinging to the telegraph support wires and enlivening the loco's exhaust, No 46229 *Duchess of Hamilton* heads for Leicester North on 29 December 1995.

Dad. I escaped briefly to have a look at Leicester depot on Christmas Eve, which housed five Class 60s and No 08473, then on the 29th to brave the frost and icy conditions to capture images of the GCR, including No 46229 *Duchess of Hamilton* exiting Loughborough Central and passing Woodthorpe with frost still clinging to the supporting wires of the telegraph poles.

No doubt in decidedly warmer climes, Duane Eddy travelled to California during December to record for the soundtrack of the film *Broken Arrow*, which would star John Travolta and Christian Slater. Closer to home, Leicester City hovered around the upper reaches of the 1st Division and finished the year on 23 December with a 2-2 draw away at Grimsby Town.

1996 began with the merger of ABB Transportation and Daimler Benz on 1 January, creating Adtranz, affecting what was left of Crewe Works. It was to be the 22nd before I was out with my camera, recording progress on the Swindon & Cricklade Railway at Blunsdon and Hayes Knoll, the two termini of the developing private railway that was aiming to recreate something of the long-lost Midland & South Western Junction Railway. Eight days later I was recording yet more work being undertaken at Brush, including remedial efforts on relatively new Nos 92002 *H. G. Wells* and 92006 *Louis Armand*.

On 4 February South West Trains was the first company to run a privatised train under the new regime, the 0510

Looking like the doors of a DeLorean DMC-12 car, J. W. Plant's Akerman EW130, a 688B 360 on-track-plant machine, works with a sister machine during track renewals at Compton Beauchamp on 21 January 1996. No 37222 stands in the background.

Twickenham-Waterloo. The 9th saw an IRA ceasefire end with the Docklands bombing in London's Canary Wharf district, killing two and causing more than £85 million worth of damage; and on the 24th the first three private trainload freight companies were launched at Marylebone station. Specifically Loadhaul, Mainline and Transrail, each had distinctive liveries and logos under the auspices of North & South Railways. This was later renamed English, Welsh & Scottish Railways (EW&SR) on 25 April, with the iconic 'three beasties' logo, designed by *Rail* reader Tom Connell. Meanwhile Paul and I had made another day trip, this time to South Wales, calling at Cardiff Cathays depot – full of on-track plant – and stations at Rhiwbina, Whitchurch, Radyr, Taffs Well and Pontypridd. Of interest was the layout at Radyr, which was shortly to be remodelled, the diminutive and utilitarian signal box at Heath Junction, and the delightful 'stub' semaphores and glorious 'Walnut Tree' signal box at Taffs Well.

A derailment and collision of a TPO at Rickerscote, near Stafford, on 8 March resulted in one postal worker dead and 19 injured. This was the first serious crash since Railtrack had been formed, but it would not be the last. The following day, George Burns died (born 1896, and just six weeks into his 100th year), and on the 13th unemployed former shopkeeper Thomas Hamilton walked into Dunblane Primary School in Scotland and opened fire, killing 16 infant school pupils and one teacher before fatally shooting himself.

Through a fellow member of Wantage Camera Club, I became friendly with Peter Best who, as mentioned earlier, was restoring ex-GWR No 4277. I was delighted and honoured to be asked to be his photographer for the rebirth of the loco and its first appearance in steam since withdrawal by BR in July 1964. Travelling to Bridgnorth on the SVR with his lady, Anthea, on 21 March, I was informed that I was driving too fast for her comfort, but I was keen to reach our goal and see the loco. I waited patiently as the loco raised sufficient steam to slowly make the first moves under its own power. It was emotional to see this once proud GWR loco alive once more. While waiting

The first time back in steam since withdrawal in 1964, No 4277 reverses out of the shed yard at Bridgnorth on 21 March 1996.

I took the opportunity to snap other locos around us in the Bridgnorth shed yard.

In the 'opposite direction', life was taken from the Gwendraeth Valley branch when Celtic Energy's Cwmmawr coal plant closed on 29 March and the primary work for the cut-down '08s', seen earlier at Pantyffynon, disappeared.

On 2 April I was back at the Rover Plant in Swindon, this time by invitation to photograph the brand-new Hi-cube wagons, looking very smart in their maroon livery, specifically ordered to replace the Cargowaggons for the motor traffic between there and Longbridge. The next two-dayer with Paul acting as chauffeur began on 23 April as we travelled north to Crewe. The Diesel Depot was first, where 61 locos greeted us, predominantly Class 47s. A small handful of '37/4s' were also present, and from these I copped No 37421 *The Kingsman*. There were 41 locos on the IED, all electrics apart from 11 diesels, which included Nos D172 *Ixion* (the former 46035 and 97403), D1842 and a cluster of six '20s'. Of the electrics, I copped four '92s' that had escaped me at Brush. Adtranz Works housed a wide variety of 37 examples of differing types, including the first manufacture of a replacement HST cab. After a while at Crewe station – where I copped No 37413 *Loch Eil Outward Bound* – we made our way to Chester, where we stayed overnight.

Day two began at Chester station, where Nos 37418, 37415 and 31233 were the only locos among units. After Mickle Trafford, where the signal box merited special attention, Shotton presented both Low Level and High Level stations, giving us scope for a variety of views. Thereafter we inspected eight of the locations on the branch, including Wrexham General, before reaching Shrewsbury, where we were met by No 47524 *Res Gestae*, seen earlier being named at Didcot. In mainly sunny weather, our camera shutters worked overtime.

In the May issue of *Railway Magazine* I had the whole page of reviews, and both supply from publishers and magazine placement was again picking up, to around five or six monthly. 5 May saw both my fifth book published, *British Railways Past & Present: The Ffestiniog Railway*, and Leicester City's last match of the season. Winning 1-0 away to Watford, they went into the play-offs fifth, later beating Crystal Palace 2-1 in front of 73,573 at Wembley and gaining a return to the Premiership. During the season, three players joined who were to become influential to the club – Steve Claridge from Birmingham City, Neil Lennon from Crewe Alexandra, and Muzzy Izzet from Chelsea.

My next outing with Paul was on 4 June, by road to Stewarts Lane depot by prior arrangement. Forty-two locos were present on shed, predominantly Class 33s and 73s, but also a handful of '37s' and Nos 47774 *Poste Restante*, 47484 *Isambard Kingdom Brunel* and 60001 *Steadfast*. Again blessed with fine, sunny weather – something we were becoming used to – we both took full advantage to add to our photographic libraries. A visit to nearby Wandsworth Road station was brief, due to a rather dodgy-looking character lurking around close by us, but we did see Nos 37037, 37042, 60073 *Cairn Gorm* and

73119 *Kentish Mercury* on the main line, and I captured my first colour slide of a full Eurostar train, with the iconic Battersea Power Station in the background. The day ended with a spotting period at Didcot ... and no cops!

Seen from Wandsworth Road station footbridge on 4 June 1996, Eurostar No 3002 heads away from London as the 1523 Waterloo-Paris Nord express. To the left, No 60073 *Cairn Gorm* climbs from Stewarts Lane shed.

Other than an out-and-back to Great Bedwyn to capture Nos 37057 *Viking* and 37051 *Merehead* — both resplendent in their new EW&S livery — on their way with guests to a celebratory event at Foster Yeoman's Somerset headquarters on 21 June, there was nothing away from home until 13 July. By then the July issue of *Railway Magazine* had published my 'Ford by Rail' article; and on the 5th Dolly the sheep, the first mammal to be successfully cloned from an adult cell, was born at the Roslin Institute in Midlothian, Scotland. Duane Eddy's latest album, *Ghostriders*, was released by Curb Records in early July in the States, but there was a considerable delay before it found release in the UK. It made Duane one of the few artists to release a new album (as distinct from compilations or re-releases) in five separate decades.

Two years after his 'birthday bash' on the NYMR, Peter Best arranged another special day out, on 13 July on the West Somerset Railway, to which Judi and I were invited. This time utilising his newly restored No 4277, the loco performed faultlessly and the day was most enjoyable. I escaped from the train briefly at Williton to take photographs ... and not missing my meal! Judi also snapped, but from the train. We had driven to the event and popped into Bishops Lydeard on the way to Minehead, noting Nos D2205 and 34046 *Braunton*. The shed at Williton formally opened the week after our visit, but already on site were Nos D3462, 08850, D9526, D2119, D7523 and D7017.

19 July saw the 1996 Summer Olympics begin in Atlanta, United States. Eight days later there was a bombing at the Centennial Olympic Park that killed one and injured 111.

August saw the publication of my latest book, *British Railways Past & Present: The Ffestiniog and Welsh Highland Railways*, including the nascent plans for the rebuilding of the latter. Between 9 and 18 August I spent time at the Swindon & Cricklade Railway, walking between Blunsdon and Hayes Knoll and recording the current status for posterity. Judi and I were back visiting the FR from 25 to 28 August, for Tammy's 18th birthday, and on the latter date the Prince and Princess of Wales were granted a divorce. The month ended with a day trip to Bath with Judi, where I was intrigued to see a floral design in a local park in the shape of an 0-6-0T steam locomotive! Back in the Premiership, Leicester City had a new manager, Martin O'Neill, who was to be very successful for and with the club.

My first major outing of September was a day trip to South Wales with Paul on the 22nd, beginning with the stabling point immediately west of Newport station. Viewed from the adjacent road and car park, it housed eight Class 37s, including Nos 37901 and 37902, together with Nos 09015, 09107, 47258 and 60096 *Ben Macdui*. The old engine shed at Barry was now home to just wagons, so it was a pleasure to renew acquaintance with

Cardiff Canton depots, South Wales & West on an upper level and the Transrail shed on the lower ground. The stand-out at the latter was No 47712 *Dick Whittington* in a gloriously shiny black-lined livery. Blessed with warm early-autumn sunshine, we savoured the delights of Margam shed and the wagon depot, Gwent Demolition and Severn Tunnel Junction station before returning home, having recorded 113 locos and one cop – No 56121 at Margam. Three days later I was back at Didcot, by invitation, to witness the arrival, by rail for the last stretch of the journey, of No 4073 *Caerphilly Castle*, sent to the GWS by the NRM for safe-keeping and possible eventual restoration.

On 23 September the Willesden Royal Mail Distribution Centre began operations, covering the UK for the Railnet system. Sadly, it became a case of the best-laid plans…! The 30th saw the unveiling of Great Western Trains' new green and ivory livery. On 13 October Beryl Reid died (born 1919), and on the 23rd O. J. Simpson's civil trial began in Santa Monica, California.

26/27 October were the dates for a 'Vintage Weekend' mini-gala on the FR, and I attended as a volunteer, manning the crossing to Minffordd yard, trying to prevent the visiting hoards from dicing with death. I also enjoyed time further up the line and savoured the sights of varied 'double-heading' over the two days.

The November issue of *Railway Magazine* contained my article 'The Redland Story', which sought to show behind-the-scenes views of the quarry outlet facility alongside the Midland Main Line at Mountsorrel. But trumping this was a trip for Judi and me to Plymouth on the 22nd. With complimentary 1st Class return tickets from Swindon, we were treated to the naming of No 43197 *Railway Magazine Centenary 1897-1997* in the presence of the editorial team. No prizes for guessing why this power car was chosen! The name was shortened to *The Railway Magazine* for 3½ years from February 2001.

My outings ended in December with a visit to what remained of 19 Shop at Swindon Works on the 9th, where some loco restoration was still under way, including Nos 4110

It is not often that you receive a phone call from a company to witness a derailment and be the only person on site to photograph it! This was the state of No 47365 *Diamond Jubilee* at Swindon Rover on 18 November 1996.

The team photo for the naming at Plymouth of No 43197 *Railway Magazine Centenary 1897-1997* on 22 November 1996. The RM team, kneeling, are Colin Marsden, Nick Pigott and Chris Milner.

Judi's ticket from Swindon for the naming of the HST at Plymouth.

For use on Great Western Trains only.

First Class Travel Pass   No. C9

0 0 0 7 9 0

Valid without an Identity Card for one single/return journey on or before expiry date shown below.

Holder's name MRS J STRETTON

Between SWINDON

and PYMOUTH   via GWT

Issued at SWINSWN by   Expiry date 30 NOV 1996

Great Western

and 9682, thence to Blunsdon to check on progress with the developing private Swindon & Cricklade Railway.

1997 proved to be an eventful year. The nature of my outings was changing, with concentration shifting from shed-bashing to trying to keep pace with the developments post-privatisation, including railway engineering works. Moreover, the face of our railway was morphing by leaps and bounds into new companies, with their own liveries; lines were closing; new locos/units were appearing or being ordered; there were unusual choices of motive power; and even a line reopening in North Wales! An early indication came on 6 January when Richard Branson took over the cross-country routes as he launched Virgin Trains, complete with a brand-new red livery with his large 'V' logo. A month later, at Leicester on 10 February, Midland Mainline revealed its teal and orange colour scheme.

On 14 January I made a rare trip to North Wales by rail, from Swindon via Crewe and Llandudno Junction, to visit the FR, maximising photographic opportunities on the way. After an overnight stay in Penrhyndeudraeth, the initial goal was achieved on the following day by seeing unrestored ex-South African Garratts Nos 138 and 143 at Dinas, on the outskirts of Blaenau Ffestiniog. Thence to Minffordd yard for *Linda* shunting

The WHR's Funky diesel exits the goods shed at Dinas on 15 January 1997 and, in the presence of the supporting Millennium Commission, breaks the banner to launch the next step, rebuilding to Rhyd Ddu by 2000.

the Garratts' water tanks, and on to the Welsh Highland at Dinas, 4 miles from Caernarfon on the emerging WHR. Here the Millennium Commission was to formally confirm its involvement in the restoration project, with speeches and the resident WHR Funky diesel breaking a banner proudly proclaiming the intention of reaching Rhyd Ddu (mid-way to Porthmadog) by 2000. The return home was from Bangor, giving a glorious round-trip for the two days.

More excitement was had during 25/26 January, when the 100-year-old road bridge over the site of Uffington station was demolished courtesy of oxyacetylene cutters. Being allowed on site as the bridge deck and two sides (held upright by cranes) were attacked was indeed a great privilege and gave me many unique photographs.

A quick out-and-back with Paul to Bicester North on 1 February, to witness Nos 33051 *Shakespeare Cliff* and 33116 *Hertfordshire Railtours* on Pathfinder Tours' 'The Crompton Crescendo', en route from Bristol to London Bridge, was

The centenarian Uffington bridge, built in 1897, is seen on 25 January 1997 with two-thirds of its decking cut away and the last section ready to be cut. Note some protection for the main-line rails beneath.

followed by a weekend's 'jolly' a week later. Travelling by rail via Woking, Clapham Junction, Waterloo and Elmers End, we explored Addiscombe station, which was earmarked for closure just three months later. Our return was through London Bridge, Mitcham Junction and Wimbledon, for another very satisfying excursion.

With weeks left to operate as a heavy rail terminus, Addiscombe has few passengers for No 466010 on 8 February 1997 for its next trip as the 1343 to Elmers End, grandly titled 'Three Counties Express'!

The next day we were back on rubber tyres for a trip south to Eastleigh and Southampton, once more joined by Neil. Among several delights was viewing the latter town's Freightliner yard and stabling point and the sight of elderly No 08077, celebrating its 42nd birthday in service. 10 February witnessed the arrival of No 3440 *City of Truro* at, and its positioning within, the new Retail Outlet Village in Swindon, to much local interest. On the 18th I was 'down south' again, still playing for the Bank's ten-pin bowling team despite having been retired for nearly three years. The venue was in Branksome and I spent time before the match at the station, another virgin location for me.

5 March saw me with Paul and Neil at new and/or rarely visited locations, with a day trip by rail from Didcot via Paddington to GOBLIN (the Gospel Oak-Barking Line, which

From being the first steam loco to reach 100mph to incarceration within Swindon's Retail Outlet Village is a real come-down. No 3440 *City of Truro* is newly in position, with building works still going on around it, on 10 February 1997.

was later electrified in 2017). After a day of diesel and electric power, including Nos 90145 at Barking and 33030 at Gospel Oak, our return was via detours to Kentish Town, St Pancras and King's Cross stations.

Four days later, the new InterCity West Coast franchise began, initially granted for a 15-year period, to be operated by Virgin Trains. Our next outing was on the 11th, returning east to the Metropolis and including locations south and north of the Thames. East Croydon was the first destination, direct from Oxford, followed by Norwood Junction and London Bridge, before we travelled under the river to New Southgate, a station that has had six incarnations since opening in 1850. Returning south, St Pancras was next, then once more under the Thames to Vauxhall and Clapham Junction before home. I collected 75 loco numbers but, again, no cops.

Reverting to steam, I journeyed on 15 March to the Buckinghamshire Railway Centre, Quainton Road, which had been well known to me during my time in Amersham. There No 9466 was in steam operating shuttles, and the weather was kind. It was also interesting to see what progress had been made on some of the other locos there. Another step in my recent shift of railway emphasis came on the 17th, when I underwent training for PTS (Personal Track Safety) certification at Westerleigh, east of Bristol, to enable me to walk the main line photographing men and machines. The day included a trip to Chipping Sodbury to train and test us on tolerances and behaviour at the lineside. You never quite become used to the sensation of being on the ground just 4 feet from an express travelling at up to 100mph!

A training session in the cess at Chipping Sodbury on 18 March 1997, showing just how close one is permitted to stand to a train travelling at up to 100mph. No 43012 speeds south as the 1000 Paddington-Swansea express.

On 21 March Rev Wilbert Awdry of Thomas the Tank Engine fame died.

April's *Rail Express* No 11 included a five-page article featuring my profile of Stewarts Lane depot, and 8 April was another exciting day. Once more with Paul and Neil, we were again travelling directly by rail from Oxford to East Croydon for a change of service to Blackfriars, then Barking and on to Shoeburyness. Another trip around the stabling point yielded more photographs of ageing EMUs before the return journey, which took in Upminster, Romford and Liverpool Street. While most motive power was in the shape of units, we did see 47 'locos', including a handful of Eurostar power cars en route. One week later, I was back inside the old 19 Shop of Swindon Works. Now visiting regularly, I was given free rein and was pleased to capture work on three ex-GWR 'Manors', Nos 7812 *Erlestoke Manor*, 7821 *Ditcheat Manor* and 7828 *Odney Manor*. I was also keeping an eye on the construction of the new bridge at Uffington, and on the 21st was back on site to complete a 'past and present' view of the structure. On the 30th I was at Hungerford to snap what I thought to be my last view of No 59003 – now devoid of name – on its way to Germany as part of the 1105 Merehead-Acton special working.

6 April was eventful for Leicester City. Reaching the final of the Coca-Cola Cup, the match, in front of 76,757 fans at Wembley, was against Middlesbrough. With the final score 1-1 (Heskey scoring for Leicester), a replay was fixed for 10 days later at Hillsborough, Sheffield. Another tight game was nearing the end when Steve Claridge latched onto the end of a Leicester attack, slightly misjudged his kick and shinned the ball into the net! Another trophy for City.

1 May was another exciting day, but for a totally different reason, as the nation went to the polls for the General Election. It was to be a seismic shift in British politics, with Tony Blair winning for Labour and becoming the UK's next Prime Minister. The following day I was again in North Wales for five days, enjoying another of the FR's wonderful Bank Holiday galas. Sadly, on the 3rd, plans for a 'Ffestiniog in the '60s' celebration went awry as *Linda* failed at Tan-y-Bwlch with big-end problems

while operating the 1155 Blaenau Ffestiniog-Porthmadog service. She was side-lined in Dduallt station until a full rescue could be mounted. On the 6th, my last day, I paused at Minffordd to photograph *Sea Lion*, *Woto* and *Conway Castle* triple-heading an 'Island Express' up the line.

The West Midlands had largely been ignored of late, but this was rectified on 14/15 May with Paul and Neil, beginning at Worcester (Shrub Hill) and its delightful array of semaphores. The top and bottom of the Lickey Incline briefly saw us at Barnt Green and Bromsgrove before we settled for a slightly longer stay at Droitwich, with its own variety of mechanical signals. Bromsgrove was revisited on the second day, followed by my first examination of the Redditch terminus, then more semaphores at Henley-in-Arden and Hatton before winding up at Leamington Spa. There was nothing in the way of great delights, but a pleasing selection of fresh locations for our cameras.

19 May was a very sad day for me, as Dad died. He had suffered an aortic rupture five years earlier but had survived. He was not the same man thereafter and, thankfully, the end was swift and he was not in pain.

31 May was the end date for two branch lines in the South East, so the Gang set sail from Oxford behind No 47805, travelling via Willesden to West Croydon. Opened in 1839, the station was the terminus of a line from Wimbledon, but, lightly used, it was to be converted for use by Tramlink. We travelled the line to Mitcham Junction and alighted to make our way to Addiscombe, via Elmers End. Opened on 1 May 1864 as Croydon (Addiscombe Road) and becoming just Addiscombe in February 1926, this once proud terminus had become run down and was to become another casualty of the onward march of Tramlink in the Croydon area. Paul did not join us on the shuttle rides from and to Elmers End, preferring to see what was operating on the Hayes branch. Addiscombe station buildings later became derelict and were demolished in 2001. Our homeward journey took in London Bridge, King's Cross and Euston.

1 June 1997 saw Ashchurch for Tewkesbury station

reopened, on the site of the one that had closed in 1971, but as an unstaffed facility with a basic waiting shelter on the two new platforms and without the architectural majesty of its forebear. This event passed me by at the time, but became important to me after my move to Ashchurch in 2007. Another new event was a speculative inter-regional service between Rugby and Gatwick Airport stations. On a gloriously sunny 2 June I travelled to Rugby to capture this new venture and the Class 319s operating it. Another innovation captured by my camera was at Bristol Temple Meads on 13 June, for the public launch of the RAC's folding bike racks in the compartment of an HST. Another good idea later abandoned!

28/29 June was to be a short weekend outing for the 'Gang of Three' – to Scotland. Setting out late evening on the Friday, we called in at Crewe, Preston and Carlisle stations before settling down in the car park of a service station just north of the border. We were rudely awakened some time later when the car behind which we had parked reversed without warning

Trying to show just how easy it is to take a bike on a train, the young lady poses at Bristol Temple Meads during the public launch of the RAC folding bike on 13 June 1997. The HST had special racks fitted inside.

and without looking! Other than the shock, thankfully there was no real damage! Motherwell depot finally allowed us access after 'polite discussions' before we boarded a train for Whifflet – opened in December 1992 – then from there to Glasgow Central, passing Mossend and Polmadie depots en route. After an out-and-back trip aboard ageing No 101690 to Paisley Canal – opened on its current site in July 1990 – Glasgow Queen Street was used for a trip to Edinburgh Waverley. More elderly units were committed to film before a journey back westwards and a visit to Carstairs prior to overnight accommodation.

We were in position at Motherwell on the early morning of 28 June 1997 to witness No 101692 in Caledonian livery forming the 0720 service to Cumbernauld, a newly introduced service. Both cars of the unit were 40 years old.

Sunday 29th dawned with access gained to Shields depot – with prior permission obtained for this tightly guarded facility – then we savoured nostalgia at Corkerhill depot. A final visit to Motherwell depot – housing 45 locos – preceded the long trek south and congestions on the M6.

My seventh book was published on 15 July, *The Counties of*

England Past and Present: Leicestershire and Rutland, my first non-railway book to achieve publication. It compared views of the two counties over the 50 years since the Second World War, with me again attempting to stand in the shoes of the original photographers. I learned many interesting and surprising things about my 'native land', not least where the phrase 'to paint the town red' came from! The book was greeted by full-page articles in both the *Leicester Mercury* and *Rutland Times*. My other non-railway manuscript, a biography of Duane Eddy, remains unpublished.

The first issue of *Rail Infrastructure* magazine appeared this month, including as its first article my feature on Westerleigh Training Centre. Judi and I enjoyed a day out at the Gloucestershire Warwickshire Steam Railway on 20 July, where Nos 47105 (diesel) and 45596 *Bahamas* (steam) were on duty; then another on 2 August in Bath, where I grabbed pictures at both stations. There were no other meaningful journeys until our next family holiday at the end of August.

This year the family holiday was on the canals. From 31 August to 6 September we journeyed aboard narrow boat *Matador* around the Warwickshire Ring, 106 miles with 115 locks. Despite some indifferent weather at times, we enjoyed the sights at Birmingham's Gas Street Basin and the experience of the flight of locks at Hatton.

Adam recalls: 'Sitting on the back of the boat in the pouring rain while you lot relaxed inside. Consoling myself only with illicit cigarettes. Also, I think that was the year Tam was sunbathing on the roof, and I deliberately ran the boat under a low-hanging tree to thwack her with the branches!'

Tammy's view is somewhat more positive: 'It was awesome! I remember listening to Banco de Gaia's *Drippy* playing loud on the boat's stereo, a very appropriate track especially when we were approaching a tunnel! Otherwise, I seem to remember that Adam and I did all the locks and it was much more fun for all because us "kids" were all grown up!'

Over the first three days I saw four electric locos and a similar number of HST sets, but no cops! While on this holiday we heard of the death of Diana, Princess of Wales. We stopped the boat and joined the national minute's silence at 1100 and Judi was reduced to tears, saying, 'And I don't even know her!'

September's *Railway Magazine* had my short piece on the FR's May 'Festival of Steam' gala; the 12th saw me join *Rail Infrastructure* editor Roger Butcher for visits to Brush and the Redland quarry outlet facility at Mountsorrel; and on the 19th seven were killed at Southall in a collision between an HST and a freight train.

October began with *Steam Classic* printing my article on the developing private Swindon & Cricklade Railway. My first outing was not until the 11th, when I travelled north to Shotton to participate in a charter at the steelworks, using No 92203 *Black Prince* to recreate the last steam-hauled iron ore train from Birkenhead Docks 30 years earlier. The day held much promise, but did not start well, with the '9F' off the rails with its rear driving wheels! There was great discussion as to how to re-rail the 86-ton monster, but it was finally achieved, delaying the proposed run-pasts for a considerable period. The rain did not help, but everyone there seemed to enjoy their time and many reels of film were exposed.

On a sodden 11 October 1997 at Shotton steelworks, No 92203 *Black Prince*, now back on the rails after an earlier problem, presents itself during a photo charter commemorating its last duty here 30 years earlier. Note the raindrops in the puddles.

The following day, 12 October, I made the short journey to the Welsh Highland Railway, ready for an upcoming event. This was also the day that Buxton closed as a fuelling and servicing point, the work going to nearby Peak Forest.

The 13th was to be the formal opening of the WHR from Dinas to Caernarfon, by the Lady Mayor of the latter town. I took photographs of the inaugural train as well as slipping over to Boston Lodge on the FR for a glimpse of No 4415, the oldest British diesel locomotive, which had recently been repatriated from Mauritius. Public trains on the WHR began on the 14th, on which date I briefly stopped at Leominster for photographs on my way home. I was back in the Principality later in the month, for the WHR Open Weekend and the FR's 'Vintage Weekend' on the 25th/26th, travelling north on the Friday. There was much to see and record, including the FR's fabled gravity train and my first sight of a Parry People Mover, inside Boston Lodge shed.

In November I was fortunate to have two more published articles: *Rail Infrastructure* No 3 incorporated one on Redland Aggregates at Mountsorrel, and *Railway Magazine* had 'Swindon Works – 1997 Style', looking at Swindon Locomotive, Carriage & Wagon Works Ltd, a four-year-old small private company carrying on the skills and traditions of the GWR within the old Works' 19 Shop. On 11 November Railfreight Distribution was sold to EWS, mirroring other areas of the newly privatised railway swiftly changing hands. In this case, Ed Burkhardt, founder of Wisconsin Central Ltd in America, galvanised the constituent parts of the new empire into a real driving force. Sadly, his tenure was not to be a long one. My only trip this month was on the 12th, when I was again inside the Brush workshops photographing the locos on which the company was working.

December brought another first for me, this time a short story and poem in *Sigma* No 2, the magazine of the Faringdon Writers' Circle, of which I had been a member for some time. My first distance outing was on the 14th, to Bitton for a visit to the Avon Valley Railway. Apart from making an acquaintance with the railway at and around Bitton, I particularly wanted to photograph the visiting ex-SR 'M7' No 30053. I had always liked the class and to see this one in steam, working top-and-tail with ex-GWR No 9600 was a joy in the winter sunshine. It was my last trip of the year.

Once again, Leicester City transferred out their leading goal-scorer from the previous year, this time Steve Claridge, who scored the winning goal in the Coca-Cola Cup. City was out of this Cup in the first round without him, losing 3-1 away to Grimsby Town. Incoming, however, was Robbie Savage from Crewe Alexandra in July, and he would go on to be a major element in the team until his departure a decade later.

To open 1998, the January issue of *Railway World* continued its four-page feature, 'Take Four', featuring photographs by a single photographer and a potted biography – and this time it was my turn! The rest of the month saw the deaths of three of my favourite people: Frank Muir on the 4th (born 1920); Sonny Bono on the 5th (born 1935); and Carl Perkins on the 19th (born 1932). On the 24th I was issued with a permit from the Laing-GrantRail joint venture, granting me track access between Princes Risborough and Bicester North for Chiltern Railways' 'Evergreen' work, and I was out on the 26th taking advantage of that at Princes Risborough and near Haddenham, photographing the track work towards the addition of a second line.

February saw the publication of my latest book – *Illustrated History of Leicester's Railways* – which did what it said on the cover! The month

My Track Access Permit for the 'Evergreen' project between Princes Risborough and Bicester North, granted to me on 24 January 1998.

also witnessed the change in my railway 'career', with more of my time spent recording infrastructure work than spotting or being out on trips. Looking back, I was fortunate in my timing. I was still enjoying everything, but now had the added spice of being granted permission to enter areas and locations that were beyond public access. As far as I could judge, I was unique in obtaining so many otherwise unseen pictures.

On the 1st I was at Bourton, east of Swindon, Haddenham & Thame (for work on a new platform) and Chinnor. On the 5th there was a demonstration at Westerleigh of a new Excavac system of vacuuming unwanted debris from the track, and on the 8th I was back at Haddenham & Thame and Princes Risborough again. There was more work between Uffington and Bourton on the 13th, 14th and 15th, with the lines closed under the engineer's possession. Over the three days, Nos D1524 (47004), 37046, 37245, 37079 and 37803 were on duty at the head of trains, and No 47702 *County of Suffolk* was similarly employed on the 21st. I was back at Haddenham & Thame on the 22nd, then, between 24 February and 4 March, I was on call for jury service in Oxford. This was my third attendance as

Not a new type of track on test at Bourton, east of Swindon, on 21 February 1998, but a temporary alignment during an engineer's possession for an intended crossover replacement.

a juror, including twice in Leicester, but this did not make the experience any easier.

I was not required on the middle weekend, so Paul and I took the opportunity to visit, by prior arrangement, the Heathrow Express depot at Old Oak Common, a facility that was normally out of bounds. On a damp and dismal 1 March we arrived at the locked gates of HEX-OH, as it was known, and it took us some time to attract attention and convince a sceptical staff member that we were to be allowed in. As well as being up close and personal with the Class 332 units, it was interesting to see No 332003 without any yellow front-end adornments! A tour of the ex-GWR shed at Old Oak was followed by a short journey towards Heathrow Airport, where we managed to gain access to the platform at Heathrow Junction. This was one of the shortest-lived stations, opened for only five months while work was under way to repair damage to a nearby tunnel, and was decidedly security-conscious! We were challenged and asked to give our dates of birth in order to identity ourselves! How/why? Stops at High Wycombe and Aylesbury ended our day.

A rare sight at the time, a unit in service without a yellow end! Inside Old Oak Common HEX-OH depot, No 332003 waits for its next call to duty on 1 March 1998.

At a press conference on 3 March, Richard Branson announced his intention to double rail passenger numbers over the seven-year life of his West Coast and CrossCountry franchises. Sadly, once more, the best laid plans… The same day the court case closed, with us giving a majority not guilty verdict. The beginning of the month also saw the March *Steam Classic* magazine publish my article on the FR's October 1997 'Vintage Weekend' celebrations, while at the other end, on the 28th, Tinsley Depot closed. Like many other enthusiasts, this was not good news to me as it was always an attractive place to visit. The month for me ended in Cornwall, from the 29th to 2 April, primarily to capture present-day photographs for a book on the Bodmin & Wenford Railway.

On my drive south, on the 29th, I called in at Laira depot, where I was given free access, before making my way to St Austell to photograph the station, and St Blazey to see the famed half-roundhouse for the first time, before finding my B&B in St Austell. After meeting up with Maurice Dart from the B&WR, we went first to Lostwithiel on the 30th, with a china clay train there being a reward. Bodmin General, Bodmin Parkway, Dunmere, Wenfordbridge, Wenford and Tresarett were subsequent destinations and I was glad of my guide, as I would not have found some of the locations without him. I was back on my own for the 31st, going to Par, Bodmin, Helland, Tresarett, Boscarne Junction, Nanstallow Halt (remains of) and Wadebridge (one of Sir John Betjeman's favourite places). Some of these locations were devoid of tracks but the nostalgia generated by the 'past' photographs in my hands was strongly evocative.

1 April saw National Power's 2½-year rail operation and its iconic blue Class 59/2s taken over by EWS, and the locos would soon lose their attractive NP livery. On the same day I started at Truro, visiting the station for the first time, before moving on to St Erth (another first) and Penzance, where Nos 153368 and 158826 were the only stock in the platforms. Here I met up with my Best Man, David, at whose house I was to stay overnight. On the 2nd he travelled with me, via a brief

detour to Newquay (for more nostalgia, but from my childhood memories), to Bodmin General, where we were caught up in a National Spring Clean campaign outside the station, with a host of local schoolchildren surrounding Great Uncle Bulgaria from the Wombles!

On 4 April Judi and I travelled to Reading to watch Tammy captain the Bangor University Octopush team, in a National Tournament, including the UK Ladies team. It was the second time we had seen her in this fascinating sport, which is a sort of underwater hockey! Sadly, in one match she was 'sent out' for foul play, and I have a picture of her sitting forlornly on the side of the pool. On our way back to Reading station we heard a steam whistle. I raced to the barriers to photograph No 73096 on its way back to Alton as the Daylight Limited Railtours' 'Western Standard' charter. Sadly, the attempt was not successful! Two days later, another Tammy (Wynette) died (born 1942).

Two weeks later would see a hectic four days, beginning with Judi and I returning once more to the FR on the 17th. The following day was gloriously sunny as we went to Harbour station in Porthmadog to witness the railway's Funky diesel, newly repainted into National Power's colours, being moved to the other end of the line to meet up with a similarly painted standard-gauge Class 59/2 on a railtour. The crowds were out at Blaenau Ffestiniog to welcome No 59205, newly named *L. Keith McNair*, on Hertfordshire Railtours' 'The Roman Nose' charter. Nos 37098 and 37377 were on the rear, to take the lead as the train returned along the branch to Llandudno Junction. Returning home on the 19th, we called in at Carrog and Llangollen, on the Llangollen Railway, to record Nos 26004 and 25313 double-heading one of the day's rosters. The following day I was back at Brush, to see progress on the re-engineering of No 47356 to become No 57001, a project commissioned by owner Freightliner. Also there was No 56009, for use as a test bed and possibly to become No 56201, but that latter step was never taken.

Beginning with the May Day Bank Holiday I spent every

alternate day from 2 to 8 May at Radyr station, with men and machines as they created a new platform and altered the whole rail layout over that period. I was again given free rein and could wander around the large site capturing images. One incident could have been awkward: I was about to photograph a man grinding a newly completed rail weld but he was not wearing a hard hat, which was illegal. I offered him my hat for the purposes of photography and was ready to press the shutter when I felt a tap on my shoulder. Turning, a representative of Network Rail asked me, 'Where's your helmet?' Over the days I visited and photographed inside both signal boxes on the site, not least the more isolated Quarry box on its last day. By the end of the works both boxes had closed and the semaphore signals had been removed, replaced by colour lights.

Mourned by many worldwide, Frank Sinatra died on 14 May (born 1915). The following day I was back on the Chiltern line, photographing 'Project Evergreen' between Bicester North and Haddenham & Thame. Then between the 21st and 24th I returned to Cornwall for more Bodmin & Wenford photographs and my first visits to Liskeard and the Looe branch. On the 23rd I was in place to see No 43056 lead the 1408 Newquay-Leeds service into Par station, an extremely rare sight, being the first time a rake of Midland Mainline HSTs had ever visited Cornwall. On the 24th I was interested to see No 6024 *King Edward I* operate on the short run between Bodmin General and Parkway.

An old name resurfaced in June, as Vic Berry set up a new

Two heads are better…!
Concentration is fixed as another
session of thermit welding is
prepared at Radyr on 2 May 1998.

On its last day of operation, 8 May 1998, the signaller inside Radyr Quarry signal box still attends to his duties, not least keeping the box neat and tidy.

scrapyard a mile or so south of his previous Leicester site. No 31217 was his first loco there and his first for cutting for eight years. He had plans but, sadly, they did not materialise. I visited Aylesbury depot on the 4th, not a common luxury, and the latest FIFA World Cup started in France on the 10th. England made it through the group stages, but were defeated in their first knockout match, 4-3 on penalties against Argentina on the 27th. Leicester City's goalkeeper, Kasey Keller, played for the USA and Matt Elliott was in the Scottish squad, but did not play a game. On the 14th I was asked by *Railway World* magazine to go to Didcot to photograph progress on the restoration of ex-GWR No 5322. I was pleased later to see some of the shots in print. I was also in June's *Steam Classic* with the article 'That was the year … 1948', a 50-year retrospective.

Much of July was taken up with further visits to the Chiltern line, but a welcome exception was on the 17th when, with another invitation from Peter Best for a special day with No 4277, we had the run of the Gloucestershire

An exceedingly rare sight at Par on 23 May 1998, as No 43056 pauses in the station with the first ever Midland Mainline HST to visit Cornwall, operating as the 1408 Newquay-Leeds returning holiday express.

Warwickshire Steam Railway as well as riding behind the loco. Another diversion was to be at Brush on the 21st, when the Works dramatically launched No 57001 *Freightliner Pioneer*. Although further conversions were completed over time, the project did not prove as successful as had been hoped. The new Freightliner livery, launched with the loco, was quickly applied to the rest of the company's fleet. The day before, John Prescott published a White Paper announcing the setting up of a Strategic Railway Authority, with wide-ranging powers, but again the ideas were not to be the envisaged panacea.

The family holiday this year was spent over late July/early August in Cornwall, in a friend's holiday cottage near Penzance. Reflecting changing patterns, there was no railway visit and the whole time was purely social, not least spending time with Best Man David and his wife Jill.

Shortly after my return I was at Tyseley depot on the 16th, photographing the ongoing restoration of Beyer Peacock's

Rolled out to great fanfare for the launch of the re-engineered conversion from No 47356, No 57001, now named *Freightliner Pioneer*, proudly stands in the warm summer sun at Brush on 21 July 1998.

first Garratt 'K1', which was destined for the WHR. The month ended with me at Newport Docks on the 26th to witness the first boatload of the new Class 66 locos. The group that had gathered to watch drew lots for which loco was to be first from the boat. It was No 66004, and I did not win! The following day I was back at Brush, where the '57' conversions were present in the form of Nos 57003 and 57004. Leicester City had mixed fortunes at the start of the new season, with a win, a draw and a defeat!

With magazine articles and the increasing number of contracts for book titles, together with infrastructure possessions and having to fit them all in with my continuing postal work, life was changing again, with far fewer 'jollies'. However, I was back in Cornwall on 19 September, visiting St Erth and Redruth, where I was in time to catch No 6024 *King Edward I* roaring south on Pathfinders Tours' 'The Penzance Pirate' Paddington-Penzance railtour. In BR days the 'Kings' were reportedly banned south of Plymouth, but rumours abounded of sightings as far south as Penzance. Indeed, my Best Man, who lived there at the time, was certain that he had seen one such instance. Obviously, that restriction had been lifted by the date of this charter. The following day I was many miles further north, at Caernarfon to witness the new WHR services from/to Dinas. The 1600 service to Dinas was an extra train added to the timetable to cope with demand, double-headed by Garratts Nos 143 and 138. You wait years for a Garratt, then two come along, but a truly wonderful sight!

The October *Classic Railways* contained my article on the Bodmin & Wenford Railway and a short article on the life of the Class 37s. My endeavours at Radyr had been positively appreciated by Railtrack and I was commissioned to undertake similar duties at Pontypridd. A much smaller contract, it was nevertheless interesting, as I had not been to the location before. On the 11th I spent time at the station and a few hundred yards on the southern approach to witness the relaying and renewing of the track and photograph, among many other aspects, No 37671 waiting to travel south with a waste train. The month climaxed with participation in the GWS's 'Photographers' Evening' on Friday the 30th, grabbing the chance for night-time photography under strategically placed floodlights, not least of No 4073 *Caerphilly Castle* positioned alongside the coaling stage.

The planned new museum in Swindon was launched on 5 November with a special event within parts of the old Works that would be affected. Two days later I was again out on track, contracted by Jarvis Infrastructure, at the western end of Reading station, where work was largely concentrated on remodelling access to the main line from Reading West. I was back again early on the 8th to capture No 66017, brand-new and on its very first duty. I also took the opportunity to photograph from the large signal gantry that straddled the rails. Little did I realise that less than two decades later the view would be transformed with the construction of a massive flyover for main-line trains heading westwards.

My next commission was a more local one, as I was on

Brand-new 'out of the box', No 66017 stands with its first duty early on the morning of a dull 8 November 1998, involved in the West Reading remodelling. The photo was taken from the signal gantry west of Reading station and was later used by EWS in some of its adverts.

hand to record the arrival of two brand-new bells for Longcot Church on the 23rd. These would increase the installation to eight and become a Mecca for bell-ringers for many years afterwards. A small celebration involving local primary schoolchildren was held in the nearby schoolyard. Two days later I was sad to hear that one of my favourite comedians, Flip Wilson, had died (born 1933).

11 December saw another after-effect of rail privatisation, when Swindon to Longbridge Rover trains were hauled for the last time by two Class 47s. Henceforth, the new '66s' were to take over. The next two days would again see me at Reading, this time at the eastern end. The work involved new trackwork on the northern half of the layout, including reinstating the dive-under to the former Southern lines while keeping the main line open for traffic. The work continued throughout the night and I caught some of this on film, despite the frequent heavy rain showers.

On the 14th I ventured to Oxford to snap preparatory work for the studied demolition of the old LNWR Rewley Road station building, which was to be transported to and re-erected at the Buckinghamshire Railway Centre at Quainton Road. Its designer, Joseph Paxton, was also the architect for the Crystal Palace. Christmas was again spent in Leicester, with Mum now on her own, but on the 28th I still escaped for a brief trip into the city, where I had my first glimpse of the new Vic Berry site. Situated close to the route of the old Great Central Railway, as had been the previous yard, this was a much smaller affair, and No 31217 was crammed in amongst all manner of redundant metalwork. Not far away, on this day, mid-table in the Premier League Leicester City drew 1-1 at home with Blackburn Rovers.

1999 began with January's *Railway World* publishing my article on the proposed new Museum in Swindon. On 8 January two trains collided outside London Bridge after one passed a

Being dismantled piece by piece, the erstwhile Oxford Rewley Road station is surrounded by scaffolding on 14 December 1998. It was destined to be re-erected at the Buckinghamshire Railway Centre at Quainton Road.

red signal. The following two days I was again at Reading for Jarvis, then 15 January saw another collision, after a landslide on the Settle & Carlisle route. There was also more work for me with trackwork at Denchworth, a couple of miles or so west of Didcot, on the 24th, and at Uffington on the 31st.

February's *Railway World* contained my article on No 5637 being restored on the Swindon & Cricklade Railway. I was out again on the main line at Uffington on the 7th and 20th, then on the 22nd Chris Green assumed the role of Virgin Trains' Chief Executive. On the 27th I travelled to the diminutive Finstock station to photograph No 66028 on Pathfinder Tours' 'The Yankee Sidewinder' charter between Worcester (Shrub Hill) and Oxford.

For the first time for many months, Paul again joined me on 14 March to enjoy a day trip to South Wales. We began at St Philips Marsh and Barton Hill depots in Bristol – the first visit to the latter for both of us – before renewing acquaintance with the two depots at Cardiff Canton. The lower level EWS shed gave me my first cop of the day, No 66034. Margam was next, with the grand total of six cops – five '66s' and No 59203 *Vale of Pickering*. While variety was sadly lacking, compared to former times, it was nevertheless satisfying to once again try to 'complete the set'! The month was quiet after that until the 27th, when I represented *Rail Infrastructure* magazine at a GTRM Autoballasting event at the Severn Valley Railway, with No 66074 hauling and demonstrating the new wagons.

On 4 April I was off to the GCR at Loughborough, then Quorn, where I was pleased to capture No 60532 *Blue Peter*. The following day I was at another preservation centre, the GWS's shed and yard at Didcot, but this time with Judi and Tammy. On a bright and mostly sunny day we all liberally employed our cameras to capture the delightful array of preserved locos on view, including old friend No 4277. Another unusual opportunity came to me on the 10th, when I was allowed to climb to the top of the bell tower of Longcot Church, to capture the present view of the village compared to one from the earliest years of the century. Without the former proliferation of elm trees, decimated by the dreaded Dutch Elm Disease, the contrast was startling!

Death was also elsewhere towards the end of the month and into May, with British TV presenter Jill Dando, 37, being shot dead on the doorstep of her home in Fulham, London, on 26 April, Sir Alf Ramsey dying on the 28th (born 1920), and Dirk Bogarde on 3 May (born 1921).

The annual FR May Day Gala was again a draw. Judi and I travelled up on 29 April to join up with Tammy and stay until 2 May. A highlight was seeing the newly built single Fairlie *Taliesin* on the 30th, in plain black livery on a test run prior to its formal launch. 2 May saw the publication of my ninth book, *British Railways Past & Present: The Welsh Highland Railway*, with me signing copies in Dinas goods shed. On the 9th I was again acting for *Rail Infrastructure*, taking photographs at Lapworth of a new FH130W road/railer.

22 May was a special day when three 'Deltics' appeared together on the ECML for the first time since 1961. Nos

One of the delights of FR Galas is the occasional runs down the line by the gravity train, with members and guests sitting on wagons filled with slate, powered purely by the ruling down gradient. Here one passes Minffordd on 3 May 1999.

D9009 *Alycidon* and 55019 *Royal Highland Fusilier* double-headed a train from King's Cross to York and return for the Deltic Preservation Society, while No D9000 *Royal Scots Grey* hauled a Victoria-Bradford VSOE Pullman charter. On the same day I was at Amersham and Chalfont & Latimer enjoying the latest 'Steam on the Met' event, featuring Nos 31625, 45110 and 9466. On the 25th I was back in Swindon, to see No 3440 *City of Truro* being taken out of the Outlet Village and No 4930 *Hagley Hall* taking its place.

At Chalfont & Latimer on 22 May 1999, LUT No 5062 on a Chesham shuttle goes round the bend!

9 June saw Great Western become the first train operating company (TOC) to relivery its stock, with Nos 43147 *The Red Cross* and 43172 in new First Group green and gold stripe colours. Seven days later I was commissioned to photograph Amey's new on-track Land Rovers at Quorn on the GCR, and the following day to capture the formalities and celebrations of the new Oxford station concourse and ticket counters.

On 19 June Paul, Neil and I were back in Scotland for

an intense weekend of 'spotting and photting'. Motherwell was again the opener, followed by Glasgow Queen Street and Central, Edinburgh Waverley and four other locations before Wigan on the way home. The latter was now an official component recovery centre and locos were in various states of undress. On 23 June No 87027 *Wolf of Badenoch* ran into a stationary Class 142 'Pacer' unit, injuring 29, none seriously. On the same day I was a visitor to the West Somerset Railway, beginning further trips over the ensuing weeks in preparation for another book; *British Railways Past & Present: The Bodmin & Wenford Railway* became my 10th book, with publication in July.

August's *Steam World* carried my article on the end of steam at Leicester, 1956-66, and on the 18th I returned to Newport Docks to see the latest delivery of new Class 66s, including Nos 66139-147 and 66503-505. On the 26th my camera captured the ongoing dismantling of the old LNWR Rewley Road station in Oxford.

Part of successful railway schemes is drumming up and retaining support. On 14 July 1999 WHR Chairman Dave Kent explains where the new railway will eventually run at Fridd Isaf curve, Rhyd Ddu, during an evening walk.

At Porthmadog, Tammy stands with her 'Prince' on 29 August 1999, ahead of the special train for her 21st birthday (on the 27th), complete with appropriate headboard.

5 September 1999 was a preservation day for me, as I visited the Swindon & Cricklade Railway – partly to view recent progress on the restoration of No 7903 *Foremarke Hall* – and then east to the GWS in Didcot, where I was pleased to photograph diminutive saddle tank No 1338 outside the shed in glorious sunshine. Later in the month the preservation/restoration theme continued with the publication of *Festiniog in Camera – 100 years 1871-1971*, my 11th book and my one and only for Challenger Publications. Still later, on the 17th and 30th, I was inside the original Swindon Museum photographing the displays before closure on the latter date.

October's *Heritage Railway* magazine published my article on the railways of Leicestershire, portraying the delights of the steam era in the county through photographs in my collection. 7 October was the next cause for excitement, with another trip to Newport Docks to see the first EWS Class 67 No 67003 unloaded. Mum had been staying with us for a few days,

On 17 September 1999, just days away from closure, the original Swindon Railway Museum displays *North Star* and Nos 9400, 2516 and W4W, with a member of staff in period dress.

so I took her with me. Being able to park within sight of the Jumboship, she could watch the events from the car while I spent time and film closer to the action. On 15 October there was a collision at Ladbroke Grove, killing 31, again arising from a train passing a red signal.

November saw weekend possessions on the main line north of Cheltenham Spa and I was on track with men and machines at Old Ends Crossing on the 7th – where Nos 37771, 56107 and 66023 were the main workhorses – and near Bishops Cleeve on the 27th, where Nos 66131, 66170, 37248 and 37716 were on duty. During the month Brendan Powell, a Longcot resident who won the Aintree Grand National on Rhyme 'n' Reason in 1988, had a fall at Newton Abbot. Trodden on by a following horse, he suffered a shattered ribcage, a punctured left lung and a collapsed right lung, and ended up in intensive care. A *News of the World* report stated that he wanted to be back in the saddle six weeks later!

During December I was inside 19 Shop of the old Swindon

Works again, on the 7th, to capture progress on Nos 9682, 4110 and 4247. The 23rd saw me granted access to the new 'STEAM' museum, to see the positioning of No 4073 *Caerphilly Castle*, the first loco installed, together with No 4248 in undercoat but cosmetically whole. On 26 December I was out on track at Bourton, east of Swindon, for more work within a possession. What a wonderful way to spend Boxing Day! Midway in the Premier League at the end of the year, Leicester City were still in the FA and Worthington Cups.

The year 2000 dawned, and we had not been subject to the Millennium Bug that had threatened doom and destruction! Whether by accident or design, the early years of the new century would prove to be busy for me and for the UK's railways, with plenty of events and colour, and advertising liveries on units in addition to varying franchisees' house colours and a multiplicity of strange and dubious locomotive namings.

Recently entombed within 'STEAM', the new Swindon Museum, No 4073 *Caerphilly Castle* is the first exhibit to be installed on 23 December 1999.

I January saw me back at Didcot where No 4144 performed on the site's demonstration line suitably adorned with a 'Y2K' headboard. The adjacent stabling point, alongside the station, rewarded me with cops of Nos 66134 and 66136 – a good start to the New Year. On the 7th I returned to Hayes Knoll on the S&CR, where No 9682 was on its first day back in steam, with the honour of being the 100th ex-Barry wreck to be restored. During the month, a turnout from the main line at South Marston, east of Swindon, was under construction to provide rail access to the nearby Honda car plant and I was on site from just before dawn on the 16th to witness and record the work. I was back again a week later to update. Sadly, although the line was later fully completed, it was hardly (if ever) used!

February began with *Heritage Railway* featuring my article looking back over 40 years since the start of the WHR restoration movement. This was followed by me travelling back to the WHR for the ongoing restoration between Dinas and Waunfawr and another forthcoming book.

And so into the new Millennium. On 1 January 2000, 4144 wears an appropriate 'Y2K' headboard as it accelerates along the demonstration line at GWS, Didcot.

Having the honour of being the 100th loco to be restored from ex-Barry scrapyard condition, No 9682 is but a short hop from its birthplace in Swindon as it steams again at Hayes Knoll on the Swindon & Cricklade Railway on 7 January 2000.

On my return, on the 6th, I visited Carrog and Llangollen at either end of the Llangollen Railway. A week later I was on site at the old Swindon Museum to witness the broad-gauge *North Star* and No 9400 being gingerly extricated from the confines of their home and winched onto a low-loader to be taken the short distance to 'STEAM'. The crowds were out in force to watch the transfers, with the road outside the museum closed to all except the low-loaders. Another eight days and I was once again at Newport Docks, to see more Class 67s unloaded. At the sidings by Newport station I copped Nos 66042, 66009, 66058 and 66081, giving me a grand haul of nine for the day – very satisfying! The death of the great Sir Stanley Matthews (born 1915) was announced on 23 February; and on the 27th Leicester City defeated Tranmere Rovers 2-1 at Wembley in the final of the Worthington Cup.

5 March was the next date for locos to exit the old museum in Swindon. Railcar No W4W and an ex-GWR Dennis fire engine were relatively easy to move, but the main struggle

With the ex-South African Garratts being taller than previous locos on the WHR, bridge heights needed attention. The lower base level can be judged here by the steel girder on the approach to Waunfawr station on 5 February 2000.

came with the length and weight of No 6000 *King George V*. The width of the road outside the museum building was such that when the loco (sans tender) was aboard the low-loader, there was no room to turn! Despite backing up slightly and utilising the independent steering of the multiple wheels, there was still the danger of the low-loader's cab taking out a shop front! A sudden burst of one of the load-bearing tyres did not help but, after much negotiating, the consist was finally able to turn into the road ... after damaging a concrete pillar between two shops! By the 21st all the exhibits had been transferred to 'STEAM' and were in their new places, albeit covered with copious layers of dust. However, now they were settled the surrounding structures could be completed. The WSR was next on the schedule, on the 25th/26th, for me to complete necessary pics for my 'Past & Present' book on the railway.

On 14 April GBRf, impressed with those operating for EWS, announced an order for eight Class 66s to cope with newly won contracts. As Class 66/7s, they would eventually total 79, the last being received in 2016, with due pomp and ceremony, in a pseudo-GWR green livery and named *Evening Star*. Four days later, on the 18th, the first Class 180 'Coradia'

With No 6000 *King George V* finally extricated from the old Swindon Railway Museum with great difficulty, the Police hope that this is short-stay parking on 13 February 2000!

125mph DMU was unveiled by First Great Western at the Old Dalby Test Track. Between 29 April and 2 May I was at the Dean Forest Railway in preparation for another book. With Judi and Tammy, I had briefly visited Coleford Junction and other locations, exploring old trackbeds on 31 March in conditions that were dry but *bitterly cold*. I do not ever remember being so uncomfortable! Apart from a small number over the next two years, this was the last time I would use b&w film.

The Spring issue of *Moorsline*, No 126, the magazine of NYMR, contained my article 'Return of 75029', covering the rebuilding of the loco by Peter Best. On 5 May I was commissioned to be at Didcot to photograph the first pieces of No 4079 *Pendennis Castle*, which had returned from Australia. There was great anticipation as GWS General Manager Mick Dean arranged the items and held the cast cabside numberplate and nameplate in turn for the camera. He found muscles he did not know he had! A few days later I received the first

An ideal way of travelling the Forest of Dean is by bike along the old railway trackbeds. On 2 May 2000 Judi arrives at what was Speech House Road station.

copies of book number 12 – *British Railways Past & Present: The West Somerset Railway*. On 15 May, Royal Mail opened a new terminal at Bristol Parkway with its own dedicated bag-handling platform. Sadly, the provision was not to last long and has since disappeared. In football, Emile Heskey became the first Leicester City player for 15 years to play in an England International; then, to continue the trend, he was sold, to Liverpool.

After many years in Australia, No 4079 *Pendennis Castle* was finally repatriated to the UK. On 5 May 2000 GWS General Manager Mick Dean displays several pieces, at the request of *Heritage Railway* magazine.

May's *Railway Magazine* carried my investigation into the dilemma of photographic collections being split or even completely disappearing with the death of photographers. I posited possible solutions and asked readers for their own suggestions. While there were some responses, sadly there was no silver bullet, no definitive way forward. I followed it up in the July issue with a case study of a collection that I rescued from oblivion. A decade later, the problem is, if anything, even worse, with digital seemingly casting thoughts away from retention/salvation of past formats.

I was frequently asked to give presentations to clubs and societies and occasionally travelled widely so to do. An example was a visit to Cambridgeshire on 17 May to talk about the emergent WHR. Travelling home the following day I made my only visits to Whittlesford and Ashwell & Morden stations, and was pleased to capture some units rare to me. On the 20th I was at Crewe Open Day, where, with several hundred others, I committed as much as possible to the camera. However, with the throng wanting their own 5 minutes looking at the exhibits, it was a waste of time trying to capture anything worthwhile. Cops of Nos 66502 and 66150 did provide some small recompense. After another visit to the GWS, to see No 4472 *Flying Scotsman* on

'Steam on the Met' was always popular with me, especially when there were rare pairings such as this at Rickmansworth on 29 May 2000. No 61572 (left) is on the 1214 Amersham-Watford shuttle, while entering the station No 62005 hauls the 1221 Watford-Amersham version.

the 27th, I made an unusual detour to photograph Nos 61572 and 62005 racing each other at Pinner during this year's 'Steam on the Met'. Thereafter the journey was to Rickmansworth, Amersham, Newton Longville (on the closed line from Bicester to Bletchley) and Bletchley.

Early in June I was awarded 2nd prize in a national competition run by Colab Ltd, a photographic processing lab in Birmingham, and received £50 and a medallion. On the 12th I was at 'STEAM' to photograph some ex-railway employees with their mannequins that would people the new museum, then this summer's trip to Scotland by the Gang began on the 17th. The usual places were revisited but I left the others briefly for a trip from Edinburgh Waverley to North Berwick for a naming late in the day. Dalmuir and Airdrie were other additions this time. Congestion on the M6 on our return journey was thankfully escaped to pay a return visit to Wigan (Spring's Branch). On 21 June the last of EWS's Class 66s – up to No 66250 – were unloaded at Newport Docks, and on the 27th I was privileged to be given unfettered access to photograph HRH The Prince of Wales as he arrived to formally open 'STEAM' Museum.

July's *Railway Magazine* published my article on the opening of 'STEAM', and *Traction* magazine carried my piece on the life and times of Vic Berry and his scrapyard. 8 July was interesting, seeing No 34027 temporarily named

On 27 June 2000 HRH Prince Charles formally opened 'STEAM', the new Swindon Railway Museum, and while the usual press was corralled inside the building I was given free rein to photograph.

Hogwarts Express on its journey to Didcot and a meeting between J. K. Rowling and some of her young fans, dressed as wizards! Another celebrity captured on film! Six days later I was in Bangor and Llandudno Junction, followed by Porthmadog on the 15th, for photographs for future books, and Carrog on the 16th on the way home. On the 18th the GWS formally displayed the now complete No 4079 *Pendennis Castle*, with the hope of eventual return to steam. The month ended with an out-and-back trip on the 29th to Leicester and Central Rivers. This latter was to be a depot for Virgin Trains, but was just a shell amidst open ground at this stage. I was having occasional problems with my car refusing to restart after a short stop during a long journey. The battery played dead and I had to enlist the help of two workmen who were thankfully nearby!

The Summer edition of the K&WVR's magazine *Push + Pull* featured my article on restoring Peter Best's No 45212.

Another celebrity: J. K. Rowling stands with some of her young wizards at the GWS, Didcot, on 8 July 2000, during the visit to the site by *Hogwarts Express*.

Newport Docks was again the destination on 4 August, to see the arrival of the final Class 67s for EWS – Nos 67027-67030. Two days later I attended Old Oak Common Open Day, which featured steam Nos 63601 and *City of Truro* together with a multitude of diesels and other exhibits, including the surprise of No 60081 in green and named *Isambard Kingdom Brunel*. I then visited Marylebone, Euston and King's Cross, and on the last day of the month it was back to Swindon Works to see progress on No 4247 and the wheels of No 35009 *Shaw Savill*.

Above: Back at Waunfawr's road bridge on 14 July 2000, what a difference the months have made.

Above right: Another view of progress: at the GWS, Didcot, No 4079 *Pendennis Castle* is back in one piece, celebrated by Mick Dean, Adrian Knowles and Richard Croucher on 18 July 2000.

Right: Heave! No 67027 sways in the breeze as it is unloaded from the Jumboship at Newport Docks on 4 August 2000.

Chapter 4
2000-2005

The first event of September was the official opening of the WHR to Waunfawr on the 15th and this prompted Judi and me to travel north on the 13th, staying with Dave Kent, Chair of the WHR, and his wife at Rhyd Ddu. Timing was not good as it was during the nationwide fuel protest and, with the blockades of oil facilities, availability of petrol was distinctly limited. We decided to spend time on the 14th with Tammy on a climb of Snowdon from Rhyd Ddu. The day dawned dull with low cloud so I chose not to take my camera. Mistake! One third of the way up the mountain the clouds disappeared and we had clear blue skies. This led me to borrow Judi's camera to photograph the train at the top. Several people at the terminus admired the Papillons that Tammy had with her, with scant belief that these small dogs had walked up! The following day, Judi and Tammy were positioned on either side of the track at Waunfawr, holding the banner celebrating the opening event that was to be broken by the official train from Caernarfon. As the large Garratt loco thundered into the platform, with special guest Dafydd Wigley MP waving from the cab, it took all of Judi's courage to stand firm anticipating the impact with the banner! Managing to find garages allowing £10 worth of petrol per car, we collected enough to return home on the 16th after witnessing a train double-headed by *Russell* – the sole remaining North Wales Narrow Gauge Railway engine in existence – and *Taliesin* – the newest loco from the FR's Boston Lodge Works.

Much closer to home, I paid two visits to 'STEAM' Museum at Swindon, one to photograph No 4247 newly in undercoat on the 22nd as it approached final restoration, then for the launch of the official museum logo on 18 October. Between

Judi looks relieved as the banner breaks and doesn't drag under the train! No 143 steams into Waunfawr on 15 September 2000, as the official launch train for the extension to this point from Caernarfon, with Plaid Cymru MP Dafydd Wigley waving from the footplate.

these dates, the last Mini built at Longbridge emerged on 6 October and the site was subsequently closed. On 17 October the 115mph derailment of a GNER train at Hatfield, due to a broken rail, thankfully only claimed four lives, but the aftermath created meltdown for the railway, with timetables suspended and the beginning of the end for Railtrack.

Work was beginning on converting the track from Asfordby past Old Dalby for electrification, to enable testing of upcoming new motive power, not least Richard Branson's planned 'Pendolinos'. I was contracted to photograph much of the early engineering work by Norex, an Irish engineering company, and my first visit was on the 27th. This was my first transfer away from b&w towards colour print film, as back-up to colour slides, and it was raining! Over the next three days I filled ten films of 36 exposures with images. On the 31st there was a slight change. I followed Henry, the company boss, down the M1 after work at Asfordby to take up position alongside the line into Euston to photograph the demolition by oxyacetylene

I was commissioned to photograph preparatory works in relation to the electrification of the line from Old Dalby. At Grimston Tunnel on 30 October 2000 work is being handled by a Mecalac 11CXi machine for engineering company Norex.

Another job for Norex was to record the dismantling of a signal gantry on the approach to Euston. In the early hours, after the last electric train had passed, sparks fly as cutting is well under way on 12 November 2000.

of an overhead gantry, in the dark after the last electric service into the terminus had passed.

November's *Heritage Railway* contained my article on the restoration of No 4277 by Peter Best; and on 1 November No 67002 *Special Delivery* ran into the back of an MGR train at Lawrence Hill station, just outside Bristol. The loco 'jumped' on top of three coal hoppers and collided with a road overbridge! Though badly damaged, the loco was virtually brand new and was therefore repaired. On the 12th I was back at Euston, again at night, driving across London to Mitre Bridge Junction to watch Henry install a signal post with the help of a road/railer, then back and forth to Willesden for other jobs.

The Hatfield disaster had highlighted the cause of track failure to be 'gauge corner cracking' and I was contracted by *Railway Magazine*, as an exclusive, to travel to Fairwood Junction near Newbury to photograph both examples of the flaws and work being undertaken to correct matters. My article on the problem and remedial work, entitled 'Operation Track Recovery', was published in the January 2001 issue of the magazine.

Leicester City were holding their own in the Premier League, but on 26 December they were trounced 6-1 by Arsenal at Highbury. Four days later I was again working for Norex, but this time in the snow at Shilton on the WCML.

As 2001 began, Sven-Goran Eriksson became manager of the England football team and stayed until 2006. Later, he would assume the position at Leicester City in 2010/11. On 7 January I was again on track, at South Marston, then Sapperton The 15th saw Wikipedia, the free online encyclopaedia, launched onto an unsuspecting world, and George W. Bush was sworn in as US President on the 20th. On the 25th I was at Thingley Junction, where 60-foot lengths of Austrian track were being flash butt-welded into 360-foot lengths, and on the 27th on-track work took me to Uffington and Baulking, where engineering trains were lined up nose to tail. I was still reviewing for *Railway Magazine* but now down to one or two a month.

With demand increasing for long welded rails following the Hatfield crash, Austrian rails were imported in 60-foot lengths and welded to 360 feet by a Sersa flash butt-welder (right) at Thingley Junction on 25 January 2001.

Another night job was in the early hours of 10 February, until daybreak in rain showers at Cogload Junction, Taunton, where the challenge was capturing sharp images despite the constant motion of track workers. On the 14th a press launch at Asfordby introduced the first 'Pendolino' and, with new motive power appearing seemingly every month, I was at Didcot on the 21st to capture one of the new futuristic-looking Class 180s. I managed satisfactory images of No 180101 on test and was also delighted by the rare sight at this location of First NorthWestern-liveried No 175101. The month ended badly for the railway when, on 28 February, an early morning crash happened at Great Heck. A Land Rover Defender towing a loaded trailer swerved off the westbound M62 motorway and ran down an embankment onto the southbound railway track. The Land Rover was hit by a southbound GNER InterCity 225 Newcastle to London King's Cross express. Ten people died.

6 March saw the start of four months of regular visits to Hinksey, on the southern edge of Oxford, to record the

Nearing final restoration at the GWS, Didcot, No 1340 *Trojan* stands inside the workshop on 21 February 2001.

initiation and progress of work to lay new sidings alongside the down main line, to aid the creation and maintenance of a 'virtual quarry', storing ballast for future engineering work. Three days later I was back at Newport Docks, witnessing the unloading of Nos 66703, 66705 and 66706, shunted by No 37419 in place of the more usual '08'. At the sidings by Newport station I was rewarded with cops of Nos 66234, 66202 and 66242. Further cops came during a visit to Leicester depot on the 25th – Nos 66177, 66210 and 66011 – and the following day I revisited 'STEAM', to view the newly arrived No 7325. The month ended with a short break at Beverley, close to Judi's brother and his family. By rail from Swindon on the 31st, with Tammy joining us, the route took in Bristol, where I copped No 67006, Derby and Doncaster. On 2 April, by prior arrangement, after recommendation from a fellow member of Wantage Camera Club, I entered RAF Leconfield and photographed the plaques and wonderful stained glass windows dedicated to railway services of the Armed Forces. The following day was spent

One of the beautiful and intricate stained-glass windows that I went to photograph at RAF Leconfield on 2 April 2001. This one was in recognition of the Royal Corps of Transport.

with Judi and Tammy touring York, including walking the boundary walls and visiting the NRM. Our return journey began at Hull Paragon station on the 4th with, sadly, no cops on the way home.

Apart from Hinksey and 'STEAM' revisits, Lydney was my only outing in April, on the 22nd, braving the rain to witness celebrations for the opening of the new Lydney Town station on the Dean Forest Railway, with flag-waving, whistles and No 5541 breaking a banner. 5 May was next, with journeys to two extremes of the compass – east to the GWS, Didcot, then west to Bristol Parkway, where I was in place to capture brand new No 220003 on test from Plymouth to Central Rivers. The following day, Judi and I had a day trip to Barry Island, looking at the fledgling preservation site while there. On 11 May, the day I was at Hinksey again, the death was announced of Douglas Adams (born 1952), followed the next day by Perry Como (born 1912).

As part of the Newport Open Day Committee's event at the Dean Forest Railway on 19 May, EWS asked me to record

Richard Branson's Virgin Trains were determined to 'empty the roads' and part of the ammunition was the introduction of new motive power for CrossCountry work. Becoming known as 'Voyagers' this was the scene at Bristol Parkway as No 220003 runs through on test from Plymouth to Central Rivers depot near Burton-on-Trent on 5 May 2001.

the presentation of a cheque for £2,600 at Norchard to Pam Dodd, fundraiser for Ty Hafan Hospice, Sully, Penarth. No 37411 had borne the hospice's name from May 1997 to February 2001 and one of the nameplates was given to Pam for display at the hospice. Several main-line locos were present, including Nos D172, 37029, 56111, 58042 and 66250. May's *Steam World* included my photograph of a young lad in a pakamac at Ventnor station in 1965. I asked if anyone recognised him and the answer came in the July issue, from his brother!

Spreading my wings somewhat, June's *Old Glory* had my review of the book *Leicester's Trams*. Paul was again chauffeur on 1 June as, with Neil and myself, he drove north to Scotland once more. Day one began in earnest at Ayr depot, a shadow of its former self, followed by calls at Kilmarnock and Wemyss Bay before the depots at Corkerhill and Shields, ending at Stirling and Perth. Day two was by rail from Motherwell to Edinburgh

An unexpected sight at Edinburgh Waverley on 2 June 2001 was Nos 31459 and 31602 double-heading the return leg of a Green Express railtour to Giggleswick.

Waverley, passing Mossend and Polmadie depots en route to Glasgow Central. While much was as previous visits, sufficient change maintained interest, not least the sight at Edinburgh of Nos 31459 *Cerberus* and 31602 *Chimaera* on the return leg of Green Express Railtours' 'Settle & Carlisle 125th Anniversary Tour' from Giggleswick.

Motherwell was again the starting point on the 3rd, at the depot this time before our brief stop at Carlisle on the way home. 24 June was the next special occasion, when I was at Asfordby to photograph one of the brand new 'Pendolinos'. What was to become just part of the WCML scene in later years was approaching space-age technology in the shape of No 390002 in the bright sunshine. 27 June was a sad day for me as Tove Jansson died (born 1914); she was the creator of the Moomins, and Finn Family Moomintroll in particular. Jack Lemmon followed the day after (born 1925), Joan Sims on the 28th (born 1930) and Chet Atkins on the 30th (born 1924).

I July saw me back on track, at Chalford, where Nos 66017

Developing on from the 'Voyagers', Virgin introduced the 'Pendolinos'. Standing at Asfordby on 24 June 2001, still on test and not yet released to the main line, No 390002, initially named *Red Revolution*, certainly looks a magnificent beast.

and 66079 were on supply and waste trains. The following week, on the 7th, I was at Sapperton again, photographing the men at work and No 66048 on haulage duty. On 11 July the months of work at Hinksey came to fruition with a staged handover by the contractors, with the backdrop of No 66157 on the first EWS train to use the new sidings. My photos of the project illustrated a feature in *Rail Infrastructure* in early 2002.

August's *Railway Magazine* contained my small piece on No 1340 *Trojan* at Didcot and a plea for funds to aid restoration. On the 16th Judi and I accompanied Tammy from Swindon by rail to Barry Island, for her to begin voluntary work on Flat Holm island in the Bristol Channel. When on our own we took the opportunity to view the emerging Barry preservation site. I copped

One of my favourite photographs of the year: from the vantage point of a tall overbridge, No 66017 constantly moves forward dropping ballast onto the new formation at Chalford on 1 July 2001, leaving a cloud of stone dust behind it.

Nos 67028 (at Bristol Parkway) and 66053 (East Usk) on the outward journey and Nos 66010 (at Cardiff Canton) and 66199 (Wentloog) on the way back. On the 29th we repeated the journey, but this time taking the boat trip to the island, partly to see what Tammy had been doing, but also to celebrate her birthday. I was fascinated to learn of the railway that had been on the island during the Second World War and to see evidence of past existence. I was also intrigued to stand on the island's southern beach with one foot in Wales and one in England, such was the boundary in the Channel!

Early September saw publication of *Colour of Ffestiniog* – my one and only book for Foxline and my first wholly colour book – but undoubtedly the major newsworthy event of the month was on the 11th, with Al-Qaeda terrorist attacks on the Twin Towers of the World Trade Center in New York. The death toll was just short of 3,000 and the world has never been the same since. In the UK, Judi and I enjoyed a few days' break in the Forest of Dean, staying in Parkend, and on the 22nd we joined a railway charter at the nearby station, with No 3205 performing 'run-pasts' with a short rake of freight wagons.

On 3 October I was again at Central Rivers depot, now complete and on the day of my visit home to a selection of Virgin's 'Voyagers'. I could photograph within the depot but not venture out into the yard – why, I do not know! This was on my way to Leicestershire, to visit Brush and Loughborough Midland station on the 4th. Eight days later I was again in North Wales, photographing further progress on the WHR

Our visit to Flat Holm island in the Bristol Channel on 29 August 2001 gave me the opportunity to trace the trackbed of the railway built here during the Second World War. The 2-foot narrow-gauge causeway is still clear to see even after 60 years.

and preparing images for a future book on the railway. The river at Bettws Garmon had caused problems as the bridge supports had suffered with age and wear from the water flow. Slightly wider than when the railway was first built, the more substantial 'seats' for the new bridge were impressive yet aesthetically pleasing.

3 November was the date for this year's SODEM – Society of Drivers & Enginemen's Road Run. Traction engines of many designs gathered in the sunshine outside the King & Queen pub in Longcot, Oxfordshire, my local. I grabbed the opportunity for some unique shots and was pleased to later see some of them in the January 2002 issue of *Old Glory* magazine. With the front cover, a double-page spread on the editor's 'Comment' page and several more inside, I was very satisfied, not least as there were many other well-known photographers in competition. It was interesting to see the copious quantities of ale being consumed.

An unusual event on 10 November saw No 5029 *Nunney Castle* stopped adjacent to the old Works in Swindon, on a run from Swansea at the head of 'The Red Dragon' railtour to Paddington, to have excessive amounts of ash removed from its smokebox! During a brief period of spotting at Compton Beauchamp, near Longcot, on the 13th, I was intrigued to witness Nos 59104 *Village of Great Elm* and 59004

Just one of my pictures of the SODEM traction engine gathering outside the King & Queen pub in Longcot on 3 November 2001 that was used in *Old Glory* magazine.

Paul A. Hammond as massive power for a rake of empties. 29 November was a very sad day, as the death was announced of George Harrison (born 1943).

On 11 December I travelled from Oxford aboard an HST powered by existing and future celebrities. At the head was No 43102, which, after arrival at Paddington, was to be named *HST Silver Jubilee* jointly by Chris Green and Colin Marsden, to celebrate 25 years of service by this iconic design. At the rear was No 43197, which Judi and I had witnessed being named at Plymouth, now merely *Railway Magazine*. The following day I was back at the GWS at Didcot to see No 1340 *Trojan* back in steam for the first time in 40 years.

My Christmas celebrations were again disrupted by a call to be out with men and machines. Initially signing in at Shilton as before, I was this time to photograph between there and Brinkworth, a total of some 7 miles. Setting out on foot along the railway I finally came upon my prey roughly half-way. The half-mile-long Track Renewal Train, which was relaying sleepers and track, was constantly on the move, and watching the system was mightily impressive. After completing the long journey to Brinkworth, I was relieved to be taken back to my car at Shilton by road! The big compensation this year, compared with 12 months earlier, was the total lack of snow.

My railway year began with the January 2002 *Heritage Railway* publishing my article 'The Light Everlasting', describing my visit to Normandy Barracks in Leconfield and containing images of the stained-glass windows. This was followed on the 8th by another visit to Lafarge at Mountsorrel – where I photographed No 66703's train being filled with ballast – and to Brush, where Nos 47845 (to become 57301) and 47827 (to be 57302) were the focus. Another conversion, No 57004, was seen among other freight locos at the close of a visit to Oxford on the 24th.

February saw HM Queen Elizabeth II celebrate her Golden Jubilee on the 6th, but the celebrations were somewhat marred three days later by the death of her sister, Princess Margaret (born 1930). The situation was then compounded on

30 March when HM Queen Elizabeth the Queen Mother died (born 1900), three days after Dudley Moore (born 1935). My railway escapades were limited in February, apart from more infrastructure work at Milton, near Didcot, on the 10th and 16th, Ardley and Heyford on the 15th, and Bicester North on 24th.

The 'Evergreen' project on the Chiltern line was also visited during March, at Bicester, Aynho and Ardley Tunnel on the 3rd and 23rd. These locations were again the focus on 22 April, to record the new up lines approaching the platform at Bicester and the layout to ease congestion at Aynho Junction. Before then, however, preservation was the lure as, on the 7th, I sampled the delights of the Dean Forest Railway at Lydney Junction and Norchard, where it was a surprise to see two of Carillion's new tampers, Nos DR 73924 and 73925, on test on

Left: The view from the top of Ardley Tunnel on 23 March 2002, as work continues doubling the line under the 'Evergreen 2' project. No 66218 heads the ballast train. Note the result of recent rain on an existing high water table.

Top right: Another view of 'Evergreen 2'. The northern approach to Bicester North is nearing completion on 22 April 2002, looking towards Princes Risborough. To the left is a new relief loop and, centre, the new up main.

Above: A third view of 'Evergreen 2', this time at Aynho Junction. No 66240 waits for the road on 1 May 2002, during a redesign of the junction. What was a single line behind the photographer was being doubled to ease traffic flows.

a newly ballasted section of DFR rail. Afterwards I took a slight detour while in the area to look in on Bill Parker's workshop at Bream. On site, in various stages of 'undress', were Nos 47160, 92203, 5521 and 30587, a truly remarkable collection for such a small venue.

On 1 May I was back at 'Evergreen' locations on the Chiltern line, but within a week I was with Judi on the Welshpool & Llanfair Light Railway for a ride behind *Countess* on the 4th, to check on progress on the WHR at Rhyd Ddu and Waunfawr on the 5th and, on the 6th, visiting Betws-y-Coed by rail from Blaenau Ffestiniog. May saw the publication of my latest book, *British Railways Past & Present: The Dean Forest Railway*, and the 2001/02 football season closed with relegation from the Premier League and the very last games to be played by Leicester City at Filbert Street, a venue I had visited many times during my youth. After 111 years, the club would in future play at the new stadium at Freeman's Wharf, half a mile or so to the south, due to open in time for the new season in August, capable of holding 35,000 and initially known as The Walkers' Stadium, acknowledging sponsorship by the local crisp manufacturer. On the 26th, I was back at Norchard in the Dean Forest for the day. On the 31st the 2002 FIFA World Cup began in South Korea. England successfully passed the Group Stage, but were beaten 2-1 in the Quarter Finals by Brazil.

Due to the paucity of loco cops – nothing apart from the occasional '66' – and the number of engineering works in progress open to me, pure trainspotting was almost a thing of the past, and June was no exception. On the 10th I was in Swindon and spent time in the Annexe to 'STEAM' Museum inspecting ancient GWR coach No 9003 that was in for restoration. Five days later I was lineside at Shrivenham to witness No D1015 *Western Champion* at the head of Pathfinder Tours' 'Western Druid' Paddington-Swansea railtour, resplendent in its recreation of the experimental 'sand' livery worn by one or two members of the class. On 27 June John Entwhistle, bassist with The Who, died (born 1944). Two days later Bampton Heavy Haulage's traction engine *Lord Nelson* and trailer trundled through Longcot, but it was sadly not to be for another mass gathering.

On 30 June I travelled early to Ardley, the temporary 'Evergreen' headquarters, planning to spend some hours examining parts of the project's progress, but was met with a very unusual sight. Although the second line had been laid for much of the length north and south of the site, neither end was connected to the system. Thus, unable to bring in a tamper to fettle the track and ballast, the decision was made to place No 66141 on this isolated 9½-mile stretch and for it to run up and down to achieve the desired result. A heavy crane was in place and the loco was in mid-air, in the process of moving to the new line. One other photographer had been invited to record the event and he was a little aggrieved that I should have been similarly rewarded, having arrived on spec!

View 4 from 'Evergreen 2'. At Ardley, No 66141 is being lowered onto the new track, which was isolated at both ends at this stage, on 30 June 2002. It would spend time running back and forth in place of a tamper, to prepare the track for main-line use.

July was to be without railways, but from the 2nd to the 5th Judi and I enjoyed an organised tour investigating the gardens of Cornwall. With some very warm weather, we both appreciated the gardens and countryside, not least the Lost Gardens of Heligan with its great variety of plants and designs.

I returned to Aynho and Bicester North on 4 August, by which time the new rail alignment at the latter was virtually complete. This was followed, five days later, with Judi and I attending an invitation-only open evening at the storehouse at 'STEAM' Museum, where many items were on show that were not normally on public display. Not least among these were impressive models of locomotives made by apprentices of the GWR Swindon Works. A further visit was made to the Chiltern Line on the 17th and the 26th. Princes Risborough was the focus on the latter date, after which I extended my scope by examining the branch line from there to Aylesbury and visiting Gerrards Cross on my way home.

September saw the return to the rails of No 67002 *Special Delivery*, after repairs to damage caused by its argument with a road overbridge in Bristol, and I was pleased to capture it in spotless condition on the 2nd heading a Royal Mail train at Compton Beauchamp, east of Swindon. Another 'phoenix' loco was ex-GWR 0-6-0PT No 5553, which was back to life outside the Annexe at 'STEAM' on the 21st. Between these two dates I was again photographing 'Evergreen' progress, at Banbury, Ardley and Bicester North on 15th.

On 6 October Judi and I went to the East Somerset Railway at Cranmore. While she stayed in the café for a coffee and chat with an old friend, I walked the line to and from Merryfield Lane and enjoyed seeing both Nos 813 and 5637 in steam. A less happy situation had happened on 3 October, when Network Rail bought Railtrack plc,

View 5 is back at Ardley Tunnel, where, on 17 August 2002, the tracks are now complete and No 168108 leads 1G32, the 1310 Marylebone-Birmingham (Snow Hill) double-unit express.

which had been placed into administration on 7 October 2001, for £500 million, plus its £1 billion debt! Also during the month, Leicester City went into administration, with debts of £30 million, much of that total due to the cost of the new stadium. Micky Adams, six months into his job as manager, was banned from the transfer market for much of the 2002/03 season, even after the club was rescued by a consortium led by Gary Lineker. However, City still managed to attain the runners-up spot and obtain a return to the top flight – albeit short-lived, as they were again relegated to the newly named Championship the following May.

20 November provided me with variety in my evening presentations to railway groups, which I had been doing for some time, when I gave a daytime talk to Stanford in the Vale WI, entitled 'God's Wonderful Railway – Then and Now'. The talk was no problem but I did find the obligatory judging of members' efforts – this time in photography – rather daunting! Nine days later, the variety was further enhanced by a visit to Waste Recycling Group's plant at Appleford, just north of Didcot. There, by request from Middleton Press, I was pleased to have such different views, but not to have captured them in wet weather and walking conditions that were more suited to wellingtons! I was back at Appleford on 7 December, but by the main line this time, seeing No 57010 on a freight after my trip to Didcot earlier in the day.

For publications, 2003 proved to be a good year for me, with three books: *Steam Locomotive Sheds* Vol 3 (in May), *British Railways Past & Present: The Swindon & Cricklade Railway* (July – with a feature on it and me in the *Swindon*

Not the prettiest of commissions! After heavy rain I could have done with wellies for my visit to Waste Recycling Group's Appleford landfill site, for Middleton Press, on 29 November 2002.

Evening Advertiser on 4 September) and *The Last Years of British Rail: 1990-94* (December). HRH The Princess Royal opened the Gloucestershire Warwickshire Steam Railway extension to Cheltenham Racecourse, but it was not so good a time in other spheres. Harassment – and even threats of arrest – of railway enthusiasts taking photographs was rife and a legacy of 9/11 paranoia; London congestion charges were introduced; tasers were issued to police officers; the M6 Toll road around Birmingham opened; and, on 12 January, Maurice Gibb (of the Bee Gees) died (born 1949). On 25 January I was at Blunsdon to see the wheeled chassis of No 7903 *Foremarke Hall* moved to the workshop at Hayes Knoll by ex-BR '03' No 2022, then, at Swindon station, I photographed the near-complete Platform 4 and No 180114 forming a westbound express.

Early February was another period of mixed fortunes, with, on the 1st, the Space Shuttle *Columbia* on its 28th flight breaking up on re-entry into the Earth's atmosphere. A much happier event was Duane Eddy being in the studio with Nancy Sinatra on the 4th, to cut *She Won't* for her next album. The track, co-written by him, had poignant lyrics and was to become one of my favourites when the CD was eventually released.

23 February saw me with Judi and Tammy at Bitton, on the Avon Valley Railway, walking the length of the proposed extension towards Bath. Then, the following day, after some months, I was to enjoy another rail journey, from Swindon to Haywards Heath, where I met up with Peter Townsend.

While not particularly pretty, I have always taken a fancy to the 'squid' frontage of the Gatwick '460' units. On 24 February 2003 No 460005 arrives at Gatwick Airport forming the 1447 service from Victoria.

We were to visit a photographer who had offered to help me with images for future volumes and, also, for Peter to discuss possibly future projects for Silver Link Publishing. Changing trains at Gatwick on the way back, I was entranced by the sight of the Squid-shaped front of No 460005 as it brought the 1447 from Victoria into the Airport station. I copped two more Class 66s during the day – Nos 66166 at Didcot and 66212 at Reading.

On 8 March Adam Faith died (born 1940), and on the 20th the second Gulf War began with the invasion of Iraq by US and Allied forces. This saw millions flock onto the streets in London to demonstrate against the UK's participation. Another musical death came on 21 April, when Nina Simone died (born 1933). Two days prior to this, I was a visitor to the Great Central Railway at Loughborough, where I was delighted to have my first sight of No 90775. A North British 2-10-0 'Austerity', on loan from the North Norfolk Railway, it had been new in 1943 as No 73652, one of an order for 150. BR acquired 25 of them, with their numbers ending at 90774.

Having been on site for the construction of Keypoint Junction, east of Swindon, I went to see the finished product of the branch line towards Honda's car plant on 5 May. Built to facilitate movement of cars by rail, it was to prove a white elephant. From there, Blunsdon was next for a walk along the trackbed to Mouldon Hill, on the outskirts of Swindon, to assess the progress of the S&CR's plans. The last week of the month was to see two major events. On the 27th I was at the GWS's Didcot site, by invitation, to record the visit of HRH The Princess Royal, who was there to see the return to use of ex-GWR coach No 9002. I was intrigued to see the diminutive No 1338 with full Royal Train headcode, as it was to transport its guest around the site. Four days later I was at Crewe Works Open Day, along with hundreds of other enthusiasts, which made it difficult to obtain decent photographs. The mix of old and new, steam, diesel and electric, included the purple-liveried No 87002, now unnamed. It was also a joy to explore the Works complex and to record it on film. From there, it was to North Wales, where I stayed for nine days, some of it spent with Tammy.

1 June found me on the WHR, the 2nd at the Llanberis Lake Railway and walking part of the WHR, the 3rd between Porthmadog and Beddgelert, the 4th at Boston Lodge on the FR, the 5th at Bangor, and the 6th at Holyhead. I had accepted a lift from Dave and Gina Kent, with whom I was staying, as they had business in Holyhead and I had never been there before. I took the opportunity to photograph both inside and out of Ty Croes signal box. The following day I went to Corris, where the formal opening of the line to

Another royal picture: HRH The Princess Royal greets the crew at the GWS, Didcot, on 27 May 2003 during her visit to inspect renovation of Royal Saloon No 9002.

Maespoeth was celebrated by No 3 shuttling back and forth, complete with large headboard. Machynlleth shed was the final visit of the day, before I made my way home on the 8th via Llangollen. On 29 June Katherine Hepburn died (born 1907); Bob Hope followed on 27 July (born 1903), and on 30 July Sam Phillips (Elvis's first record producer) died (born 1923).

An honour for me came on 16 July, when I was requested by both Network Rail and the Strategic Rail Authority to be the official photographer for the opening of the new Platform 4 at Swindon. Formalities were hosted by Richard Bowker of the SRA, together with John Armitt, head of Network Rail, and Chris Kinchin-Smith of First Great Western. Happily, all went

Progress on the WHR is obvious from this view of Fridd Isaf curve, Rhyd Ddu, on 3 June 2003. These were the first trains into and out of Rhyd Ddu station and were stabled there for safety, away from the station site, which was nearer the road.

Another railway that was progressing after many idle years and lack of early support was the Corris. Here Corris No 3 proudly returns to Corris from Maespoeth on 7 June 2003, the official opening day.

Another opening: Platform 4 at Swindon on 16 July 2003, when I was the official photographer for the Strategic Rail Authority. Left to right are John Armitt (Network Rail), Richard Bowker (SRA), and Chris Kinchin-Smith (FGW).

well and NR and SRA were pleased with the images.

This year saw my 60th birthday and, to celebrate, Judi and Tammy treated me to and joined me on an Inside Track holiday. Based in Carlisle, in a hotel next to the station, we were to spend four days exploring various nearby railways. Setting out from Bristol Parkway on 1 August, we met up with the rest of the party at Oxenholme. By coach to Ribblehead, then rail from

Settle to Carlisle, and with our luggage going by coach to the hotel we were off to a good start. Unhappily, Judi and Tammy were allocated rooms at the rear of the hotel, overlooking a yard where staff congregated for a smoke and where empty bottles were thrown into a skip. Nor did they enjoy a wedding party one night into the early hours underneath their bedroom! Happily, the days' events and the weather by and large were more successful.

The Ravenglass & Eskdale Railway was first on the 2nd, followed by the Lakeside & Haverthwaite Railway, a boat trip to Windermere Lakeside station and rail to Oxenholme and our coach. We were fortunate to have the coach stop to see No 60009 *Union of South Africa* at Shap on our way back to Carlisle. My birthday, on the 3rd, took us to the Leadhills & Wanlockhead Railway, then an ex-industrial complex at Dunaskin. Then it was coach to Dumfries and back to Carlisle by rail. I was treated by many in the evening for my birthday and I rather fancy I drank too much, but I was still in fine shape for our last day. This incorporated a visit to the South Tynedale Railway at Alston, then Hadrian's Wall before boarding the train home at Penrith. Sadly, because of excessive heat, the UK's rails were suffering and our journey was slow, not helped by our coach on the 'Voyager' not having air-conditioning and us being seated in the full sun for most of the journey! Still, it did not spoil the overall appreciation of Inside Track's provision and organisation.

Another variety of experience courtesy of Middleton was my visit to the Moreton-in-Marsh Fire Service College. I had not been aware of this facility and was intrigued to see its many acres on 14 August, laid out for all sorts of fire eventualities, including buildings, an aeroplane and No 73126 and carriages straddling a level crossing, complete with overhead catenary. Afterwards I detoured on my way home to visit Fenny Compton signal box, which was due to close shortly afterwards. Three days later I was on track again, at Bicester Town, where rails were being replaced and rebuilt on steel sleepers. Little did I know that a decade later the sparse facility here would be

Another job for Middleton Press produced yet another visit to an obscure location. The Fire Service College at Moreton-in-Marsh was a complete unknown to me before the invitation and I was fascinated at the facilities. On 14 August 2003 No 73126 straddles a level crossing with mock colour light signal and OLE equipment in situ.

completely rebuilt and renamed Bicester Village, to recognise the nearby shopping outlet.

September began with *Heritage Railway* including 'Steaming back to Swindon', my look at the progress of the S&CR and the debut of No 7903 *Foremarke Hall*, now fully restored. My next railway outing was with Judi to North Wales on the 13th. Travelling by rail from Swindon, via Birmingham New Street, we would spend the next five days in the Principality, again staying with Dave and Gina Kent in Rhyd Ddu. The immediate goal was attending the WHR's 'Super Power Weekend' on the 14th, and our location was the prefect base, as the railway negotiated sinuous curves on its approach to the station, skirting the foothills of Snowdon. The weather was good and we delighted in seeing Garratts Nos 138 and 143 top-and-tail shuttles from Caernarfon, as well as the FR's *Prince* recreating sights from the past. On the 15th Judi insisted that we climbed Moel-y-Gest, the peak looming over Porthmadog. Happily, the weather was still good, but my legs certainly did not feel the same when we reached the top! For the final three days we played tourists, visiting friends and favoured locations in the area, with little in the way of a railway diet. Home on the 18th was by way of Shrewsbury and Newport.

The railway fix was suitably satisfied on the 21st when I was official photographer for the S&CR's weekend, celebrating the return of No 7903 as well as the opening of the extension enabling the railway to escape from the confines of Blunsdon over the River Ray bridge, immediately south of the station. I was instrumental (if you will excuse the pun) in Sir George Martin officiating and cutting the ribbon. He was given a cab ride on and allowed to 'drive' *Foremarke Hall*, and he would afterwards say that it was an ambition he had long held. The following weekend I paid my second visit to the ESR at Cranmore, again walking the length of the line to Merryfield Lane Halt.

October's *Backtrack* magazine saw my first reviews, further spreading my outlets. Most of my month was again spent on line, on the embankment alongside the A420 on the eastern approach to Swindon and at Wantage Road, where infrastructure trains were nose to tail. On 24 October British Airways' Concorde made its final UK flight, and

At Blunsdon on 21 September 2003, Sir George Martin is captured unveiling the next extension of the S&CR, in front of the newly restored No 7903 *Foremarke Hall*. This was my last colour film before I went digital!

5 November saw the same in the US; it then transferred to its final resting place, a museum in Seattle.

Early in November I took what was to be an important photographic step, by buying my first digital camera – a Canon EOS 10D from Jessops in Swindon. I had been warned that it was a steep learning curve from film to digital but, used as I was to EOS film cameras, especially the '5' with its eye-focussing facility, I found little difficulty. The 10D was near the top of the range when I bought it, but it was quickly superseded by a newer model, something that I have been faced with ever since. After practice, my first digital images were taken on a very wet Leicester (London Road) station, when I really tested its forgiving characteristics in dubious light conditions. These were also put to good use the following day during visits to Lafarge, Mountsorrel, and the Great Central Railway in Loughborough, then, on the 21st, at St Pancras, where I wanted to capture some shots of the country end of the platforms before subsequent transformation.

Not stunning, but this was my first digital photograph, taken in pouring rain at Leicester on 18 November 2003, showing No 43071 on the rear of the 0837 Nottingham-St Pancras express. A good test of digital capabilities.

On 13 December, Saddam Hussein was captured by the US Army.

2004 marked 120 years since the birth of what became Leicester City, and there was a suitable range of merchandise on sale to celebrate. Following re-evaluation of its business, Royal Mail decided to end its rail TPO services, with 9 January seeing the last run, ending the sorting of mail on trains in the UK after 166 years. On the 18th I returned to the GCR to photograph Nos 61264 in service and 78019 and 69523 on shed, and to record the view east from the shed yard towards the Midland Main Line and the southern end of Loughborough Midland station. This was a period of my near abandonment of the railway, and 26 February was virtually the only contact of the month when Judi and I accepted an evening invitation to 'STEAM' Museum to join a farewell party for Curator Tim Bryan, leaving after many years to take up a position at

Another test of digital was the use of 1600 ISO and 15th of a second at f5.6 to adequately produce this portrait of No 4073 *Caerphilly Castle* in low artificial light on 26 February 2004. Note the 'Cheltenham Flyer' headboard.

the Motor Museum at Gaydon. As well as the formalities and photography, Tim and his successors, Judi, Tammy and I enjoyed a tour of 'STEAM' free of the public. No 4073 *Caerphilly Castle* looked magnificent in spotlights with the 'Cheltenham Flyer – World's Fastest Train' headboard.

March's *Organic Gardening* had an article on our Longcot garden by gardening expert Jenny Steel, and *Heritage Railway* published 'The Ffantastic Ffiftieth', my celebration of 50 years of the FR. On the 4th I accepted another invitation, to photograph the new HST driver simulator at St Philips Marsh depot, taking the opportunity to record other items while there. I also visited Barton Hill depot and the station at Filton Abbey Wood, of which I would see much more over coming months.

Modern driving simulators are a real boon to the railway industry. At St Philips Marsh on 4 March 2004 a member of FGW staff tries out an HST simulator, with realistic track and lineside displays.

Filton Abbey Wood had become a bottleneck on the northern route from Bristol Temple Meads, and plans were designed to ease matters by creating a new dedicated line to Cardiff and the opening of a third platform. I was back on site on the 26th to record preparation and early works. The following day was away east, at Chorleywood, familiar ground when I lived at Amersham, to see on-track works. A

My first London Underground engineering outing, at Chorleywood on 27 March 2004, saw me refused access to the track, with the potential danger from two live rails, but shots from the platform more than made up for this … and I was safer!

major difference here was the four-rail London Underground electrification; as a result I was not permitted onto the track, merely having to photograph from the platform, but it was interesting seeing different models of machines.

Celebration of a different kind was the opening of the GWSR to Cheltenham Racecourse on 2 April, with No 3440 *City of Truro* complete with 'The "Truro" Partnership' headboard recording support from *Steam Railway* magazine and the NRM. A week later Judi and I were in Porthmadog to sample the delights of the brand new 'Talking Train' launched by the FR. The proposal was for on-the-move information about what passengers could see from the train, by using supplied handsets to give recorded data at points highlighted by strategically placed numbered signs. It was a bold move, and reaction was uncertain, probably due to it being such an innovation, and it was not continued. While in North Wales, we enjoyed a further two days of playing trains on the FR and WHR.

On 15 April I was at Stroud station to record the naming of HST power car No 43143 *Stroud 700*, celebrating the town's foundation in 1304, and on the 29th I was in Birmingham for Personal Track Safety (PTS) training. Taking place several storeys up in a high-rise building overlooking New Street station, I took the opportunity to take some unusual views of the location.

May's *Railway Magazine* published 'Tim Calls Time', a small piece by me about Tim Bryan, renowned railway author and founding curator of 'STEAM' leaving to go as Head of Collections at the Heritage Motor Centre at Gaydon. The month also saw publication of two more books, *British Railways Past & Present: The Welsh Highland Railway* Volume 2 and *The Last Years of British Rail 1980-84*. I was now also reviewing for *Railways Illustrated* with a pick-up in reviews again, and I regularly appeared in three magazines. As so often over recent years, Judi, Tammy and I spent time at the FR's and WHR's annual May Day Gala, this year from 1 to 6 May. At the end of the month NRM presented 'Railfest' to celebrate 200 years since the first steam locomotive journey.

Famous deaths at this time were Ronald Reagan on 5 June

Close to 70 years since closure, the old FR trackbed on the northern approach to Dduallt still held signs of old sleepers on the curving level ground to the right of the walkers on 3 May 2004.

(born 1911), Ray Charles on 10 June (born 1930), and Marlon Brando on 1 July (born 1924). June was very hot and between the 14th and 17th I was scouring the county of Leicestershire for photographs for another book. It was hot outside the car but resembling an oven inside, and I ended each day at Mum's like a wet rag. During this month my many visits to Filton Abbey Wood monitored the relentless and impressive progress, and the blockade here gave me the rare opportunity on 24 June to photograph, from Fishpool Bridge in Bristol, diverted trains on the usually freight-only line from Avonmouth. Later in the day I also captured No 31454 on 5Z34, an empty stock working from Castle Cary after taking Glastonbury Festival revellers from Swindon. Four days later the same loco, together with No 31128, was recorded on the 1024 service from Westbury bringing the slightly less excited throng back again.

With works completed at Filton Abbey Wood, the new Platform 3 was formally recognised by No 150243 being named *The Filton Partnership* by one local and three railway dignitaries at the station on 2 July. On 7 July I was again at Cranmore, this time to photograph the 'unveiling' of No 30075, a look-alike of a BR 'USA' tank, and the 18th saw another unveiling, of a statue in Longcot churchyard, at which I was the official village photographer. It was a good occasion to make contact with

I was involved with photographing the station developments at Filton Abbey Wood and the creation of a new line to Cardiff. No 66211 slowly negotiates the new line, with the Kirow crane support train, on 19 June 2004, as the first train to use the line.

To celebrate completion of the works at Filton Abbey Wood, No 150243 was named *The Filton Partnership* at the station on 2 July 2004. Senior figures from the Partnership pose for their portrait, holding a replica nameplate.

some from the village who were strangers to me.

August was to see the 'Gang of Three' make a now rare two-day outing, beginning at Loughborough on the 21st. Next was Knottingley, where I copped No 66565, Doncaster (Nos 66571 and 67026, allowing me to clear the class) and Barnetby (Nos 66611 and 66083). Day two began at Immingham, where 93 locos were on shed! Many were in store, including my last wanted '56' – No 56086 – but I also copped Nos 66607 and 66615. Not a great haul from so many, but a satisfying visit nevertheless. A brief stop at Rugby on the way home provided me with another cop, No 66508, in a bay platform. August closed for me with a return to 'STEAM' to witness the arrival and unloading of No 50033 *Glorious* for a brief stay in the museum Annexe.

On 6 September I was out locally at Compton Beauchamp to capture an unusual combination of diesel No 66227 double-heading with steam No 5051 *Earl Bathurst*, returning the steam loco to Didcot after the previous day's Past Time Rail's 'The Torbay Express' railtour. Five days later and Judi and I were once more at the WHR's 'Super Power Weekend', especially appreciating the first sight of No K1, the world's first Garratt, in steam at Dinas on the 11th. The following weekend No 3440

City of Truro was giving rides alongside the old Swindon Works, on specially laid track courtesy of *Steam Railway*. The weather was very good and the crowds appreciative of the gesture. On 20 September Brian Clough died (born 1935), followed by John Peel on 25 October (born 1939); the latter, especially, was a sad day for me.

Hardly the 'Cornish Riviera Express'! On specially laid temporary track, part-funded by *Steam Railway* magazine, No 3440 *City of Truro* runs alongside the remains of Swindon Works on 19 September 2004.

September and October were bridged by me at preservation sites at Cranmore and Wallingford, on the 26th and 2nd respectively. The latter presented a bonus in the presence of Class 08s *Lion* (ex-08022) and *Unicorn* (ex-08060); both had belonged to Guinness after their BR career and were still in their black livery with the Guinness logo. Early in October Micky Adams resigned as Leicester City manager, Craig Levein taking over. He was sacked after 15 months, with little success on the pitch, and Rob Kelly appointed in his place.

On 9 October I began the day photographing No 73096 showing plenty of smoke as it accelerated away from Didcot on Daylight Railtours' 'The Gloucester Javelin' railtour from Alton to Newport, before I travelled to Radley for more

All smiles from Alan Titchmarsh and David Shepherd as they share a joke on the occasion of a rededication of the latter's No 92203 *Black Prince* at Toddington station on 18 October 2004.

infrastructure work. The GWSR at Toddington was another preservation centre in focus on the 18th, when I was invited to photograph the dynamic duo of David Shepherd and Alan Titchmarsh rededicating the former's loco No 92203 *Black Prince*. There was much jollity as the latter sprayed the loco's nameplate with champagne, Formula 1 style! Another invitation was honoured on the 26th, when I was at Toton depot to shoot No 58009, recently reliveried in brash orange and yellow for Seco-Rail, ready for its transfer for work in France. While at the depot I was blessed by seeing the brand-new and at the time unique Nos 66951 and 66952. I had to be careful with my camera, as I had been given strict instructions not to take any photographs other than of the '58'! The month ended with me capturing the heavily graffitied 'Thumper' No 207203, which had arrived in a siding to the east of Swindon station en route to its new home at Blunsdon.

Especially and uniquely invited by Seco-Rail, I was at Toton depot on 26 October 2004 to photograph No 58009 bedecked in its brand-new orange and yellow livery, in preparation for shipping to France and work on a new TGV line.

On 16 November the Government published a White Paper proposing a smoking ban in public places, but despite widespread support it was 2008 before it finally applied to pubs, bars and restaurants. Two days later The Hunting Act 2004 received Royal assent, banning hunting of wild mammals. Around the same time, the world's tallest bridge, the Millau Viaduct over the River Tarn in the Massif Central mountains in France was officially opened. Having seen a time-lapse film of its construction, I could say it was truly magnificent and awe-inspiring.

It was 4 December before I was out again, travelling to Gerrards Cross to view early works on the proposed tunnel for Tesco, immediately south of the station. That done, I ventured to Beaconsfield station for a few record shots, then to W. H. Smith to check on magazines. Imagine my surprise at seeing Geoffrey Palmer sitting at a table selling a poetry book for charity! He was very friendly and accommodating and allowed me to take his photograph, but 'I don't smile!' The following week I was back at the S&CR, to photograph Father Christmas at Hayes Knoll and to walk as far as possible towards Cricklade, to judge the plausibility of the railway extending northwards.

You never know who you will meet! Entering W. H. Smith's shop in Beaconsfield on 4 December 2004 I was met by Geoffrey Palmer OBE selling a book of poems – for charity, and not by him – and he was pleased to pose for his portrait.

2005 would see another three books published – 'British Railways Past & Present' volumes on Leicestershire (in February, my 10th release) and the Ffestiniog Railway, Volume 2 (in May), and *The Last Years of British Rail 1985-89* (October).

As it was now nearly 50 years since I first used a camera (Dad's) on railways, I was relaxed taking railway images, but less so outside my comfort zone. Thus I took opportunities for different subjects and, on 8 January, accompanied by Judi and Adam, I visited the Bristol 'Earth from the Air' exhibition. Admittedly I was merely snapping other people's work, but the challenge to succeed remained. The following day the challenge was back on track, at Moulsford, Cholsey and Steventon on the GW main line, but an unexpected bonus was the offer of a lift from Cholsey back to where I had begun at Moulsford on a Geismar people-carrier. Akin to four low-slung chairs within a frame on rail wheels, the sensation of speeding along the main line, just inches from the ground, was exhilarating, even if it was only about 15mph! The 22nd and 23rd saw me again out on track, at Shrivenham on both days, and on the 29th to Tilehurst, west of Reading, where I was to photograph No 66605 and Network Rail's HOBT (High Output Ballast Train). Arriving at 2330, as agreed, there had been staff infringements that had delayed matters. I took photographs of as much of the train as I could, lit by the station lights, before it was finally decided, at nearly 0100 on the 30th, that I should abandon the idea! It was a long frustrating drive back home.

I was now contracted to produce a book on Oxfordshire, so on 5 February I was out and about in the county taking the

Another unique request saw me at Tilehurst station on 29 January 2005. Earlier problems had upset original plans and I was not allowed on to the station until 2330! Eight minutes later, No 66605 is captured at rest with the High Output Ballast Train rake. Ongoing problems prevented any access to the track and I was finally relieved of duty an hour later.

'present' shots, beginning at Carterton, where the new view of the old station site was straight into a brick wall! 19 February saw me at Steventon, near Didcot, where the main line was again under the engineer's possession. Nos 66210, 66140, 66167 and 66127 were all on duty with rakes of various wagons. The following day Hunter S. Thompson died (born 1937). Probably unknown to the majority, his writings for *Rolling Stone* magazine were always stimulating and controversial, and his book *Fear and Loathing in Las Vegas* is like no other I have read and has remained one of my favourites since first published in 1972.

One appeal of the GWS, Didcot, is the 'Transfer Shed', illustrating the period in the late 1800s when standard and broad gauges coexisted. *Fire Fly* stands on the broad-gauge side of 'Burlescombe' on 3 March 2005.

Over the weekend of 5 and 6 March No 3440 *City of Truro* was guest of honour at Blunsdon, with the weather improving on the Sunday to bring sunshine to views of the loco operating shuttles between Blunsdon and Hayes Knoll. Margam was my next destination, on the 23rd, at the request of *Rail Infrastructure* magazine, to photograph Network Rail's new TRT (Track Renewal Train). Its length necessitated that it be split in the sidings near the depot, but the open area and more fine weather led to satisfactory photographs and, as a bonus, it enabled me to view various locomotives in store. Elsewhere, in the spring and early summer, James Callaghan died on 26 March (born 1912); on 9 April HRH The Prince of Wales married Camilla Parker Bowles in a civil ceremony in Windsor's Guildhall; on 7 July four coordinated bombings in central London killed 52 and injured more than 700; and Edward Heath died on 17 July (born 1916).

Nostalgia was high on the agenda on 7 April, when I called in at Syston station. After serving the public it had been an industrial site, but this was about to end, the land being sold for housing. I recalled my two years of going to school in Loughborough from these buildings and was sad at their condition. However, I was relieved to know that they were not to be demolished, but taken down brick by brick to be recreated by the Midland Railway Centre at Butterley. Mum was with me, as we were en route to visit ex-girlfriend Gill (see Volume 1), but she could not fully understand my reverie at these old buildings!

My final view of the public approach to Syston station on 7 April 2005, just weeks before it was dismantled. I wallowed in memories as I was allowed to take the views.

From 28 April to 3 May Judi and I were again visitors to the FR's May Day Gala. The visual delights were as plentiful as ever, but on 29 April I was particularly pleased to see *Merddin Emrys*, freshly back in steam, standing outside Boston Lodge shed, its immaculate temporary black livery shining brightly in the sunshine, and ex-Darjeeling loco No 19, with coaches, crossing the Cob in more fine weather on 4 May.

In temporary black coat, *Merddin Emrys* still looks magnificent back in steam, standing outside Boston Lodge works on 29 April 2005.

At the request of owner Seco-Rail, I was back at Whatley Quarry on 12 May to photograph their brand-new tamper No DR 75406, which was on test before being used on the main line. Through to the end of June, my next photograph of real note was of No 31601 in its 'Wessex Red' livery, operating out of Swindon on the route to Westbury on the 26th. This was followed on the 30th with another naming. Unlike in steam days, the quality of some of the names adorning diesels and electrics left much to be desired and such was the case with No 43009 when it was 'blessed' with *First Transforming Travel* at Swindon station!

3 July 2005 will always be a special day for me. The news media had been awash with the story and images of the collapse of the Tesco tunnel at Gerrards Cross. The idea had seemed simple: with no land available in the town centre for the new store, it was decided to utilise the railway cutting immediately south of the station. The plan was to have a concrete half-arch planted on either side of the railway and 'stapled' together at the crest. The sides and top of the tunnel would then be filled and covered with soil and the store built on top. Unfortunately, with the sides only partially filled, soil was placed on top, which, after saturation by heavy rain, caused one of the segments to collapse inwards. All media coverage had shown the new hole from the top, but Network Rail refused me access to copy this. So, chancing my arm, I approached the station, which was closed to the public, asking for access to the platforms. My PTS certificate served as validity

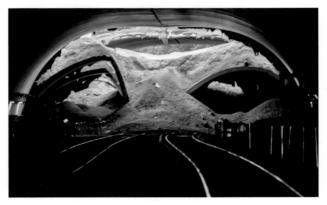

My most valuable photo, of the collapsed Tesco 'tunnel' on 3 July 2005. Taken hand-held through the tunnel from the southern end of a Gerrards Cross station platform, this shot was used by several national newspapers, including front page on *The Guardian*, together with BBC TV and ITV for slots in their 10 o'clock news programmes. It earned me more than £1,300.

and I was warned that I would be gobsmacked by the view through the tunnel. I was! Hand-held, I took zoom shots into the tunnel of what looked like the upper half of the face of a giant, with huge eyes and the tracks disappearing into it, as the spoil covered the ground. One of my photographs was used by *Railway Magazine* and, immediately after publication the London *Evening Standard*, *The Scotsman*, *The Sun*, *The Daily Mail*, *The Times*, *The Guardian*, *The Bucks Free Press*, the BBC and ITV (both for the *10 o'clock News*) all wanted to use it. The *Evening Standard* did a full page spread on 9 August and *The Times* used it twice; then on 25 August *The Guardian* used it for its 'G2' front page. In total, that one photograph earned me in excess of £1,300. Talk about being in the right place at the right time!

13 July saw me photographing the new layout and decor at Marylebone station – very different from my previous visit some 20 years earlier – and between the 14th and 17th I was out savouring the delights of Oxfordshire, for my next book, visiting many small hamlets that were totally unknown to me. Closer to home, literally from my bedroom window, I rejoiced in good weather to photograph the Red Arrows performing over the house on the 21st! Each year they appeared, to

The one year (of many) that the Red Arrows displayed over our house, during nearby Shrivenham College's passing-out day. This was the formation over Longcot on 21 July 2005.

celebrate the passing-out parade at nearby Shrivenham Military College. So often the weather was unkind for photography, but this year the sun shone and I spent a mad period dashing back and forth between the front and rear bedrooms!

This chapter closes with my day's trek on 21 August to Gerrards Cross, to see what progress was being made on repairing the tunnel damage, then to Kintbury and nearby Hampstead, where it was again a case of mixing with men and machines.

My newly acquired Ford Focus, seen on the approach road to Shipton-under-Wychwood station on 24 July 2005. I would own it for ten years, finally selling it when it had done 235,000 miles!

Chapter 5
2005-2010

September 2005 proved to be a special and exciting month. On the 1st Judi and I met up with Inside Track at Waterloo to begin our journey to Bruges by Eurostar from one of the International platforms. This was the start of five days of enjoyment and thrills sampling the city and its canals as well as trams and trains in other parts of Belgium, including Ostend and Brussels. There were highlights on each day, but enjoying a boat ride on the canal at Bruges in the sunshine, then the company of Judi's cousin Liz and her family, who lived in Brussels, on the 2nd were but two. Another was a run-past on a bridge over a river at Balgerhoeke by the steam train on which we travelled for the day, followed by a cab ride enjoyed by Judi. Travelling by rail from Swindon to and from Waterloo, I had copped Nos 66523 and 66507 at Reading on the 1st and added No 59204 at Acton on the 5th on our return home.

17 September was pleasurable as I received £350 from *The Guardian* for my cover shot of the tunnel collapse at Gerrards

My one and only visit to the Eurostar platforms at Waterloo was for an Inside Track holiday, based in Bruges. No 3320 is on our train, waiting to leave on 1 September 2005 for our journey as far as Lille.

At Balgerhoeke, between Eeklo and Maldegem, No TKP 6281 (a Polish loco from 1963, restored in 2001) treats us to a run-past on 4 September. Judi would later have a cab ride on the loco.

Cross. The following weekend I was honoured to be the subject of a 'Meet the Author' event at Bridgnorth station bookshop, with two sessions over the 24th and 25th. A selection of my books was available with me pen in hand ready to sign. I was also allowed some time to escape for a ride on and to photograph the trains and to have the real privilege of meeting and photographing Jenny Agutter at Kidderminster during the afternoon of the 24th. She was signing copies of the new Silver Link Publishing illustrated edition of *The Railway Children*, and her popularity, with a queue of around 100 yards waiting for a signature, put my event well and truly in the shade!

With the threat of closure looming, I took a last opportunity to photograph what remained of the workshop inside the old 19 Shop of Swindon Works on 7 October. This was followed between the 15th and 18th by a return visit to North Wales for the FR's Autumn Gala and to examine the latest progress on rebuilding the WHR. The freedom granted

Celebrity Jenny Agutter poses with some of her fans at Kidderminster on 24 September 2005, signing copies of an illustrated edition of *The Railway Children*. Such was the demand for her signature that she went way past her planned session timing, but was happy to satisfy her public.

by digital photography, compared to previous visits when still employing film, was put to good use with the myriad of possible subject matters. On our way home, by way of Corris, we took the opportunity to revisit the Centre for Alternative Technology (CAT) and to photograph the short water-balanced funicular railway.

David Lloyd George stands at Porthmadog with members of FROCS (Ffestiniog Railway Occasional Costume Section) on 15 October 2005.

November was quiet railway-wise apart from two events. The first was at Swindon station on the 9th, when FGW MD Alison Forster and Anne Dixon, representing the National Trust, jointly named No 43169 *The National Trust*. The second was a Sunday trip to Bargoed in the South Wales valleys on the 20th to record the men laying tracks to an amended design at the station, including a new holding siding for terminating trains. Finding space in the station car park was like being part of a jigsaw puzzle! Two days later, Angela Merkel became the first female Chancellor of Germany and, on a less happy subject, George Best died on the 25th (born 1946). On 28 November I sent confirmation to the DVLA that Judi's car, her Peugeot 305 Estate, had gone to a scrapyard, and asked for a refund of unused tax – this was eventually received.

December's *Railway Magazine* included my short article on the final closure of Swindon Works, following the Great Western Railway Heritage Trust being given notice to quit the

Another exclusive assignment came on 20 November 2005, with the 'orange army' hard at work at Bargoed creating a new track layout to relieve a bottleneck at the station created by the previous arrangement.

old 19 Shop. On the 3rd I was back at the Dean Forest Railway to witness the celebrations for the reopening of the line to Parkend, with No 9681 doing the honours, complete with a large headboard, hauling the railway's DMU set as passenger accommodation – a fitting occasion marking the hard work of staff and volunteers. On Christmas Eve, back in Leicestershire to be with Mum over the holiday, I went into the city to photograph the large Upperton Road that had straddled both the Great Central main line until 1969 and the southern part of Vic Berry's scrapyard site. It was due to be demolished for road alterations and I was sad at the thought of this landmark disappearing. I was even sadder at the announcement that the magnificent former Great Central lattice girder bridge at Braunstone Gate was to go, to satisfy the whims of De Montfort University and against the wishes of so many in the city. It was the sole remaining example in Leicester, and one of very few in the country.

The headboard says it all: 'Parkend at Last!'. No 9681 rests at the station on 3 December 2005, having brought the 1129 'members only' train from Norchard, being the first passenger train there since 1929.

One last, large piece of tangible evidence of the Great Central Railway in Leicester is seen on 24 December 2005. Much loved by many in the city, it was later demolished against outcry and campaigns to save it.

2006 was another good year for me, with a total of six books, taking my total to 29, and January's *Heritage Railway* contained my article on the ancient and unique Boston Lodge Works of the FR. On 3 February the 1890s-vintage Derby Locomotive Works was demolished. It was one of the first plants in the UK to mass-produce diesels, including the famous 'twins' Nos 10000 and 10001 in the late 1940s. Later in the year the Strategic Rail Authority was wound up, its functions passing to the Department for Transport. My first outing of the year was to 'Focus on Imaging' at Birmingham's NEC on 26 February.

March's *Heritage Railway* published my article on the heyday of steam at Swindon Works. On the 3rd I answered a request from *Rail Infrastructure* magazine for photographs of a 'ballast shoulder'. Specifically showing a curving track, with the ballast built up to contain any outward forces, I travelled to Didcot North Junction and collected several images. Sadly, the article for which the shots had been taken never finally materialised. Two days later I was at the site of Bath Green Park station, now a Sainsbury's car park, for the special visit of ex-S&DJR No 53809. Displayed on specially laid track and sponsored by *Steam Railway* magazine, it was there to commemorate 40 years since the closure of the station on 7 March 1966. The rest of the month saw me on a day trip to the GCR, at Loughborough Central and Quorn, on the 10th; to the DFR, at Lydney and Parkend, on the 25th; to Whatley Quarry by invitation, to photograph Seco-Rail's new tamper on the 28th (and taking the opportunity to snap the elderly No 08032); and finally enjoying an evening out to see Neil Innes at the Swindon Arts Centre on the 31st.

April began for me on the 3rd at Shrivenham, where I was in place to capture No 43004 *First for the Future*, resplendent in yet another FGW livery, at the head of 1Z30, the 0912 Paddington-Penzance FGW management train comprising carriages Nos 44049, 40752 and 41003 and power car No

I had an urgent request for photographs of a 'ballast shoulder', where the ballast is built up from the surrounding ground to support the track. I visited Didcot North Junction, where the curve displayed this uplift, and took shots, including this one of No 180101 approaching from Oxford on 3 March 2006. The article to accompany it was never written!

Another event part-sponsored by *Steam Railway*, and using more temporary track, took place on 5 March 2006, in what is now Sainsbury's car park at Bath Green Park, where No 53809 'celebrated' 40 years since the end of the S&DJR. 'Gone but not forgotten.'

43009 *First Transforming Travel*. It was highly unusual to see such a short HST set performing this official duty. Two days later I was not pleased to learn that Gene Pitney had died (born 1941). By this time Judi and I had separated after many years of friction, and she had moved to Wales. On the 14th I travelled to Castle Caereinion to see where she lived – next door to daughter Tammy and her partner Kevin – and took the opportunity to pay a brief visit to the nearby Welshpool & Llanfair Light Railway to witness No 823 *Countess* at work.

The May *Railway Magazine* carried a two-page feature of 'past and present' pictures from my just released Oxfordshire book, and the same month's issue of *Heritage Railway* used my report on potential ideas for restoring rail traffic into Faringdon by mixed-gauge from Uffington. Ever ambitious, the idea sadly failed to progress. 6 May saw me again travelling to visit Judi and Tammy, taking the opportunity for a brief break of journey at Stokesay, near Craven Arms, and to photograph at a new location. 11 May brought mixed emotions; I spent much of the day on DFR, photographing at various locations in glorious sunshine, ahead of a second book on the railway, but my happiness was tempered when I heard that Floyd Patterson had died (born 1935). He was an American boxer whom I once met and whose autograph I obtained as a young boy in short trousers on Leicester London Road station!

On 19 May I was back again on the DFR, but for a much more special reason this time. HRH The Princess Royal arrived at Lydney Junction to be met by railway dignitaries, and was then transported to Parkend behind No 7802 *Bradley Manor*, the largest steam loco to visit the line. Met by local children, she then performed the duties of formally opening the station and the railway's extension. On the 28th I was at Wallingford, signing copies of my Oxfordshire book and taking the opportunity to travel the branch to Cholsey behind ex-GWR saddle tank No 813. The month closed with me at Loughborough Midland and being granted permission to

Another view of HRH The Princess Royal, at Parkend on 19 May 2006, formally recognising the extension of the Dean Forest Railway. Her train was hauled by No 7802 *Bradley Manor*, the largest steam loco to visit the line.

photograph the site of the old Great Central overbridge at the southern end of the station. Long demolished, the restored GCR had great plans to reinstate it and I wanted a 'before' shot, from a vantage point now out of bounds to the public.

I June was another unusual outing for me, when I joined other invited press and interested parties to witness at GEFCO, Rockingham, Northamptonshire, a demonstration of Holdfast's 'rubber highway'. The premise was to make roads out of branch lines, with the possibility of maintaining light rail services, and the idea was demonstrated by several brand-new Peugeot 307s driving on, off and along the specially treated track at the site. Eight days later the 2006 FIFA World Cup began in Germany. England were knocked out in the quarter finals by Portugal, 3-1 on penalties. The rest of the month saw the release of the first six of a series of 'Railways & Recollections' books authored by Silver Link's Peter Townsend and me from the photographs of the late Ray Ruffell. Moderately priced books incorporating facts and figures outside the railway world, they were slow to sell initially but later gathered pace and, at the time of writing, have amounted to more than 80 titles. Elsewhere I was back and forth to the DFR collecting more material for the next book until the 22nd, when I enjoyed a day out on the Mid-Hants Railway, courtesy of a social club in Faringdon.

An interesting day out was to GEFCO at Rockingham, Northamptonshire, to view a Holdfast 'rubber highway' demonstration on I June 2006. To make roads out of branch lines, with the possibility of maintaining light rail services, the innovative idea was to serve both road and rail.

July's *Heritage Railway* included my article on possible future plans to extend the DFR, and on the 4th I had yet another unusual request – to photograph drain clearance on the railway at Oxford station. Sadly, the timings given me by the drain company proved inaccurate and the task had finished by the time I arrived. However, I was shown what they had done, how it was done, and then had the dubious delight of seeing the men being hosed down following their exertions. On the 7th Syd Barrett died (born 1946). On the 19th there was a 'blast from the past', when Paul, Neil and I had a day out to Andover, Winchester, Romsey and Southampton Millbrook. With gloriously sunny weather, it was almost like old times. Three days later, the GWS held a low-key Open Day to show off No 6023 *King Edward II*, cosmetically complete in early BR blue livery, standing proudly on the site's turntable. Not yet ready to steam, it still looked magnificent.

August's *Railway Magazine* featured my short piece on the Holdfast 'rubber highway'. Between the 2nd and 10th I was travelling to byways in north Gloucestershire to collect images

Yet another strange request was to photograph drain clearance just north of Oxford station on 4 July 2006. Sadly, I was given wrong timings so missed the action, but I did see mission accomplished!

Partially cut after withdrawal, it was thought that No 6023 *King Edward II* would never be restored. Happily, this proved not to be the case and, cosmetically restored at the GWS at Didcot on 29 July 2006, the only extant single-chimneyed 'King' waits to be returned to steam.

for the first of three books on the county. The 3rd was my 63rd birthday, but celebrations were dampened when I heard that Arthur Lee, of the group Love and one of my all-time favourite singers, had died (born 1945). On the 19th I was back on old ground, with men and machines at Amersham station. The weather was changeable and a couple of very heavy showers were viewed from shelter on the platform. The month closed with four days visiting the track realignments at Wootton Bassett.

September and early October were busy, largely with photographing locations in north Gloucestershire and on the WHR, in readiness for future books. The latter also gave me the chance to capture the first and last Garratts built by Beyer Peacock, Nos K1 and 143, standing together outside the engine shed at Dinas in the sunshine on 8 September. Slotted in between these duties was photographing West Wycombe locations for *Modern Railways* magazine on the 10th; recording

Rain stopped play! At Amersham on 19 August 2006 No 66719, in Metronet livery, endures a heavy shower, while all humans have run for cover.

the arrival of No E6003 *Sir Herbert Walker*, sans cabs, at Hayes Knoll on the 16th; and on the 25th fulfilling a commission from Seco-Rail to photograph demonstrations by its Medium Output Ballast Cleaner (MOBC) at Risca, on the Ebbw Vale line, which was to be restored to passenger workings. The second half of October saw Judi and I join up in North Wales on the 14th for a walk along and beside the new WHR in Beddgelert

Another exclusive invitation took me to Risca to watch No DR 76601 *Olwen* demonstrate its capabilities as a Medium Output Ballast Cleaner. This Seco-Rail demonstration on 25 September 2006 was part of the reopening of the Ebbw Vale branch to passengers.

Forest. I was again in the Principality on the 29th for a ride and photographs on the WLLR, being especially satisfied to capture Nos 822 *The Earl* and 823 *Countess* double-heading a Welshpool-Llanfair Caereinion train to celebrate 50 years since the closure of the line by BR.

31 October to 3 November were four days of superb late-autumn weather and real delights at being on site at Cae Pawb, on the outskirts of Porthmadog, to watch the construction of a new flat crossing. Highly unusual, permitting the narrow-gauge WHR to cross the standard-gauge Network Rail line on the level, it was employing 'Grandfather Rights', reinstating the facility that had existed until the closure of the old WHR in the late 1930s. I was also in position to capture an exclusive shot of the very first railed vehicle to use the layout, a standard-gauge road/rail machine. The next invitation was to record the latest progress on the new build of No 2999 *Lady of Legend* by the GWS at Didcot on 18 November, utilising many parts from

A true exclusive: having been on the ground for the works to reinstall the WHR crossing at Cai Pawb, Porthmadog, I was in position to capture this PW150es road/rail vehicle as the very first rail machine to cross the new arrangement on 1 November 2006.

New builds were the fashion in the early 2000s. On show at the GWS, Didcot, on 18 November 2006 is the progress in creating No 2999 *Lady of Legend* from No 4942 *Maindy Hall*.

ex-Barry wreck No 4942 *Maindy Hall*. The volunteers had made great strides in the recreation, and it almost looked ready to steam as it stood proudly in the sunshine.

December's *Heritage Railway* included my article on the latter days of the Severn & Wye Junction Railway. The rest of the month was uneventful for me, but Christmas Day was no doubt an unhappy time for many families when James Brown died (born 1933).

1 January 2007 saw Bulgaria and Romania join the European Union. Five days later, in spells of heavy rain, I was part of a party from the S&CR digging out the remains of what had been a bridge at Farfield Lane, within sight of Cricklade, examining possible obstacles to a further northern extension of the railway. On the 21st I was back on the WHR, this time with the management team from Silver Link Publishing, spending time viewing volunteers relaying track in Beddgelert Forest, then walking the trackbed back to the village of Beddgelert for refreshments.

As Ecclesiastes 3:1 says, 'There is a time for everything and a season for every activity under heaven.' I was feeling that this could apply to me when, for the first time since 1955, I went for two months – February and March – without a railway 'fix'. This was due to me seriously trying to sell the house in Longcot, as living in a five-bedroom house on my own was becoming

223

untenable; also I needed to be able to give Judi her half of the financial settlement. Finally a sale was agreed with a condition that I be out by (an early) Easter, so that the purchaser and his family could be in and settled in time for the new school term. My focus thus had to be on preparing for removals, and Judi gave up five weeks of her new life to come back to help me.

On 6 February Frankie Laine died (born 1913); one week later ex-Portsmouth chairman Milan Mandarić bought Leicester City, reportedly for around £6 million; and on the 23rd a tragic Grayrigg rail accident saw 'Pendolino' No 390033 *City of Glasgow* come off the track at 95mph due to the condition of some points. The fact that there was only one death was testament to the strength of the train. Happily, at the time of writing (2017) there have not been any further fatalities due to accidents.

On 25 March I left Longcot, the early move out leading me to stay with Mum for three weeks until completion on the Ashchurch house in April. An early delight in my new surroundings was seeing an MoD train in Ashchurch loop and to discover this addition to main-line spotting on my doorstep.

My next book, *British Railways Past & Present: The Dean Forest Railway* Volume 2, was published and heralded with a book signing at Norchard on 7 and 8 April, with a satisfying level of interest. On the 11th Rob Kelly was sacked as Leicester City's manager, with Nigel Worthington being appointed to the end of the season. On the same day Kurt Vonnegut died (born 1922); I very much enjoyed his science fiction. In May Martin Allen was given City's job for the new season, but lasted for just four games, to 29 August. Gary Megson was then in post, but for just six weeks to October! Frank Burrows and Gerry Taggart then shared the position as caretaker managers to the end of the season. My first photographs after the move to Ashchurch were, perhaps not surprisingly, of an MoD train, on 18 April.

On 7 May I was back in Longcot, to cast my vote in the General Election, as I had not had time to alter residential details. My first railway outing after the move was to North Wales, to participate in the four-day 'FR 175' Gala, between the 25th and 28th, celebrating that distance in time since the very first horse-drawn trains had run in 1832. Several of the trains bore a specially designed large headboard. There were many special events, with three of the days dedicated to Victorian times, the 1920s and the 1960s. Many of the staff dressed appropriately and drew highly complimentary comments, not least volunteer Michelle Littleford dressed as a 1960s Jean Shrimpton lookalike! Back home, now being just 7 or so miles from Toddington, I paid my first visit to the GWSR on 1 June, paying to walk lineside and thoroughly enjoying the freedom to capture locos hard at work, including No 4771 *Green Arrow*.

On 11 June I visited 'STEAM' to witness No 50033 *Glorious* being brought out of the Annexe, just short of three

As part of the FR's 175th celebrations, three days were allocated to different periods of the railway. On the third day, 28 May 2007, one of the railway's volunteers represented the 1960s as a Jean Shrimpton lookalike, complete with long blond wig.

Part of Ashchurch's history, the old goods shed stands abandoned on 2 June 2007. Happily, it was to find rescue as part of the GWSR's rebuilding of Broadway station.

years since I photographed it going in. Castle Caereinion and Llanfair Caereinion were then my next ports of call to witness the arrival of Resita No 764-425, a Romanian loco brought in to boost the WLLR's motive power. Sadly, it was not an unmitigated success and was subsequently sold on; it has since returned to Romania. An unusual sight at Ashchurch on 29 June was four Class 87 electric locos passing through the station – Nos 87026, 87008, 87006 and 87007 –behind diesel No 47828 *Joe Strummer*, operating as 0Z87, the 1130 Oxley-Worcester movement to Long Marston.

During the summer CrossCountry Trains were short of available HST sets and had therefore 'borrowed' one or two from the ECML and MML. It certainly provided variety on 7 July, to see Nos 43119 *Harrogate Spa* and 43077 with 1E46, the 1032 Paignton-Newcastle express, at Homedown near Ashchurch. With the very dark GNER livery, they were affectionately known by some as 'Darth Vaders'! The 11th was another day for photographing Gloucestershire for a forthcoming book, this time concentrating on a horizontal central slice of the county. Craven Arms was next, on my way to Welshpool on the 17th, followed by Cossington, Rothley and Loughborough between the 27th and 31st. No 4141 was a pleasing sight in the surviving former Great Central station on Loughborough Central-Leicester North trains and, despite being an ex-GWRT loco, not seemingly out of place.

Another sad day for me was 4 August, when Lee Hazlewood died (born 1929). He had been instrumental (pun intended) in furthering Duane Eddy's career, being his producer for the first five years of hits as well as being a quirky singer/songwriter in his own right. He rescued Nancy Sinatra's career with his production of *These Boots Were Made for Walking*. Two days later the 'Gang of Three' were out roaming again, beginning at Barnt Green, then visiting Droitwich Spa and Worcester Shrub Hill, with the semaphore signals at the latter two locations particularly admired. Other than beginning to explore local vantage points, the rest of the month's images were merely to record shots in and around my new station.

Semaphores give extra interest to the railway, especially when they are the more unusual 'stub' versions as seen at Droitwich Spa on 6 August 2007. No 150102 restarts 2S52, the Central Trains 1357 Worcester Shrub Hill-Shirley local.

I renewed my travels on 1 September to see No 6233 *Duchess of Sutherland* at Heyford at the head of 1Z33, the 0839 Solihull-Bristol Temple Meads Pullman charter. This was special as it was the first time I had seen the loco since its incarceration at Bressingham Museum and in steam since BR days. Much of the rest of the month was dedicated to photographing locations for my next book, before going back to Wales. Accompanied by Judi, I paid my first visit to the preservation centre at Llynclys on the 27th. Two days later we travelled to Gobowen to capture Nos 37410 *Aluminium 100* and 37417 *Richard Trevithick* on Pathfinder Tours' 'The Lakeland Coast Express', before going to Llanfair Caereinion for more shots of Nos 822 *The Earl* and 823 *Countess*. October was again close to home until the 31st, when I was again in Leicestershire, with camera, at Loughborough Central station and lineside at Cossington.

At a dull Gobowen on 29 September 2007, 'Growlers' Nos 37410 *Aluminium 100* and 37417 *Richard Trevithick* restart from the scheduled stop of Pathfinder Tours' 'The Lakeland Coast Express'.

November was a busier month, travelling to Market Harborough on the 9th to record the tight curvature at the station that was causing Network Rail problems, then 'back home' to Thurmaston and nostalgic memories the following day. On the 16th, by invitation from Peter Best, I was at his site in Stanford-in-the-Vale to photograph his work on No 4277, which was largely in bits in preparation for a further return to steam. Meanwhile, on 14 November 'HS1', the 68-mile high-speed railway between St Pancras International and the Channel Tunnel, was opened. On the 17th I joined a private charter on the GWSR to enjoy a day with a specially weathered No 65462. Initially with dull, cloudy conditions as we assembled at Winchcombe, the day brightened considerably and by the time we were being treated to run-pasts at Defford Straight the sun shone brightly. One of my shots made the front cover of *Railway Magazine* a couple of months later and was used in the design of my business cards.

22 November saw Ian Holloway appointed as Leicester City manager. He was the first City manager for more than 50 years to win his first league game – 2-0 against Bristol City –

Another of my favourite photographs is this branch-line view that could be from almost any era. On 17 November 2007 No 65462 steams along the Defford Straight, between Toddington and Winchcombe, during a rail charter. This shot made the front page of *Railway Magazine*.

but it was sadly downhill from there. On 30 November Evel Knievel died (born 1938), through illness not injury, despite his dangerous lifestyle.

I and 15 December were pleasurable days despite dull and/or inclement conditions, as I returned to the delights of being out on track, 3 miles north-west of Aylesbury, where a semi-abandoned single branch line out of the town was in the process of being re-fettled and groundwork prepared for a new 'Aylesbury Vale Parkway' station. Sadly, on the second visit there was a challenge to my IWA (Individual Working Alone) certification, as I had missed a mid-term assessment, and this led to me losing that benefit and returning to just an ordinary PTS (Personal Track Safety) authorisation. This greatly restricted my abilities to go where I wanted to obtain desired images and made me reconsider my options.

On 10 December Led Zeppelin reunited in London for their first show in 25 years, then two days later Ike Turner died (born 1931). On the 16th Dan Fogelberg also died (born 1951), another of my favourite singers.

Another preparatory site at which I was present was this one, in readiness for the opening of Aylesbury Vale Parkway station. On 1 December 2007 Nos 75204 and 76306 engage in more ballast cleaning for the £11 million interchange 3 miles north-west of the town.

2008 was the International Year of the Potato! It was also another good year for my books, seeing a further six published, taking my tally to 35. Reviewing outlets had changed over the past 12 months or so, and the focus was now on *Railway Herald* from 2007 into 2008, with occasional ones elsewhere.

On 11 January Sir Edmund Hillary died (born 1919), and on the 25th I drove to North Wales to enjoy three days of photography on the developing WHR, ready for Volume 3 of my books on the railway. With access to the tracks before trains started running, it was both fascinating and exhilarating to walk the length of the Aberglaslyn Pass, including through the tunnels on the route. I journeyed back on the 28th, with a brief stop at Craven Arms for photographs and refreshments. Thereafter, February was wholly local-centric.

1 March broke the 'silence', with a trip to Thurmaston to photograph No 71000 *Duke of Gloucester* on the steam leg of

the Railway Touring Company's 'The Cheshireman' railtour, from Leicester to Chester. Little did I think, 50 years earlier, that I would ever see this magnificent locomotive at my childhood spotting place. Fifty years was also relevant seven days later, when it was that length of time since Duane Eddy's first record, *Moovin' n' Groovin'*, had entered the US charts on 3 March 1958. Over the three days 14-16 March, I was at Minehead station, partly book-signing and partly escaping to enjoy the sights and sounds of the West Somerset Railway Gala. Another three-day jaunt was back to North Wales from 14 to 16 April, collecting Judi from her new home on my way up, then enjoying accommodation in Beddgelert, which was almost becoming a second home. The main interest at this point was the installation of tracks across Britannia Bridge and into Harbour station at Porthmadog, something I never thought I would see over the 40 years since my first visit to the location.

The second half of April was eventful. On the 19th it was a treat to see No 60019 *Bittern* speed through Ashchurch for

For the reintroduction of the WHR into Porthmadog, new tramway-section track was laid across Britannia Bridge and into Harbour station, causing some disruption, as seen here on 14 April 2008.

Tewkesbury station on Kingfisher Railtours' 'The Severn Valley Phoenix' railtour from Kensington Olympia to Kidderminster. Two days later I was in Portishead, to undergo another PTS refresher course, needed every two years, then on the 27th I drove to Cheshire. Since splitting with Judi there had been something of a hole in my life and I had tried a couple of on-line dating sites, meeting one or two of the contacted ladies. This day I was to meet one from Chester and we agreed that I would park at Bache station and we would then catch the train into Chester. Despite having spoken several times on the phone and exchanged photographs, the day did not go as either of us had anticipated and the afternoon ended with us agreeing to go our separate ways. From there I drove to Beddgelert, where I spent another couple of days photographing both WHR and FR.

During the past 12 months I had been introduced to and joined TYMCARS (Tewkesbury YMCA Railway Society), and on 3 May was part of an arranged visit to the extensive layout at Long Marston, where lines of diesel and electric locos were

A sight to gladden the heart: No 60019 *Bittern* roars through Ashchurch for Tewkesbury station on 19 April 2008 with Kingfisher Railtours' 'The Severn Valley Phoenix' from Kensington Olympia to Kidderminster.

Leaving Loughborough Central, No 70013 *Oliver Cromwell* – with 'whiskers' – accelerates the 1200 service to Leicester North on 5 May 2008.

the subject of interest. The following day was not so happy. Leicester City drew 0-0 against Stoke City away and were relegated to the third tier of League football for the first time in the club's 124-year history. The 16th was Judi's 60th birthday. We had asked what she would like to do for the special day, and 'To go to Barcelona' was the rather surprising reply from someone who hated crowds, cities and general urbanity. However, she wanted to see Gaudi's architecture, so as a family of six we went to self-catering accommodation arranged by Adam not far from the incredible Sagrada Familia, flying out from Bristol on Wednesday the 14th and returning on Saturday the 17th. Between our return and the month end I was at the GWSR (twice) and the DFR.

On 2 June Bo Diddley died (born 1928). Five days later I was signing three new books at Alison's book shop in Tewkesbury: two new 'British Railways Past & Present' volumes on North Gloucestershire and Central Gloucestershire, and *British Railways Steam: The Final Years 1965-1968*. During the

Judi enjoying her 60th birthday in Barcelona with the family on 16 May 2008.

summer Nigel Pearson was appointed Leicester City's next manager, tasked with taking the club back to the Championship – which he did in the first season! Top of the division by November, two successive hat-tricks by Matt Fryatt – on 29 November at home to Dagenham & Redbridge in the FA Cup and on 6 December at home to Southend – were highlights. June also saw me upgrade my camera to a Canon 40D, with my 10D going as a gift to Judi as her first digital camera. However, firmly wedded to slides, she mastered neither the camera's functions nor the downloading and saving process, so the camera saw little use.

Coincidentally, as with the 10D, my first shots 'in anger' with the 40D were at Leicester station, as I went to the city on the 15th to collect Judi's cousin Liz. She had always wanted to visit Cornwall and had travelled from Brussels, where she lived, for me to act as chauffeur for a week's investigation of the county. We stayed with some friends of my Best Man, close to Penzance, and, with predominantly warm and sunny weather, began to tour the area, beginning at Launceston and Bodmin on our way down on the 16th. The Eden Project and the Lost

Gardens of Heligan were on the 17th, followed by rail to St Erth and St Ives on the 18th, where our plans were disrupted. After walking for about an hour along the cliff from St Ives, we turned to return; I gave her my hand as support on a steep part of the path, lost my footing and fell forward. Concerned for my new camera around my neck, I landed head first onto Cornish granite, splitting my face open just beneath my right eye. Fortunately my glasses and camera were spared, but the gash was deep — and we still had an hour's walk back to St Ives. My white handkerchief quickly turned red as I attempted to staunch the bleeding. From the surfers' headquarters in St Ives I was taken to Penzance hospital for stitches. We continued our holiday the next day, to St Michael's Mount and Minack Theatre, but neither my confidence nor facial features were enhanced by the experience. We travelled home on the 20th, where Mum was rather perturbed at my injury.

At the Launceston Railway on 16 June 2008, Liz undertakes her rehearsal for a job as fireman.

Not least because of my accident, July was quiet until an evening trip on the 19th to the DFR with TYMCARS, for a fish and chip supper. Two days later, the first of several outings by Cheltenham Camera Club, giving members exclusive access to venues for photography, took us to the sole remaining back-to-back houses in Birmingham. With the public excluded for the day, we had free rein to explore and photograph. Glorious weather helped both here and later as we walked around the city before the return home. I was particularly interested to see the revitalised and smartened Moor Street station, together with ex-GWR No 2885 on show in a terminal platform. This would later be removed when Chiltern Trains decided it needed the facility for services to Marylebone.

4-8 August saw me again in company with Judi in North Wales, visiting both the FR and WHR before going to Wellington and exploring the Tanat Valley and Ironbridge on the 6th. Afterwards I travelled home by way of Leominster for more shots of the location. I was again in the area on the 26th, at Codsall and Craven Arms, on my way to join the family for a ride behind No 76079 from Machynlleth to Pwllheli and back to celebrate Tammy's birthday.

September was a busy month, kicking off with the weekend of 6th/7th attending the WHR's 'Garratt 50' event. At least 50 of the type were present at Dinas, ranging from the original and several models of No K1, the very first to be built, down to much more diminutive sizes of various shapes. Sadly it rained for much of the two days, not least when 15-inch and 7¼-inch scale models stood alongside the real No K1 in Dinas yard. On the 19th I was on the SVR, enjoying sunshine that draped Nos 813, 5542, 7812 *Erlestoke Manor* and 7714 either on shed or at work. The following day was non-stop – beginning at Ledbury to catch No 40145 at 0832 on Pathfinder Tours' 'The Torbay Whistler', the 0630 Tame Bridge Parkway-Kingswear, then back to Bridgnorth for a guided tour of the shed at 1215, and finally to Oswestry for 1400, to be reserve photographer at a friend's wedding. I eventually escaped at 1800 to drive to my overnight accommodation. The 21st was again spent at the SVR before a drive to Mum's, to enable me to capture No 60163 *Tornado* on the GCR in 'undercoat grey' livery, gathering speed at 0945 at Woodthorpe heading for Leicester North.

The Gloucestershire Warwickshire Steam Railway had long held aspirations to extend from Toddington to Broadway, and over the years was making slow but steady progress. On 2 October I made the first of many trips to Broadway and the trackbed from the Toddington headquarters, recording constant development. The rest of October and November were very quiet, with just short local outings. On 4 November

A sight for sore eyes: a Class 40 on the mostly single-line Worcester-Hereford route! In mist and blindingly bright early morning sunshine, No 40145 restarts from the Ledbury stop with Pathfinder Tours' 'The Torbay Whistler' on Saturday 20 September 2008, on its way from Tame Bridge Parkway to Kingswear.

US Senator Barack Obama was elected as the 44th President of the United States, becoming the first African-American to hold that office. Later in the month Duane Eddy was inducted into the Musicians Hall of Fame in Nashville with, among others, the Crickets and Booker T. and the MGs. My only visit of any length was between 5 and 8 December, when I was again on the FR and WHR, calling in at Craven Arms on the way there and back

   2009 began with January's *Railway Magazine* hosting two pages of 'past and present' photos from my two Gloucestershire books in its 'All Change' series. It also started with the first snow of the year on the 4th. Sadly, from a photographic point of view it was not particularly heavy and the bright sunshine of the 5th rapidly introduced a thaw. I did, however, take the opportunity for some shots locally, both on and off the railway. Patrick McGoohan died on 13 January (born 1928); while being very well known as TV's *Danger Man* he is, for me, best remembered as 'Number Six' in *The Prisoner*. Fifty years after it was first broadcast, it is still one of my all-time favourite drama series.

My one trip of note in January was on the 19th, photographing at the local station after meeting an old friend for a meal in Didcot. To close the month, on the 31st I attended the launch at Blunsdon of a new-build plan to construct and recreate a 'Galloping Gertie', a 2-6-0 tender locomotive that once ran on the M&SWJR. It was an idea warmly received by attendees, but sadly very little has been heard of it since.

Since my move to Ashchurch I had become aware of the Cheltenham Gold Cup week, around the middle of March. The influx of thousands of racegoers led to increases in rail services, not least direct trains from London. On the 13th I was at Cheltenham Spa station to witness No 67030 arriving at 1119 with 1Z58, the 0805 Euston-Cheltenham special. The station car park was off-limits to cars, being given over to a fleet of double-decker buses operating shuttles to the racecourse. On the 19th

On the last day of its visit to the Great Central Railway, Sunday 22 March 2009, 'Q6' 0-8-0 No 63395 rests on shed at Loughborough (GC) just before its next turn out on the line.

a biographical article on me appeared in the *Leicester Mercury*, featuring one of my latest books, *British Railways Steam: The Final Years 1965-68*. Appropriately, I was back in Leicestershire on the 22nd, at Loughborough Central sheds to photograph No 63395, a rare visitor away from its home on the North Yorkshire Moors Railway.

The following day the 'Gang of Three' were out once more, with Paul and Neil meeting up with me at Tamworth (High Level). After spending time on the Low Level platform, during which I photographed DRS-liveried No 66418 on the 0438 Coatbridge-Daventry Intermodal service, transporting sugar for the Russell Group, we caught a train to Crewe. During 2 hours there, notebooks and cameras were employed to record a wide variety of types and colours, including Stobart Rail-liveried No 66414 on a northbound freight. Stafford was our last port of call, with the sun still shining and blessing our pictures at this open location. The month ended with the sight at Ashchurch of No 950001, an all-yellow Network Rail Class 150 conversion. Comprising cars Nos 999600 and 999601, it was operating as 2Z08, the 0659 Derby RTC-Bristol Temple Meads test train, via Westerleigh Oil Terminal. Pausing in Ashchurch loop to allow passenger services to pass, it gave plenty of time to compose its portrait.

Between 10 and 13 April the destination was another Gala on the FR and WHR. A highlight was Garratt No 87 in near white livery on Caernarfon-Porthmadog rosters, but the standout for rarity was my day's detour to the Corris Railway, to witness shire horse 'Truman' demonstrating the ancient art

Demonstrating potential dangers at level crossings, a Class 170 unit speeds into Gloucestershire at Northway on 7 April 2009.

of horse-drawn railway shunting. With the gauge being just 2ft 3in there was hardly room for the horse to fit between the rails! On 11 April Susan Boyle sang *I Dreamed a Dream* on TV's *Britain's Got Talent* and was an immediate and totally unexpected worldwide sensation, being viewed over 200 million times on YouTube!

To help mark the 150th anniversary of the Corris Railway, horse-worked freight trains were demonstrated at Maespoeth over the weekend of 11/12 April 2009. On Saturday the 11th horse 'Truman' was employed, encouraged by his owner Ian Cryer, author and illustrator of the 'Rachael, the Railway Horse' series of children's books.

Public services from Caernarfon through to Beddgelert on the WHR began in time for the 2009 Easter weekend celebrations. Blessed with glorious weather on the railway for all three days, newly restored Garratt No 87 arrives at the new southern terminus on Sunday 12 April 2009, with the 1000 train from Caernarfon. Note the appropriate tank front decoration.

2 May was a satisfying day. Leicester City ended the season top of their division, seven points clear of second place, guaranteeing Championship football again for 2009/10. It was also the day I travelled to photograph the Amey/Colas possession at Puxton, near Worle, where the northbound track was being relaid. Further, it was the day that my new 'British Railways Past & Present' book, Volume 3 on the Welsh Highland Railway, was available in the shops. A week later I joined Peter Townsend at Harrowden Junction, north of Wellingborough, to see No 70013 *Oliver Cromwell* at the head of 1Z61, the 0814 London Victoria-Sheffield Steam Dreams' 'The Palatine' railtour. Originally planned to go direct to Manchester, there were gauging problems at a couple of locations, causing diversion

No 70013 *Oliver Cromwell* restarts from a long stop at Harrowden Junction on 9 May 2009, having arrived there some 30 minutes early, and receives friendly waves. Originally Steam Dreams' 1Z61, 'The Palatine' railtour to Manchester, it was renamed 'The Cathedrals Express' and rerouted for Sheffield, via Harringworth Viaduct and Syston East Junction.

via Corby to Sheffield. It had arrived 30 minutes early at the junction and was held until released, still 18 minutes early. This gave me time to position myself to capture it gathering speed following its restart.

On the 16th and 17th I was back at the WHR, mostly at Beddgelert where, on the latter date, I had to be quick with my trigger finger. Waiting to photograph No 143 as it arrived with the 1000 train from Caernarfon, I noticed four sheep dozing at the side of the line. Not anticipating what was about to happen, I was fortunate to manage to capture the sight of the four of them suddenly waking up and making a dash for it across the tracks in front of the large locomotive bearing down on them. They were lucky not to end as lamb chops!

Woolly jumpers! Sheep have safely grazed at Beddgelert station since trains stopped running there, on the old Welsh Highland Railway, more than 70 years ago … but no longer! Their continued presence at the station is causing the new railway headaches and one can see why in this view. On Sunday 17 May 2009 four of the animals play 'chicken' as Garratt No 143 arrives with the 1000 departure from Caernarfon, with the crew anxiously watching the road ahead.

My next book was to be another 'Past and Present' look at the Severn Valley Railway, and I therefore spent 12 to 15 June at many of the locations between Kidderminster and Bridgnorth. I was back again on the 20th, when I was fortunate to be in the right spot to witness No D444 *Exeter* fail at Hampton Loade with brake problems. Ascertaining that No D8188 was to travel up from Kidderminster to rescue loco and train, I walked a few hundred yards to a lineside vantage point to capture the pairing as they eventually headed south. The 27th was to give me another unexpected sight. Having arranged a meal and ride on the GCR with Mum and cousin David, we arrived at Loughborough Central station to find it renamed 'Cemetery Junction'! A film written by Ricky Gervais and Stephen Merchant, named after a district of Reading where the action takes place, was filmed at Loughborough with an incredibly realistic retail building added to the platform for the duration. On the 25th Michael Jackson died (born 1958).

For part of the forthcoming film *Cemetery Junction*, written and directed by Ricky Gervais and Stephen Merchant, Loughborough Central station was 'converted' to the eponymous station. This was the view on Saturday 27 June 2009, shortly after filming had ceased, with a noticeable change to the northern end of the station very visible.

I was in the company of Peter Townsend and Paul Morris on 25 July for my one and only visit to Rushden station. The sole intermediate station on the Higham Ferrers branch, closed on 13 June 1959, it was now a museum, café and club house for the Rushden Historical Transport Society. I enjoyed good company, beverage and the sight of No 31206 standing proudly in the platform with coaches.

8 August saw Leicester City back in the Championship, without a sponsor but with '125' incorporated into their

badge for the season, celebrating the club's 125th anniversary. All began well, with the first five results being three wins and two draws. Five days later, Les Paul, the innovative guitarist and inventor, died of complications from pneumonia aged 94 (born 1915). On the 21st my travels took me to Bridgnorth, Welshpool and Llanfair Caereinon, but it was the following day that was the anticipated highlight. By invitation, I joined a small group of enthusiasts to sample the privately run monorail layout a few miles north of Blaenau Ffestiniog. Never having been close up to the arrangement before, I was fascinated by the technicalities of the system, the loco and the honour of a ride around the location.

On 9 September the entire Beatles catalogue was rereleased as digital remasters, including original artwork for

With the threat of eviction from his home looming over owner Richard Morris – who had only recently had a triple bypass operation! – the monorail system on his adjoining land was also under a cloud. On what could be the last public operations for some time, a private charter enjoyed fabulous weather conditions to view the layout on Saturday 22 August 2009. The sole steam loco, *Monoloco*, an 0-2-0ST completed in 1998, poses for its portrait between demonstration runs.

first time since 1987. Seven days later I was out and about again. Since moving to Ashchurch in 2007, I had never spent much time exploring locations in a wider circle from home, but on the 16th I took the opportunity occasioned by a stock move from Long Marston to venture into Worcestershire. Normal fare was anticipated at Abbotswood, but I was rewarded by NR's 'yellow banana' NMT heading south as 1Z15, the 0650 Derby RTC-Swindon Cocklebury Yard. No 43013 led, one of the few HST power cars with buffers, with No 43062 on the rear. I met a TYMCARS member there and we then both travelled to nearby Norton Barracks to witness grey-liveried No 56311 hauling 0Z57, the 1300 Long Marston-Crewe stock move comprising Nos 87013, 87014, 87004 and 86401 *Northampton Town*.

Back in Leicester on the 20th, I took some final shots of the fated Braunstone Lane girder bridge ahead of demolition, before making another foray to the SVR on the 24th for the Autumn Steam Gala. The day started dull but brightened as the morning wore on and the afternoon was wall-to-wall sunshine. This contributed to some very pleasing portraits lineside south of Bewdley of Nos 813 and 4936 *Kinlet Hall*, the latter late in the afternoon on the 1622 Arley-Kidderminster turn.

3 October was the date of a rare reunion of Judi's extended family, with contingents from Brussels and Luxembourg coming to a venue in Oadby, Leicestershire, in addition to those from many points of the UK compass. As usual my camera was put to good use. Adam assumed the role of DJ and even included some of my favourite tracks among the dance tunes. On the 14th I repeated my visit to the SVR and the weather echoed the previous trip, although this time the sun was not as cloud-free. However, this did not spoil my first view of one of the growing breed of new-builds in the form of the frames of No 82045 at Bridgnorth.

The 23rd was a reunion of sorts as the 'Gang of Three' met up again, beginning at Birmingham New Street. Rugby, Nuneaton, Stafford and Crewe were the destinations and included my first ride in a Class 350 electric unit. Despite the reduction in motive power over the years and my success in seeing as much as possible of what was left, I still managed to cop Nos 66574 and 66301 at Nuneaton during our 2-hour stay. Crewe also gave me two – Nos 90049 and 66415. Later, I was pleased to photograph No 92005 *Mozart* on 4O10, the MX 1218 Trafford Park-Southampton EWS Intermodal duty.

Most 'Pendolino' services roar non-stop through Nuneaton station. One such is seen at 1217 on 23 October, forming an unidentified service to Euston approaching at speed in the bright autumn sunshine.

On 26 October I purchased a Canon G11 camera for £499, including £250-part exchange of my G10, having become disappointed with its focussing. Known as a 'bridge' camera – mid-way between an SLR and a 'point and shoot' – the G11 was small enough to be a back-up in my pocket or to sit in the car in case of need.

I had recently joined the LMS-Patriot Society to support the new-build of an unrebuilt 'Patriot' 4-6-0, long extinct since BR days. I joined the Members Day at Llangollen on the 8th, to see the frames and proposed nameplate of No 45551 *The Unknown Warrior*. Adopted by the British Legion as its memorial engine, it was hoped to be complete in time for 2018 and the anniversary of the end of the First World War. Seven days later

I was on track with the works on the line at Bredon, a few miles north of Ashchurch. That was my last outing of note in 2009. On 20 December Rage Against the Machine took the Christmas No 1 slot in the UK with *Killing in the Name*, after a massive Facebook campaign to prevent the winner of *The X Factor* from taking top spot again!

2010 was a good year and a bad year. For me, it was another good year with a further six books published, but elsewhere there were earthquakes and other disasters. On 12 January a 7.0-magnitude earthquake hit Haiti, devastating the nation's capital, Port-au-Prince. With a confirmed death toll of more than 316,000, it was the seventh deadliest on record. 27 February saw an 8.8-magnitude earthquake in Chile, triggering a tsunami over the Pacific that killed at least 525. This earthquake was one of the largest in recorded history. On 14 April volcanic ash from one of several eruptions beneath Mount Eyjafjallajökull, an icecap in Iceland, disrupted air traffic across northern and western Europe; and six days later the Deepwater Horizon oil drilling platform exploded in the Gulf of Mexico, killing 11 workers. The resulting Horizon oil spill, one of the largest in history, spread for several months. Further disastrous events followed during the year.

January began for me in Leicester, with the family, to celebrate Mum's 90th birthday on the 3rd. Soon after my return home, Gloucestershire was carpeted with snow, which lasted for more than a week. On the 7th I was out with the camera on my local line, capturing trains leaving snow clouds behind them. Two days later I was there again to see No 5043 *Earl of Mount Edgcumbe*, wreathed in smoke, with 1Z71, the 1044 Tyseley-Gloucester WCRC-operated charter, 'Ken's Birthday Express'. One of the shots received a 'Commended' award in a Cheltenham Camera Club competition later in the year. January was also a good month for me with the 'birth' of the Ashchurch, Tewkesbury & District Rail Promotion Group (ATDRPG), which featured in the local press following its first public meeting on 23 February.

January had another fillip, with the arrival of the powerful

Class 70s from across the Atlantic. This enabled me to start copping locos again, seeing and photographing No 70002 at Ashchurch on 4Z70, a Rugeley-Stoke Gifford rake of empty Freightliner Heavy Haul coal hoppers on the 19th. On the 30th it was back to Leicestershire for the GCR's 'Lostock & Several Smoking Barrels' three-day gala. In bright sunny weather I captured several pleasing images, but among my favourites was 'Jubilee' No 5690 *Leander* in MR red livery at the head of a rake of iconic 'Windcutter' wagons. On 20 February

The family celebrate and are keen to enjoy the feast on 3 January 2010 at Birstall on Mum's 90th birthday.

the sun disappeared seconds before Nos 4965 *Rood Ashton Hall* and 5043 *Earl of Mount Edgcumbe* burst through Ashchurch for Tewkesbury station, double-heading as 1Z43, 'The Great Western Incursion' Tyseley-Didcot special.

5 March was the first day of the SVR's 'Spring Steam Reunion Gala', and I was there for the three-day event. Especial delights were No 61994, a long way from its Scottish home, and a variety of locos working hard on an extensive timetable, mostly in sunshine. The 13th was another delight, being invited to partake in Brian Morrison's 80th birthday surprise party at Quainton Road. Brian had been a guru for me over many years and I learned much from his photographic eye. It was an honour to be among so many renowned railway photographers and publishers. On 9 April I drove to the WLLR, to take part in a

Making a delightful vision, wearing a 'Ken's Birthday Express' headboard, No 5043 *Earl of Mount Edgcumbe* speeds south through the wintry Gloucestershire countryside past Northway, as 1Z71, the 1044 Tyseley-Gloucester WCRC-operated charter, on Saturday 9 January 2010.

private charter before the weekend of 10/11 April, which would see the last workings of ex-Sierra Leone No 85 on the railway before expiry of its 10-year boiler certificate and placement in storage. It was a good-humoured affair and shutters sounded like machine-gun fire! The following day Judi and I explored past railway sites in and around the Tanat Valley. 29 April saw me at Quattro Rail's compound in Brownhills, to complete my latest PTS refresher course.

I May saw the opening of Tryfan Junction station on the WHR, but incredibly I was the only person present to record the 1000 Caernarfon-Hafod-y-Llyn arrival, the first train to stop here for around 75 years! The official party arrived on that train! The same day saw the launch of the FR's 'Quirks &

After No 61994 had stalled on Eardington Bank earlier in the day on 5 March 2010, its departure as the 1150 train to Kidderminster from Bridgnorth was delayed. The crew discuss the situation.

Curiosities Gala', where all manner of weird and wonderful items of motive power were on show, including a Land Rover on 2-foot-gauge rail wheels. Also on show was the new Boston Lodge-built *Lyd*, a replica of a Lynton & Barnstaple Railway loco. The football season closed on 2 May; Leicester City ended fifth and in the play-offs against Cardiff City. Scores were level at 3-3 after two legs, but Leicester lost 5-3 on penalties – so nearly straight from League One to Premiership! Manager Nigel Pearson left for Hull City after a disagreement with the owner.

    A day in hot summer sunshine was my treat at the GWSR on the 5th, as was the sight of No 8476, a Stanier 8F built by North British for the War Department during the Second World War as No WD348. Becoming LMS No 8274 before going to Turkish Railways as No 45160, it was repatriated to the UK in 1989. On 11 June Duane Eddy was presented with a Mojo Magazine Icon Award at the Mojo Awards Dinner. While in the UK he appeared on Jonathan Ross's Saturday show on

A truly historic moment, and only me there to record it! With the new platform completed at Tryfan Junction on the WHR, a party of construction volunteers and other interested individuals were conveyed by train to the site on Saturday 1 May 2010. In its new blue lined livery, Garratt No 87 enters the station with the 1000 Caernarfon-Hafod-y-Llyn service, being the first passenger train to stop here for around 75 years!

Radio 2 and Clive Anderson's *Loose Ends* programme on Radio 4. 12/13 and 19/20 June saw the S&CR's 'GWR175 Steam Gala', over two weekends, with the stars being Nos 3717 *City of Truro* and 5322 from Didcot. The 24th heralded the beginning of research for the third part of my *British Railways Past & Present: Gloucestershire* trilogy, and on the 26th, under a relentless sun, I was walking the DFR track between Norchard and Parkend.

Preparing to run across the Cob to Porthmadog during the FR's 'Quirks & Curiosities Gala', this ex-Statfold Barn Railway Land Rover adds variety to the fare on offer.

Enjoying a brief run out of Norchard shed yard, and a recent arrival
from Bill Parker's Flour Mill, *Rocket* provides real variety during the
DFR's 'Severn & Wye Railway Festival 2010', celebrating 200 years of
the S&WR on Sunday 27 June 2010.

City of Truro was again on show, as was a working replica of
Rocket on the 27th, a recent arrival from Bill Parker's Flour Mill
for this 'Severn & Wye Railway Festival 2010', celebrating 200
years of the S&WR.

On 5 July I travelled to Great Malvern station as a
representative of ATDRPG, to meet a manager from London
Midland Trains and discuss possible future collaborations. The
following day the 'Gang of Four' was reunited for a trip to
Rugby, Nuneaton, Crewe and Stafford, recreating our previous
usage of a West Midlands Day Ranger ticket. 7 July saw Paulo
Sousa as the new Leicester City manager – he was sacked
on 1 October after a poor start in the Championship! On 10
July I was photographing the annual Tewkesbury Medieval Fair,
celebrating the battle of 1471.

Enjoying our days out, the 'Gang of Four' met again at
Peterborough station on 3 August before travelling by rail to
Grantham, Nottingham and Derby. Seeing motive power and
liveries from the other side of the UK from Ashchurch was

Welcome to the past: Gordon, (Sir) Aubrey, Matt and Sandra at Tewkesbury Medieval Fayre on 10 July 2010.

The penultimate outing of 'The Cambrian' steam special in 2010 crosses the threatened Pont Briwet over the estuary. No 44871 heads the 1005 Machynlleth-Pwllheli service.

a delight, as were two cops, at Nuneaton – No 66714 – and Peterborough – No 66723. With an engineer's possession of the main line, I was on track at Cheltenham on the 8th to photograph Nos 66618, 66585 (both cops) and 66615 on infrastructure trains. As well as enjoying sharing Tammy's birthday on the 27th, we had a delightful day as a family climbing the hilly nature reserve on the outskirts of Penrhyndeudraeth. Overlooking the estuary and Pont Briwet bridge, I was equally satisfied to record No 44871 on the penultimate outing of 'The Cambrian' steam shuttles of 2010, the 1005 Machynlleth-Pwllheli service, as it crossed the bridge in bright sunshine.

Chapter 6
2010-2015

September proved a busy month, with the first four days completely occupied with excursions around South Gloucestershire and Bristol, old photographs in hand, in preparation for my next 'Past and Present' book. Day one began at Chipping Sodbury, then I travelled westwards to Severn Beach, while Day two concentrated within Bristol, at St Philips Marsh depot and the sites of Barrow Road shed and Fishponds station. Temple Meads to Avonmouth was the focus on the 3rd, with Stapleton Road to Temple Meads completing the quartet of trips on the 4th. Although concentration was on photographically recreating the past, many trains were seen but, sadly, no cops. There were interesting conversations along the

way, however, including a 'female Paul Simon', a young American guitarist 'sitting on the railway station' at Montpelier on the 3rd.

On the 9th I was with Peter Townsend, attending a meeting at Barnstaple by rail, where we met Tim Maddocks, a Network Rail employee, with

The massive biomass hopper at Bristol Bulk Handling Terminal at Avonmouth dominates the skyline, dwarfing the view of No 66162 at St Andrews Road with a rake of empty coal hoppers on Saturday 11 September 2010.

whom I would later work on projects. On the return to Exeter, for a coffee before returning home, I had a brief but pleasant conversation with Andy Burnham, then Labour's Shadow Secretary of State for Health. Photographs in the sunshine at St David's station and a cop of No 66599 at Taunton nicely wound up the day.

Two days later I was back in the Bristol area for the book, then on the 13th I was at Honeybourne to join Tim and others from Network Rail as they surveyed work needed for the forthcoming redoubling of the North Cotswold line. Discussions with Peter and Tim at Exeter had determined that a book to cover this work was desirable.

Approached by Colin Marsden to assist with photographs of two Class 08s, needed for a proposed book, on the 18th I travelled to Birmingham, by prior arrangement, to snap No 08616 in an individual livery at Tyseley depot, and No 08805, in blue, at Soho depot. I had another appointment on the 22nd, at Broadway Tower. I was wanting to spread my photographic wings to portrait work and had agreed a photo shoot at the location with a young lady willing to be my 'guinea pig'. The sun shone brightly and the shoot went well, a point acknowledged by her chaperone. On 4 October Norman Wisdom died (born 1915).

Part of the North Cotswold work was replacing a single-track bridge near Honeybourne with one catering for two. Between 30 September and 2 October I was on site to witness the detailed and impressive task of removing the old bridge and wheeling a pre-cast replacement into place on a low-loader, manually controlled by an operator on the ground with a key pad. Watching him manoeuvre the massive structure forward, change the angle of approach, then lower it into the prepared cradle, with just millimetres to spare, was awe-inspiring.

On 2 October Duane Eddy was onstage at the Royal Festival Hall in London, then, six days later, he appeared at the Jack Daniels 160th birthday celebrations at Clapham Grand, together with Jarvis Cocker and Richard Hawley. On the 13th he was at the Grand Opera House, York. While in the UK he

The wonders of modern science! The new 150-ton double-line bridge, east of Honeybourne as part of the Cotswold line redoubling, is slowly positioned into the space created for it on Saturday 2 October 2010 by the man with the 'games console' strapped around his neck, controlling the 32-wheeled low-loader! The space under the bridge will be filled (hopefully) in the future by the northern extension of the GWSR on its run to Honeybourne station.

appeared on *Later with Jools Holland*, then spent time recording a new album in Sheffield with Richard Hawley's band, virtually live as he had been for his earliest recordings. Elsewhere, Sven-Goran Eriksson was appointed manager of Leicester City on 3 October.

Much of the rest of the month was spent photographing the North Cotswold line, until I made another journey to the WHR on the 30th and 31st. This weekend was to see the first trains run between Caernarfon and Porthmadog with the completion of the line, and red-liveried Garratt No 138 was greeted by many hundreds on arrival in Porthmadog. I managed to find a location to record the event where there were just a handful present. When the train was due we were deluged by a hailstorm, driving me back into my car. The train was late arriving due to a farmer driving his tractor onto the track in protest, further north, but this was to prove a blessing as the sun shone brightly when the train finally arrived! After this frenetic period, November and December were virtually devoid of interest, apart from a brief visit to Worcester Shrub Hill's signal box and sidings with Tim on 10 November.

History in the making. The first complete train from Caernarfon to Porthmadog, over the revitalised WHR, crosses Snowdon Street behind Garratt No 138, nearing its destination, on Saturday 30 October 2010.

2011 was another good year for me, with four more books published: *British Railways Past & Present: Bristol and South Gloucestershire* and *Ffestiniog Railway Recollections* in May and, later in the year, *British Railways Past & Present: The Cotswold Line: Worcester to Oxford*, together with a Limited Edition hardback version that included an extra 32 pages. The highlight for me in early January was being allowed access to the security-controlled Portbury Docks, near Bristol, to photograph two ex-Stanier 8Fs days after their repatriation from Turkey. After a frosty night, the sun shone brightly on Nos 45166 and 45170 and their tenders on low-loaders prior to their travels inland.

I was again graced by sun on the 29th when I travelled to the GCR at Loughborough for its winter gala and to the Midland station for an update on the rebuilding at the north end of the station.

On 10 February Vichai Raksriaksorn, of the King Power Group, part of the Thai-based Asia Football Investments consortium, was appointed as new chairman of Leicester City, to fill the vacuum left when Milan Mandarić took over at Sheffield Wednesday the previous November. My camera lay dormant for much of this month, not being picked up in earnest until 7 March, when I was out at Charlbury and Ascott-under-Wychwood to capture progress on the North Cotswold line redoubling. Elsewhere, 11 March saw a 9.0-magnitude earthquake and subsequent tsunami to the east of Japan, killing 15,840 and with another 3,926 missing. On the 15th protests began in Syria against Bashar al-Assad, sparking a civil war; Jet Harris, a founder member of the Shadows, died on the 18th (born 1939); and on the 23rd Elizabeth Taylor also died (born 1932).

1 April was the next injection of excitement, when Judi and I joined the first 'Snowdonian' train. Only possible with the completion of the WHR to Porthmadog, the railtour ran from Porthmadog to Blaenau Festiniog and back to Minffordd, where locos were changed. Thereafter, the itinerary was a non-stop run through and past Porthmadog and on to Caernarfon. The day then ended with a return to Porthmadog, giving participants the honour of two through journeys over the 40 miles of both the FR and WHR. Fairlies *Taliesin* and *Earl of Merioneth* handled the first leg, with *Merddin Emrys* and *David Lloyd George* taking over at Minffordd to haul the rest of the journey.

The 9th, 15th and 16th were devoted to more photographs along the North Cotswold line before spending three more days from the 23rd on the FR and WHR for another gala. I was delighted to photograph Mallet No 9 at Beddgelert on Saturday the 23rd, visiting from the Statfold Barn Railway. This turned out to be my only photograph of this type of loco, as it failed while operating the 1010 Rhyd Ddu-Porthmadog shuttle, suffering with hot-box problems. The FR's *Lyd* took over for the rest of the gala, masquerading as BR No 30190, in recognition of its design as a Lynton & Barnstaple Railway loco.

On 29 April Prince William and Catherine Middleton were married in Westminster Abbey. The following day our son Adam married his fiancé Claire Bowring at a much more interesting location – Bristol Zoo! During preparations, Adam and some male friends recreated the iconic Abbey Road crossing picture on the road outside one of the Zoo's entrances. The day after, while some of us were recovering from the wedding celebrations, news was released that Osama bin Laden had been killed in Pakistan. My only photographs of note in May were on the 2nd – recording garden sculptures as exhibits at Showborough House in Worcestershire – and out on track at Charlbury and Ascott-under-Wychwood on the 30th (in pouring rain) and the 31st (marginally better conditions).

With the North Cotswold line redoubling work coming to

Adam and friends try to recreate the Beatles' iconic *Abbey Road* image on 30 April 2011, outside Bristol Zoo, the location for his wedding later that day.

fruition, I was part of the celebrations on 6 June, on board No 166207 from Charlbury to Ascott-under-Wychwood, where the new second platform was formally opened. Despite having this extra platform for the first time for many years, this wayside station would still only have two stopping trains a day. More views of many of the stations affected by the recent works were obtained on the 14th.

On 20 June Duane Eddy's *Road Trip* was released in the UK, his first album for 25 years. To celebrate he was in the UK for a brief tour, beginning on 21 June at the 100 Club in London. I travelled to the capital that day, checking in to overnight accommodation before making my way to the club. Backed by Richard Hawley's band, he put on a great show in front of a packed crowd who thronged around him afterwards for autographs and conversations. The following day I took the

My Duane Eddy ticket for the 21 June 2011 100 Club performance in London.

Looking like a huge railway slug (!), No 332004 arrives at Paddington on Wednesday 22 June 2011 forming a service from Heathrow.

opportunity for photographs at King's Cross, St Pancras, Euston, Marylebone and Paddington stations, including the wonderful statue of Sir John Betjeman on the St Pancras concourse. I copped No 66844 at Didcot on my way home. Later in the week, on Sunday the 26th, Duane wowed a crowd on the West Holt Stage at the Glastonbury Festival, many of whom had probably never heard him before.

2 July was my next 'road trip', to the GCR, Loughborough Midland station and lineside at Cossington. The following day I acted as chauffeur to Liz, visiting from Brussels, around east Leicestershire and Rutland. A two-day excursion by rail from Ashchurch to Penzance on the 12th and 13th saw me enjoy an overnight stay with David, my Best Man, and his wife Jill. I broke the journey home on several occasions and grabbed more chances of photographs at not frequently visited locations. On the 16th the direction was totally the opposite as Judi, Tammy and I journeyed to Aberdeen to attend a family wedding the following day. Adam and Claire were supposed to be with us, but Adam had fallen ill on the 16th. As well as the wedding, I photographed at Edinburgh Waverley and Aberdeen stations, the latter by prior arrangement as I was warned of the strict policy of no photographs without permission. Even then, it took some perseverance for my authority to be accepted!

On 30 July Leicester City had a taste of international football, losing 2-1 to Real Madrid in a pre-season friendly at the King Power Stadium. On the same day I was intrigued but delighted to see the Groundhogs scheduled to perform at a local fete, in a field at Meifod in mid-Wales, close to Welshpool! Despite suffering a stroke in 2009, lead guitarist Tony

Still playing after all these years, Tony McPhee of the Groundhogs performs at a local event in Meifod, mid-Wales, on 30 July 2011.

McPhee was still on good form and, with some replacements to the original line-up, the performance in the warm summer sunshine was hugely enjoyable. The following day I made use of my time in the area to travel on the WLLR behind No 822 *The Earl*.

August saw the completion of much of the North Cotswold work and led to me spending much time on and around the line. On the 9th I had the honour of being given access to the machinery controlling the semaphore signals underneath Moreton-in-Marsh signal box, followed on the 12th by another honour, when I was delighted to be part of a group allowed to enter and inspect the railway tunnel underneath Mythe Road on the outskirts of Tewkesbury. The line that had once run from Ashchurch to Great Malvern had closed exactly 50 years earlier. Other North Cotswold line visits occurred on the 14th, 19th, 22nd and 31st. Of these, the most exciting was standing on the brand-new footbridge at Honeybourne at

A historic moment on the opening day after completion of the Cotswold redoubling! At precisely 0600 on Monday 22 August 2011 No 43098 heads the first train into the new Platform 2 at Honeybourne with a non-stop up working.

precisely 0600 on Monday 22 August, as daylight made its first tentative appearance, to witness No 43098 head the first train into the new Platform 2 with a non-stop up working, becoming the first HST set EVER to grace this route. When the previous up platform was removed 40 years earlier, the HSTs were but a dream!

The first excitement in September was on the 17th, when No 5043 *Earl of Mount Edgcumbe* pulled into Worcester Shrub Hill station at 0822 on the Vintage Trains' 'Cathedrals Express' Tyseley-Paddington railtour, organised by FGW to celebrate the completion of the North Cotswold re-doubling. Many rail celebrities mingled with members of the public and the train even contained BBC's Kevin Connolly, who was to report on the event and with whom I had a conversation in the corridor of the leading coach (not for broadcast!). Seeing the delight on Theresa Villiers's face at both Moreton-in-Marsh – on the footplate – and at Paddington, at the end of the journey, was truly satisfying, as was the sight of the 'Castle' standing proudly

Theresa Villiers and Bob Meanley are aboard No 5043 *Earl of Mount Edgcumbe* on Vintage Trains' 'Cathedrals Express' at Moreton-in-Marsh on 17 September 2011.

at the buffer stops at Paddington. Two days later, more delight was on the faces of the schoolchildren at Highley station, on the SVR, as they waited with their mock gasmask boxes for No 92212 to whisk them away from the threats of wartime! A trio of delights was completed, again on the SVR, as ex-Caledonian Railway No 828 stood in its superb blue livery at Kidderminster, bathed in bright autumn sunshine.

October's *Railway Magazine* contained my article 'The Tracks of our Years', looking at the redoubling of the North Cotswold line. I had been requested by Colas Rail to photograph one of its new diesels being part of the work at Dr Day's Junction, to the north of Bristol Temple Meads station. After signing in and being inducted as to the work and movements of machines, I was on site at 0900 on the 9th to snap No 66847. Once that was done, the Colas manager disappeared and I continued photographing the rest of the work, being allowed to go where my fancy took me, even down to Lawrence Hill. Another '66' into the camera was No 66744, recently renumbered from 66843. Eight months later it was named *Crossrail*, in recognition of the new line being built under London.

October was proving eventful, as I was asked to go to

Due to begin its very last shift at 2355, No DR 73257, the last '07' tamper operating on Network Rail's system, receives some preparatory attention from Tommy Toomer (left) and Gary Lloyd (right) 20 minutes earlier at Salisbury on Thursday 13 October 2011. After its night's work, it will be moved to Balfour Beatty's compound at Ashford, awaiting its fate.

Salisbury to photograph the last of Balfour Beatty's older generation of tampers as it prepared to travel to its final job. Sadly, I was not needed until 2300 hours, so spent some time photographing the night scenes at Salisbury station. Having completed my assignment by 2340, I returned to my car and drove back home. I declined the offer of spending the whole night with the machine, recording its last duties out in the countryside!

On the 21st I indulged in broadside panning shots of No 6024 *King Edward I* at 0955 from a field at Ashchurch as it worked 5Z60, the 0848 Kidderminster-Bristol (Barton Hill) train via Newport and Severn Tunnel. Four days later Sven-Goran Eriksson left Leicester City, by mutual consent, after initial promise and big spending. Nigel Pearson returned from Hull and hopes were high for the season.

On 9 November I attended an ACoRP presentation in the MPs' dining room at the Houses of Parliament, where the speakers were Mark Hopwood, MD of FGW, and MPs Theresa Villiers and Ben Bradshaw. As the gathering was not until after lunch, I took the chance to photograph at Charing Cross station and along the Thames, including the London Eye. This was my first view of the iconic structure. I was pleased to cop No 66413 at Acton on my way into London. Three days later London Midland's 'Farewell 150' tour took place, at 0750 from Birmingham Snow Hill, a celebratory last run of Class 150s through Droitwich and up the Lickey Incline. I was at Droitwich Spa and Bromsgrove

With a crew member gazing back, No 150001 'banks' No 150106 as the pair begin the attack on the Lickey Incline, forming the London Midland 'Farewell 150' tour on Saturday 12 November 2011.

to capture both locations for posterity. That task completed, I drove to Derby to attend a members' meeting of the LMS-Patriot Society, held in the Roundhouse, refurbished from the old MR engine shed.

December was taken up with fleeting visits to Moreton-in-Marsh, Bath Spa and Gloucester. The bestselling album for 2011 was *21* by Adele, which was the No 1 album for 18 weeks between 5 February and 30 July; she also had the bestselling single, *Someone Like You*.

Although I had not given up writing, and more books were scheduled, 2012 was the first year since 1994 that I was without a new title. However, other things were on my mind, not least that Mum was now 92, so I sat her down in the conservatory of her bungalow on 16 January to video her. I asked about her early life, meeting Dad, the war, etc, and, as she has since died, I am eternally grateful for the effort. Two days earlier I had been at Wanstrow, on the Cranmore branch from Witham, at the request of Colas Rail, to photograph No 47727 *Rebecca* and 47749 *Demelza* top-and-tailing the 6Q70 from Westbury, formed of five Autoballaster wagons. The movie capability of my camera was again in use at Loughborough Midland on the 15th, on one of my many visits to the station as the extensions and alterations to the platforms took shape.

Another regular set of photographic records was begun on 17 February, capturing the site close to the railway line at Northway that was to become new housing. Two deaths this month were Whitney Houston on the 11th (born 1963) and ex-Monkee Davy Jones on the 29th (born 1945). On a very blustery 27th I again employed movie mode to record a lineside view of No 37259 and its throaty roar on 1Q13, the Derby RTC-Exeter Riverside Network Rail train. A northbound 'Super Voyager' also snuck into the frame.

1 March was a day to which I had looked forward as I was to join a select group for a walk through Chipping Campden Tunnel. Dawning very misty, the warm sunshine quickly burned this off and we had clear conditions for our expedition. Though double track, the bore gave a more restricted feel, which added

to the awareness that we had limited time to complete the tour before the passage of the next service train.

Loughborough was not the only station seeing platform alterations, and on the 12th I was inspecting the FR plans at Harbour station, Porthmadog, for the widening of the Cob embankment at the town end to create land for the proposed joint FR/WHR station – very much a case of thinking outside the box! The following day, 246 years since its first publication, *Encyclopædia Britannica* discontinued its print edition. On the 18th, while she was still mobile and with memory largely intact, I took Mum to the 13th-century St Peter's Church at Belgrave, Leicester, where she and Dad had married on 30 May 1942. The weather was damp, as was the grass, but she had not visited the site for many years and was happy to wallow in nostalgia. Another venerable location was visited on the 20th, when I photographed Brunel's original train shed at Bristol Temple Meads, after a tip-off concerning plans for its redevelopment ahead of the proposed electric IEP high-speed trains.

From 23 to 25 March I accompanied the two Peters from Silver Link Publishing to the West Somerset Railway Spring Steam Gala. The weather was glorious and, in addition to my part in book-signing sessions, I took full advantage

Making a stormy exit, Nos 7828 *Norton Manor 40 Commando* leads No 6960 *Raveningham Hall* away from Minehead with the 1200 train to Bishops Lydeard on Saturday 25 March 2012, during the WSR's Spring Steam Gala.

for photographs, especially of the relatively new turntable at Minehead. Being up close and personal to Nos 6024 *King Edward I* and 70000 *Britannia* on this was most satisfying. A short trip to Watchet also gave opportunities for boat pictures. The month climaxed with a day at Bristol, soaking up atmosphere at Temple Meads and Parkway.

On my way to North Wales for the 2012 FR May Day Gala, I broke the journey at Craven Arms on 4 May and timed it well to snap No 67001, the former *Night Mail*, roaring through on the 1615 Cardiff Central-Holyhead cross-country express. The following three days were dry, but only the 6th produced sunshine. This did not detract, however, from the sight of *Earl of Merioneth* with a large circular headboard reading 'Dinas-Portmadoc 1832 1982 Porthmadog- Blaenau Ffestiniog', celebrating 180 years since the birth of the FR and 30 years

With a storm gathering behind, *Earl of Merioneth* accelerates across the Cob out of Porthmadog on Sunday 6 May 2012 during the FR's 'Blaenau 30' Gala, as the 1015 service bound for Blaenau Ffestiniog, with one of the original 1982 headboards. 'Order! Order!' was often heard from the then Speaker of the House of Commons, George Thomas, who was a great supporter of the railway, and his words grace the headboard.

since restoration of services to the top end of the line. *Lyd* in pseudo-SR livery was also a delight, as was the gravity train, both on the 6th. For the 7th I moved to the WHR at Beddgelert before travelling south to the Corris Railway. Nos 3 *Sir Haydn* and 7 double-headed the 1300 train to Maespoeth and return with all-female crews for the day.

On 9 May *Railway Herald* No 314 featured my article on 30 years since the FR had reopened to Blaenau Ffestiniog, but a greater delight for me came three days later. Duane Eddy opened his latest UK tour at Market Harborough Leisure Centre, ably supported by Nell Bryden, a somewhat surprising venue but none the less enjoyable. In a sports hall, rather than a seated venue, the audience were as welcoming as ever and, after the show, one of Judi's cousins and Peter Townsend had their photographs taken with the man. The partisan crowds

The first night of Duane Eddy's latest UK tour, 12 May 2012, at Market Harborough Leisure Centre, performing with Richard Hawley's band.

A ticket for the performance.

were also out in force on the tour's last night, at Warwick Arts Centre on the 28th. While the tour was under way, Donna Summer died on the 17th (born 1948) and Robin Gibb on the 20th (born 1949).

On 10 June it was Judi's turn to have the limelight, being invited to Fat Boy Slim's mother's 80th birthday party. Judi looked stunning as I took her to the Oxfordshire venue; I then went to Oxford station for photography. At the appointed time I returned to collect 'Cinders' and was invited into the gathering, having the honour of meeting Norman Cook and his wife Zoë Ball. The following day we were back at the FR, where on the 12th I photographed an old standard-gauge Metropolitan Railway carriage frame, rescued from a field. The historic Boston Lodge Works had secured a contract to refurbish it, and fabrication of the body was to follow later. The visit's raison d'être was preparation for my next book on the railway, and the weather through to the 13th was very kind.

Another site visited regularly was the rebirth of Broadway station, as volunteers from the GWSR crafted this phoenix to rise from the ashes of the long-closed railway. By 19 June the platforms and the railway footprint between them were taking shape. Another book on which I was working was to cover the redoubling of the South Cotswold line from Swindon to Kemble, and together with co-author Tim Maddocks I visited St Mary's, Sapperton Tunnel and Beards Crossing, near Stroud, on the 20th.

Possibly the sporting highlight of the year for the UK came in July with Bradley Wiggins becoming the first British cyclist to win the Tour de France cycle race. An even greater highlight for me, however, was on the 7th, as I joined a TYMCARS trip to visit Shrewsbury's iconic signal box. Towering above the southern exit from the station, its 180 levers were truly breathtaking and its length longer than a cricket pitch! To be allowed free access for photographs was a real honour. The day was rounded off by a booked visit to RAF Cosford Museum.

Attending an ACoRP event in Manchester on the 18th gave me the chance to photograph at Piccadilly; and a model railway

Just some of the 180 levers in Shrewsbury signal box, Saturday 7 July 2012.

exhibition at the SVR on the 21st did likewise at Kidderminster. On 18 August Scott McKenzie died (born 1939), with Neil Armstrong following on the 25th (born 1930). A two-day trip to see Judi presented my first view of the emergent railway preservation centre at Oswestry station on the 21st. Rumours had circulated of electrification of the Midland Main Line, so on the 26th I was at Syston and Cossington capturing some 'past' views.

Back at home on 1 September, I captured vintage Nos 31601 and 31602 hard at work on 6Z31, the 1107 Chaddesdon-Cardiff Tidal Sidings scrap steel working, and No 67016 working 1Z96, the 1735 Worcester Shrub Hill-Victoria returning VSOE special, both just into Gloucestershire and speeding south. Four days later the brick-by-brick demolition of the old goods shed at Ashchurch was nearing completion, with the material bound for Broadway for use at the new station on the GWSR. I visited the preserved railway at Shackerstone and Market Bosworth on the 15th and was delighted at the sight

Arrival at Transilvania (sic) International Airport, Tirgu Mures, for the SARUK party's trip to Romania, 26 September 2012.

of *The Blue Circle* giving 50p brake van rides. Formerly at Snodland Cement Works, this unusual 1926 Aveling Porter 2-2-0WT with flywheel was resplendent in bright blue livery.

Over the three days from the 21st to the 23rd I was 'incarcerated' at the Engine House at Highley on the SVR for a book-signing session during the railway's Autumn Gala. I did, however, escape for moments to witness several of the trains passing close by and was delighted to see Nos 30120 and 31806 double-head the 0936 Bridgnorth-Kidderminster train on the first day. Day two's highlight was the 1888-vintage ex-LNWR 'Coal Tank' No 7799 (ex-58926) on a brief visit to the line.

The 'big one', however, was to come on the 26th, when, in company with a group from the Welsh Highland Railway, I flew from Luton Airport for an eight-day visit to Romania. There as members of SARUK (Sibiu-Agnita Railway UK Division!), we were to aid volunteers on a narrow-gauge railway, who were trying to restore the line that had been closed in 2000. Very reminiscent of the WHR in its early restoration days, the work was familiar even if the language and surroundings were not! Much hard work was accomplished and 'a good time was had by all' in 30-degree heat beneath clear blue skies.

Normality seemed mundane after this, but a moment of excitement came on 30 October when No 7903 *Foremarke Hall* did the honours with the 'Cheltenham Spa Express', the

John Keylock and Alasdair Stewart of the SARUK party prepare to experience 1st Class Romanian rail travel on 27 September 2012 at Agnita.

1030 Toddington-Cheltenham (Racecourse) train, as the first passenger-carrying service over the reopened Chicken Curve. On the northern approach to Winchcombe on the GWSR, the line had been closed by a landslip and the volunteers had worked long and hard to rebuild it. As a sort of celebration, Silver Link Publishing held a two-day book-signing session at Winchcombe station on 3 November. Sadly, the weather was not wholly kind.

Being a member of the Cheltenham Camera Club I was used to competition challenges of different kinds, but the one requiring shots at a market was intriguing! I visited the local markets in Tewkesbury and Leicester on 14/15 November and the concentration on visuals made me more aware of the extent of different fare on show. However, my entries in the Club's competition were without success! 23 November saw the introduction of ticket barriers at Cheltenham Spa station,

At Chicken Curve, Winchcombe. No 7903 *Foremarke Hall* hauls the 'Cheltenham Spa Express', the 1030 Toddington-Cheltenham (Racecourse) train, as the first passenger-carrying service over the reopened curve on 30 October 2012.

not welcomed by locals. The same day Larry Hagman died (born 1931), followed by Dave Brubeck on 5 December (born 1920), Sir Patrick Moore on the 9th (born 1923) and, on the 11th, Ravi Shankar (born 1920). The year ended on a positive note for ATDRPG with the fulfilment on 10 December of a five-year dream, the inauguration of Ashchurch's first direct train to London. Sponsored by Gloucestershire County Council for a year as a trial, the 0521 Worcester Shrub Hill-Paddington HST – one of only two HST sets to run via Cheltenham to London – was to stop at Ashchurch for Tewkesbury at 0544. The group gathered in the freezing cold of the first morning to offer goody bags to any intrepid travellers. The trial was a success, with the roster later taken into the timetable.

2013's first trip was on 2 January, by rail from Ashchurch for Tewkesbury to Leicester for Mum's 93rd birthday. It was to be her last in her bungalow; the onset of dementia and general frailty meant that she was no longer safe on her own. Briefly sampling a coffee of dubious quality in the buffet at a sodden

Leicester London Road station on my way, I was delighted to see the passage of four Class 20s, top-and-tailing new LUT stock. One of them was, to my delight, No 20905, the last of the '20/9s' needed by me.

11 January was the date of the official launch for the proposed redoubling of the line between Swindon and Kemble. MPs and railway dignitaries assembled for speeches on a pleasantly sunny day and there was much networking and anticipation. The next two days saw work begin on the main line alongside the sidings immediately south of Ashchurch for Tewkesbury station. This would be completed during the following weekend in the midst of snow storms! Snow was still around when I travelled to Leicester on the 26th, to visit the old engine shed and gain access to the now private facility, with permission, for photographs.

16 February proved to be an eventful date for the ATDRPG. Through contacts within Network Rail, the group had been offered the 70-metre strip of land between the up platform at Ashchurch for Tewkesbury station and the neighbouring Children's Nursery, with a view to converting it to a community garden. Perhaps foolhardily the offer had been taken up and a

Kemble dignitaries – three MPs and three railway officials – gather after the launch of the redoubling to Swindon on 11 January 2013.

The ATDRPG garden 'before' on 16 February 2013. It would take 3½ years to complete Phase 1!

gate was finally installed to give access. It would presage the start of much hard work to clear the site of weeds, brambles and buddleia, some near 6 feet high, and the setting up of working parties on the second Saturday of each month. The call went out for volunteers.

5 March saw me take advantage of our 0544 train to London to photograph the display at Paddington of *Princess* from the FR, advertising the delights of the North Wales railway. The startled looks on the commuters at Paddington was something to behold. A real bonus for me, on the return journey, was copping No 66230 at Pangbourne, the last '66' I needed from those still in this country. The month also celebrated the 10th anniversary of the Heart & Soul Choir in Tewkesbury, which I had joined in 2008.

The GWSR organised a tourism day annually for interested parties such as hotels and B&Bs, and on the 18th I joined the crowd and enjoyed a presentation at Toddington, a tour of the engine shed and a ride to Cheltenham Racecourse and back. Nos 4270 and 35006 *Peninsular & Oriental S. N. Co* were nearing

To celebrate 150 years of the Ffestinog Railway, *Princess* was taken to Paddington, and is seen here at 0831 on 5 March 2013.

completion inside the shed. The next date of major interest was the 27th, when members of the Cheltenham Camera Club had a privileged visit to Morgan Motors in Great Malvern. To see cars with wooden frames being hand-crafted was fascinating and intriguing, and led to attractive photographic opportunities. The global destinations of some of the cars were enlightening.

A view inside Morgan Motors, Great Malvern, during a private visit by the Cheltenham Camera Club on 27 March 2013.

8 April saw two deaths of note: Baroness Thatcher (born 1925) and Annette Funicello (born 1942). Not so well known, this US actress and singer was very popular in the 1960s and came to my attention as the very attractive young lady pictured on Duane Eddy's album *Girls, Girls, Girls*. On 22 April Ritchie Havens died (born 1941), and four days later George Jones (born 1931); a friend of Duane Eddy and, to my mind, probably the best country singer ever, George ironically died on Duane's birthday! The month also saw the publication of my first book for around 18 months, the third volume of my 'British Railways

Past & Present' series on the Ffestiniog Railway, celebrating a century and half of the steam railway out of Porthmadog.

As so often in recent years I visited the FR's Spring Gala, making a slight detour on my way to North Wales on 2 May to photograph at Craven Arms. A departure this time, however, was to spend time at the level crossing to the north of the station, which ended with an invitation into the crossing signal box. I took full advantage of photographing within the box together with a handful of trains from the elevated vantage point. The weather was glorious, but by the first day of the 150th Anniversary Gala on the 4th it had deteriorated to rain, creating poor conditions to capture the demonstration of horse-drawn wagons at Harbour station, Porthmadog, and the show of strength of eight members of the local Rugby Club

Top left: No 34067 *Tangmere* accelerates out of Melton Mowbray on 14 April 2013 with 1Z67, the King's Cross-Matlock Peak Rail 'The Peak Forester', running 12 minutes late.

Left: Renumbered as No 6015 *King Richard III* to celebrate the discovery of the King's body in Leicester, the loco is about to set off at 2025 on 19 April 2013 with the King Richard III Society's Dining Special to Loughborough Central.

Above: Eight-man horsepower! *Princess* is manhandled across Britannia Bridge, Porthmadog, on 4 May 2013 by local rugby players.

hauling *Princess* across Britannia Bridge by rope! It took until lunchtime on Monday the 6th for the sun to really show its face, as Garratt No 138 crossed Britannia Bridge with the 1000 train from Caernarfon.

The football season finished on 4 May, with Leicester City ending in sixth place. The team had been in the top six for much of the last ten months, but in the play-offs they lost 3-2 on aggregate to Watford after missing a last-minute penalty! A hopeful sign for the future, however, was the signing this month of Jamie Vardy from Fleetwood Town for £1 million, a non-league record transfer fee. On the 16th I was out and about on the South Cotswold Line with Tim, beginning at Kemble and making our way to the outskirts of Swindon, capturing images for our next book.

'I can see it, Mummy!' The excitement grows as mother and son wait for No 175112 forming 1V57, the 1040 Holyhead to Cardiff Central service at Craven Arms on 14 June 2013.

On 1 June I was back in Leicestershire making full use of the bright summer sunshine at Cossington to record trains in advance of the much-rumoured electrification plans. In recent months FGW had reliveried several of its HST power cars, with varying degrees of visual success! On the 5th I was at Cheltenham Spa for my first glimpse of No 43148 parading a gaudy advert for 'The new HP ElitePad: The tablet built for business'. Proclaimed to be for Windows 8 Pro, it was soon to disappear. On the same day *Railway Herald* No 364 published my article on the FR's '150 Years of Steam' celebrations. Ten days later I was accompanied by Judi to the latest LMS-Patriot

Society's Members Day at Llangollen Railway, where we were shown the latest progress on the new build of No 45551. 16 June was Father's Day, which was celebrated with a trip on the WLLR. Standing on the balcony of the rear coach, I photographed along the whole route, unencumbered by trees.

On the 21st I had an appointment with a local estate agent at Mum's bungalow, to initiate a sale process as she had moved into a residential home in Loughborough earlier in the month. The thought of selling her home of 42 years was not a happy one, but her dementia had reached the stage that she had no idea where she was and her memory was virtually nil. Happily, she did still remember me and the family. During this period there was the summer launch of the GCR's appeal for funds to support proposals to create 18 miles of preserved line by rejoining Leicester and Nottingham with the reinstallation of a bridge over the Midland Main Line at Loughborough, together with the creation of a new museum at the southern end of the line at Birstall.

July's *Railway Magazine* featured my article on the 762 Club's plans to create a new build of *Lyn*, an original Lynton & Barnstaple Baldwin loco that carried the number 762 under SR rule. The 25th was the second day of the two-day National Track Plant Exhibition, at Long Marston. The weather was hot and sunny and the day was further blessed when No 66850 was named *David Maidment OBE* by the man himself. The following day the loco travelled through Ashchurch with 7Z56, the 1055 Long Marston to Westbury train, returning stock from the Exhibition.

3 August was a very special day, my 70th birthday. My family had asked what I wanted as a celebration and they had pulled out all the stops for a birthday trip on the WHR, in a Pullman car filled with family and friends. They had also arranged for the loco, Garratt No 87, to have a suitable headboard – which I still retain! The sun shone brightly, all went without a hitch and, to quote Lou Reed, 'Just a perfect day'! I spent the next few days back in Birstall, gradually emptying Mum's bungalow ready for its sale. Much of the rest of the month, between the 12th and

My 70th birthday train, hauled by No 87, receives some TLC at Caernarfon before returning to Porthmadog, complete with headboard, on 3 August 2013.

A laminated invite to my 70th birthday party.

Stunning scenery & steam
to celebrate
John's special birthday

SATURDAY 3rd AUGUST 2013
Welsh Highland Railway

The view from the cab of No 66717 *Good Old Boy* in Kemble Tunnel on 13 August 2013, operating as 6W81, the 1005 Kemble to Bescot Up Engineer's Sidings empties and running 59 minutes late.

My one and only visit to Sir William McAlpine's railway at Fawley Hill on 18 August 2013, with No 31 climbing the steep incline with a full consist of passengers.

29th, was spent concentrating on photographs of the South Cotswold line, but a delightful break from this was a visit to Sir William McAlpine's standard-gauge railway at his home at Fawley Hill, Buckinghamshire. Another hot sunny day, there was much to see and I was delighted and honoured to meet the man himself and be taken to his house, as he thought he had some of my books! On 31 August Sir David Frost died (born 1939).

In September the £550 million extension to Lewis Cubitt's 1852 trainshed at King's Cross, with its iconic semi-circular roofspace, finally opened. The 28th was the day of the latest Cotswold Line Promotion Group's FGW HST trips, this time to Swanage. I took my 1st Class seat at Evesham and settled in to enjoy the ride to the seaside. All was well until we reached Corfe Castle on the preserved Swanage branch. Late the previous day, Network Rail had decided that platform clearance beyond there was insufficient for the HST set to reach the terminus, so we detrained and joined a hastily rearranged steam special to take us the rest of the way. For those of us of a certain age, this was in fact a bonus, as we were hauled by 1946-vintage No 34028 *Eddystone*, a resident of the Swanage Railway. Despite dull weather the opportunity to explore Swanage and its railway was given maximum attention. An added bonus was cops of Nos 70017 and 70008 (outward) and 70020 and 66954 (homebound) at Southampton.

It is amazing what one discovers when clearing a house, and the contents of Mum's bungalow were no exception. On 4 October I came across, among elderly artefacts, a Victorian blouse coat with velvet sleeves and an intricate bodice design liberally decorated and buttoned with jet.

Tim and I were continuing with the South Cotswold photographs and on 17 October we encompassed Stonehouse to Standish Junction and back towards Gloucester. 12 November brought more excitement, but of a wholly different sort. Following rescue from an Essex pond, the nameplate of 'A1' No 60127 *Wilson Worsdell* was receiving TLC at a private site before being offered for sale. At the time of my visit, only the 'W' of the first name was showing signs of returning to showroom condition after 15 hours of hard work. The main thrust of my visit to the individual involved, however, was to view his ownership of the nameplate of ex-LNER 'Footballer' No 61665 *Leicester City*. Many years earlier, when the loco was withdrawn, I was offered the plate by BR for £13 10s, but Dad would not lend me the money to buy it. To be fair, his weekly wages were less than £10 at the time! I had long regretted the loss and paid homage to my near miss and photographed it for posterity.

On 21 November I was out to see another blast from the past, in the guise of the new build of long-lost No 45551,

The nameplate from No 61665 *Leicester City* that could have been mine!

Not really suitable for parking during the Tewkesbury floods, seen on 9 January 2014!

now to carry the name *The Unknown Warrior*. To be blessed by Salvation Army Chaplain Major Nigel Tansley in a short service, en route to the Warley National Model Railway Exhibition the following weekend, the loco was at the National Memorial Arboretum, displaying progress to date, including the name-bearing splashers that I had sponsored. The early days of December continued the preparatory work on the South Cotswold line book, this time focusing on the area near Swindon. Peter O'Toole died on the 14th (born 1932), then on the 31st I photographed the recently erected memorial plaque in Tewkesbury High Street, positioned next to the sole remaining pillar of the first station in the town.

    After a busy 2013, I was anticipating more of the same for 2014, but things took an unexpected turn. I was again in Leicester for Mum's birthday (her 94th) on 3 January, and shortly afterwards was in Tewkesbury to photograph the flooding that had taken place there between the 9th and 13th. I then made a return visit to Loughborough Central to see the appearance of No 92214 (bearing the name *Cock o' the North*) and the unveiling by Nicky Morgan MP of a plaque celebrating the NRHA 'Station Environment Award', rewarding the GCR for the restoration of Loughborough station and canopy, on Friday 24 January. On 27 January I had a panic phone call from Judi. She was not feeling at all well, so I went to mid-Wales to be with her. She was not able to function properly and I finally secured an emergency appointment with her GP. He was not happy, so the following day we attended Shrewsbury Hospital. After several tests she was diagnosed with brain cancer, with multiple secondaries, but they were unable to establish the primary. They never did find out and I would spend much of the

Truly turning the clock back, complete with Station Master greeting the train, No 45041 draws into Rothley station on Mothering Sunday, 30 March 2014, with 2B14, the 1230 Leicester North-Loughborough Central roster.

rest of the year travelling back and forth together with trips to Shrewsbury and Stoke hospitals.

February saw the Ebola virus epidemic begin in West Africa, eventually killing at least 11,300 people. Shirley Temple died on the 10th (born 1928) and Sir Tom Finney on the 14th (born 1922). Tony Benn died on 14 March (born 1925), on which date I was back at the GCR to see a new-build diesel brake tender under construction by RVP (Railway Vehicle Preservations) at Rothley, by which time Judi was going through radiotherapy but was responding well. The GWSR 'Tourism Day' was on the 24th and those of us present were graced with good weather.

On 10 April Leicester-born novelist and playwright Sue Townsend died (born 1946), and four days later 276 Nigerian schoolgirls were kidnapped by terrorist organisation Boko Haram. Meanwhile, volunteers on the Ashchurch for Tewkesbury station garden were working miracles, and on the 12th laid the full 70 metres with black light-suppressing material. I managed to fit in some trips for the South Cotswold line book with my visits to Judi, and on the 14th saw Colas-liveried Nos 70803 and 70805 on the redoubling work, the latter being a cop.

To slightly lift my spirits, on 5 May Leicester City were crowned winners in the Championship, claiming their place back in the Premiership, and 35,000 fans lined the celebratory street parade. The season included 21 consecutive matches without defeat, with the team being promoted as early as 5 April and acknowledged champions on the 21st. They ended with a massive 102 points and 31 wins out of 46 matches. Shortly afterwards I brought Judi to Tewkesbury to go to The Roses theatre to see Ruby Wax on stage. I had bought Judi a copy of Ruby's book *Sane New World* and we were interested in seeing what she had to say. We took the book with us and the evening ended with Judi, Ruby and myself chatting for around 25 minutes, discussing how Judi was coping with her illness. Ruby was very impressed with her attitude and wrote a superb dedication in her book for Judi. After our return to Wales, I took Judi to the FR on the 17th because she wanted to participate in the latest gardeners' work party, as she had done so often before. I took the opportunity for photographs! Four days later I made my one and only visit to Church Stretton and spent a relaxed time snapping the various trains at the station.

I June was another new experience for me, watching fledgling blue tits emerging from the nesting box outside my kitchen door. Being so close, around 6 feet from the nest, it was fascinating watching the mother bird encouraging her chicks as one by one they plucked up courage to jump from the box. Two days later I went to Fladbury, on the North

At Llanerfyl on 21 April 2014, despite radiotherapy Judi is still able to enjoy a walk in the sun.

Cotswold line, to witness No 70810 (a cop for me) on 6Z70, the 1438 Bescot Up Engineers Sidings-Long Marston train of ballast wagons. Freight was rare on this line, but even more so was a '70/8'. On 5 June a Sunni militant group called Islamic State of Iraq began an offensive in northern Iraq, and on the 9th Rik Mayall died (born 1958).

A family get-together was arranged for the 15th at Ludlow, roughly halfway between the homes of Adam, Claire and me and those of Tammy, Kevin and Judi. The day was warm and bright but, sadly, Judi did not feel up to it. Happily, on the 18th she felt better and, with me and Tammy, enjoyed a very pleasant walk through Dyfnant Forest.

With the deadline of our next book approaching, Tim and I spent time mopping up the final photos on the South Cotswold line on 2 July, between Oaksey and Stonehouse. A week later I meandered around parts of Cheltenham Spa, capturing views for a book to be produced on the town by the Cheltenham Camera Club. Thankfully, several were used in the book. On the 16th I was again with Tim for the final selection of shots, then on the 19th I was with Judi at Llangollen for the latest LMS-Patriot Project Members Day. It was to be the last time we would have a day out together.

Real evidence of progress was made at the Ashchurch for Tewkesbury station garden on the 24th, when a large sign explaining the project and giving contact details was unveiled close to the station waiting shelter. Three days later I was pleased to be back at the old engine shed site at Leicester, to photograph the first locos on site for a new operator.

A young blue tit spreads its wings for mother outside my kitchen door at Ashchurch on 1 June 2014.

With Judi's condition deteriorating, outings became restricted but I did manage to record interesting movements at Banbury on 16 August, due to a blockade at Watford Junction. This meant that not only did the line through the station see unusual motive power, but also several diverted trains doubling up and, on one occasion, even three services all running as one. 1Z10, the 1005 London Euston to Birmingham International express, consisted of three 'Super Voyagers', providing 15 coaches! On the 18th I had a full set of solar panels fitted to my roof and looked forward to the forecast income. Lord Richard Attenborough died on the 24th (born 1923). What was probably Judi's last normal outing was a visit to Chirk Castle, with Tammy, Kevin and myself, on the 27th, Tammy's birthday.

1 September was a day of celebration for the South Cotswold line and I recorded No 43005 as the first HST power car to emerge from Kemble Tunnel on the second line.

The following day saw a TYMCARS visit to Long Marston, with permission to wander around the large acreage photographing the many locomotives, including electrics. The weather was gratifyingly kind. On the 7th raised beds appeared in ATDRPG's station garden. Initially just five, the final total rose to 14. Ian Paisley died on the 12th (born 1926). The 20th saw the CLPG's latest HST outing, this time to Plymouth, although I decamped

The ATDRPG prepares the sign for unveiling on 22 July 2014.

at Totnes to meet up with Tim and his wife for lunch. The trip was another hugely enjoyable one.

On the 21st, early into Leicester City's 2014-15 Premiership season, the club broke records, with a 5-3 defeat of Manchester United. At the time of writing City are still the only team to have beaten United in the Premiership after being two goals adrift; and they scored four times in the last 30 minutes, having been 1-3 behind! Sadly, thereafter they didn't win again until 28 December – 1-0 versus Hull City – and ended the year bottom of the table!

Early in October Tammy and Kevin were due to have a week's holiday in Derbyshire. Knowing the state of Judi's illness,

Fifteen coaches formed 1Z10, the 1005 London Euston to Birmingham International express, on Saturday, 16 August 2014 with No 221010 on the front and No 221117 at the rear, due to weekend blockade at Watford Junction. It is seen passing non-stop through Banbury.

On a completely new stretch of track, following the completion of the Swindon-Kemble doubling project, No 43005 emerges from Kemble Tunnel forming 1G29, the 1136 London Paddington to Cheltenham Spa express, on a dull Monday 1 September 2014.

they took her with them and she had what was probably her last really happy time. The next truly special day was on the 17th, when HRH The Princess Royal was at Kemble station to formally 'open' the completion of the doubling project between there and Swindon; the rest of the line to Gloucester was already double. On 25 October Jack Bruce, bassist with Cream, died (born 1943), followed by Acker Bilk on 2 November (born

HRH The Princess Royal unveils the plaque to formally open the redoubled route from Swindon to Kemble at the latter station on Friday 17 October 2014, watched by Patrick Hallgate, Western Route Managing Director, Network Rail.

1929). On Wednesday 5 November No 168219 formed 1V98, the 0958 Banbury to Morris Cowley MAT special working, crossing the River Thames on the freight-only Cowley branch to transport dignitaries for a show of intent for reintroducing passenger workings to the route. Finally, on 20 November, I had cleared and cleaned Mum's bungalow and it was now ready for inspection by prospective buyers.

Back with Judi at the beginning of December, I took time out to travel by rail to Newtown for my only visit. It was nothing to write home about, but it did give me the chance of photographing at a new location. Joe Cocker died on the 22nd (born 1944).

By Christmas Leicester City were at the foot of the Premier League – could they survive, as only two clubs before had stayed up after being bottom at Christmas? Ready for present-giving time, the South Cotswold book was published – *British Railways Past & Present: The Golden Valley Line: Swindon to Gloucester*.

2015 was a topsy-turvy year in all manner of ways. On 3 January Tammy and Kevin drove from Wales to Loughborough to join me in celebrating Mum's 95th birthday, then drove back again. The next day Tammy went to see Judi in the Welshpool hospital where she now was, but arrived 10 minutes after she had died. I returned home on the 4th via photographs at Market Harborough, and received the news from Tammy moments after my arrival. The whole family was obviously upset, not least at her going when just 66, but we were all relieved that she was spared further suffering. Her green burial, on the 17th, close to Welshpool, was a truly memorable day as all present wished to celebrate her life rather than mourn her loss. No sombre colours were allowed.

Formed by a Chiltern Trains Class 168 DMU, 1V98, the 0958 Banbury to Morris Cowley MAT special, crosses the Thames east of Kennington Junction on Wednesday 5 November 2014.

Enjoying Brunel's easy gradients, No 61306 *Mayflower* has no problems with Steam Dreams' 'St David's Day Cathedrals Express' from London Paddington to Cardiff Central as it passes Shrivenham on Sunday 1 March 2015.

From 30 January to 1 February I froze with Peter Rowlands (Silver Link's sales manager) at Loughborough Central station, attempting to look cheerful for a book-signing on the platform! 1 March was my next outing, to Shrivenham, east of Swindon, to join a gaggle of anticipating photographers. Enjoying Brunel's 'billiard table', 'B1' No 61306 *Mayflower* was the attraction with Steam Dreams' 1Z61, the 0858 London Paddington to Cardiff Central 'St David's Day Cathedrals Express'. On the 10th I drove to visit Judi's burial plot and made use of passing through Welshpool to photograph Network Rail's yellow-liveried No 97304 on the 0910 Crewe to Dovey Junction Down Loop. Sir Terry Pratchett died on the 12th (born 1948). Now being less stressed, I took a day off from routine on the 18th to spend time in the sunshine at Banbury, hoping but disappointed not to see a new Class 68.

On 21 March Leicester City lost 3-4 away to Spurs, were still bottom of the Premier League, and were considered a

With No 66754's name *Northampton Saints* in place, in recognition of the club's achievement as Aviva Premiership Rugby Champions of 2014, the celebratory group, complete with cup, stand for their portraits at Wellingborough Railhead on Wednesday 22 April 2015. Left to right, they are Dylan Hartley, Club Captain and England cap; Martin Hill, Chairman of GRS Ltd; Jim Mallinder, Club Director of Rugby; and John Smith, MD of GBRf.

'Pacer' No 142073 departs from Cheltenham Spa as 2L59, the 1345 Cheltenham Spa to Maesteg return inter-regional stopper, on Wednesday 13 May 2015.

'dead cert' for relegation, accumulating just 19 points from 29 matches and being 7 points from safety, but … they won all their matches in April, the first time the club had won four in a row in the top flight since 1966! May continued with one draw and three wins, leading to seven wins from their last eight games and ending 6 points clear of relegation. This 'Great Escape' was the first time that a club at the bottom of the Premiership in early April, with so few points, had survived.

The age of the 'Pacer' was increasingly being reported to

Double-headed 'Spam Cans' is a rare sight as Nos 34007 *Wadebridge* and 34092 *Wells* leave Gotherington with the 1420 Cheltenham Racecourse-Laverton roster during the GWSR's 'Cotswold Festival of Steam' on Saturday 23 May 2015.

be ending, so on 8 April I went to Cheltenham Spa to record an example that regularly worked the service from Maesteg. In warm spring sunshine No 143605 left as 2L59, the 1345 service to Maesteg – nothing special to look at, but one for the library. I had not ventured out to photograph for an upcoming Middleton Press book for some time, so took the opportunity of a free day to go to Nuneaton on the 14th for such a task. In time I was fortunate to have images used in other publications. On the 22nd I drove to Wellingborough for several firsts.

'Pacer' No 142074 pauses in Platform 7 at Cardiff Central on Monday 8 June 2015 as 2V25, the 1245 Coryton to Radyr local, alongside real progress being made with the track for the new Platform 8.

Invited by *Modern Railways* to cover the event, it was the first loco naming I had attended other than at a railway station, the first loco named after a rugby football club, the first naming of a Class 66/7 that I had witnessed, and the first time I met John Smith, the MD of GBRf.

Just three weeks old, newly opened on 17 May and extending the line from the nearby Parkway station, Ebbw Vale Town plays host to No 150250 as it waits for its passengers to board on Tuesday 9 June 2015, forming 2F24, the 1037 Ebbw Vale Town to Cardiff Central service.

In front of invited guests, No 66754 was given the appellation *Northampton Saints*.

The following day a wildflower meadow was laid in the station garden. Effectively grass turf impregnated with wildflower seeds, it gave us an instant creation and enhanced the entrance area of the garden. Tammy eventually identified 20 different species of plants. On 30 April Ben E. King died (born 1938), followed by B. B. King on 14 May (born 1925).

On 13 May I captured another variant of 'Pacer' at Cheltenham Spa when No 142073 operated the 1345 service to Maesteg. A week later I travelled by rail to Nottingham to meet up with a long-lost friend and again employed my camera to advantage. An exciting visual on the 23rd was the sight of two 'Spam Cans', unrebuilt Bulleid 'Pacifics', operating on the GWSR. Among a myriad of other enthusiasts, I was happy to photograph Nos 34007 *Wadebridge* and 34092 *Wells* on the 1420 Cheltenham Racecourse-Laverton train during the railway's 'Cotswold Festival of Steam'.

The railway press had alerted me to two events, close in location and date, and I determined to cover both. First was a trip to Cardiff Central on 8 June, to see progress on the creation of a new Platform 8 but also to commit to the library more shots of 'Pacers', as well as whatever else was in action. The following day it was by road to the brand-new Ebbw Vale Town station, where I recorded No 150250 arrive and depart as 2F24, the 1037 Ebbw Vale Town to Cardiff Central service. Both days produced published views.

Progress on ATDRPG's station garden, 11 July 2015.

Now sadly without Judi, Tammy was my companion for this year's LMS-Patriot Society Members Day at Llangollen on the 27th, and again, as in most years, we were graced by fine weather for the tour of the engine shed, then the ride along the line with lunch. The following day Ian Allan OBE died (born 1922); without him, thousands of trainspotters would not have flourished, including me! A memorial service celebrating his life and achievements was held on 23 November. On 30 June Nigel Pearson was sacked as Leicester City manager, with Claudio Ranieri appointed as his successor. There was little general expectation of success or a tenure beyond weeks. But how wrong can people be…?

On 10 July Omar Sharif died (born 1932). Four days later I had the 'delight' of driving along the M25 to reach Dartford, where I was to attend a PTS refresher course. Arriving at my overnight stay during the early-evening rush hour, after a brief stop at Stone Crossing station I grabbed an hour after a quick meal to visit Dartford's station. Given permission to photograph, the location and the electric units were all new

With a 'Multi-Coloured Swap Shop' of coach types and liveries in tow, No 68004 *Rapid* is appropriately named as it hurries into Heyford on Saturday 18 July 2015 with the 0542 Newport (South Wales) to Carlisle Pathfinder Tours' 'The Lakes & Border Explorer' express railtour.

During the first week of the six-week blockade around Bathampton Junction, a rake of JNAs forms part of the consist of the 6W43 engineer's train (left) at the western entrance to Box Tunnel on Wednesday 22 July 2015, as work continues to lower and relay the down main line.

to me and I thoroughly enjoyed myself creatively, as well as taking 'record shots'. On my way home the following day I was trapped by roadworks and forced through the Dartford Tunnel and back over the adjacent bridge. This cost me a penalty of £70, which I did eventually reclaim after a written complaint. I was at Heyford on the 18th to grab a shot of my first Class 68. With a 'Multi-Coloured Swap Shop' of coach types and liveries in tow, No 68004 *Rapid* proved to be appropriately named as

Inside Box Tunnel, 29 July 2015.

it hurried through the station with the 0542 Newport (South Wales) to Carlisle Pathfinder Tours' 'The Lakes & Border Explorer' railtour.

Following the success of the books on the two Cotswold lines, Network Rail approached Tim and me to do something similar for the electrification between Swindon and Bristol. So, on the 22nd, we signed in with TPOD 1 (Temporary Period of Disruption) at Shockerwick, east of Bath. After photographing at Bathampton Junction, we were taken along the track to Box Tunnel and my first experience of being inside this iconic structure. Seven days later, from the Corsham end, we had a walk through the complete near-2-mile tunnel – another item deleted from my bucket list!

A moment of joy and relief as David Allan (Chair of SARUK) congratulates Mihai Blotor (leader of the Friends) on the safe delivery of the 1911 Hungarian 0-8-0T, ready for the weekend's rides, at Cornatel on Friday 25 September 2015.

On 1 August Cilla Black died (born 1943). Four days later Tim and I walked the track to Dundas Aqueduct, near Limpley Stoke, and photographed on and under another of Brunel's creations. 8 August saw Leicester City's first match of the 2015-16 season, for which the bookies had quoted odds of 5,000-1 against the team winning the league, the same as finding Elvis Presley alive! Several supporters had the foresight to put money on it and struggled to hold their nerve as the season progressed and City moved upwards! On the 12th I was again with Tim, at Bathampton Junction, where we had the freedom to walk through the works – I later succeeded in gaining two magazine front covers from this day – and on the 19th we did similarly eastwards from Bath Spa station.

I was at Swindon station on 15 September for another naming. HRH The Duke of Gloucester pulled the curtain by No 43023 to reveal *Sqn Ldr Harold Starr One of the Few*, commemorating 75 years since the Battle of Britain. On the 19th Leicester City achieved a ten-game unbeaten run, including the end of the previous season, the best since 1976. Between the 22nd and 29th I was back in Romania, once more using muscle on the emergent Sibiu-Agnita railway around Cornatel. On the last day, I photographed at Luton Airport Parkway station as I waited for my train home. The train to Leicester, where I would change, was packed, but I did manage to find a seat. However, when the guard checked my ticket I could not find my Senior Railcard and was forced to pay a £30 penalty. I had left it at home!

On 3 October Tim Maddocks officiated, as representative of Network Rail, to formally recognise the closing of Phase 1 of ATDRPG's station garden. During 2016, after further small improvements, including a replica running-in sign and mock level crossing gates, the garden was entered in ACoRP's national competition, and received a Silver Award at an Awards Dinner in Southport – true reward for all the hard work of the volunteers. My Ford Focus, which I had owned for ten years, had reached 235,000 miles and I thought it time to change. It was sold for £600 and, on 15 October, I took possession of an

'09' Peugeot 307SW for £3,500. Having become used to petrol again, it quickly became a comfortable and reliable friend. 26 October saw the new Oxford Parkway station opened, on the line to Bicester.

On 28 November Jamie Vardy scored for the 11th match in a row, creating a new Premier League record and netting a

Towards the end of Phase 1 of ATDRPG's station garden, Tim Maddocks of Network Rail does the honours in cutting the ribbon on 3 October 2015.

Seen on the return run from Avon Riverside on Sunday 20 December 2015, Bill Parker's No 5521, masquerading as London Transport No L150, operates the 1030 Bitton-Bitton via Oldland Common and Avon Riverside Santa Special alongside the footpath/cycleway.

total of 13 in those games. Early in December I bought a new camera, a Canon 7D Mk II, and used it first on the Avon Valley Railway on the 20th, not least to capture Bill Parker's No 5521

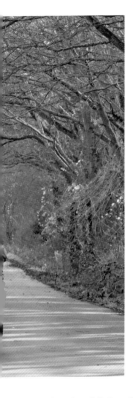

masquerading as London Transport No L150, operating the 1030 Bitton-Bitton via Oldland Common and Avon Riverside Santa Special. The picture was the first to be published from this camera. The day before, Jimmy Hill died (born 1928).

So, my 60 years ended with Leicester City at the top of the league, the first Premiership team to be bottom one Christmas and top the next! The team went on to win the league for the first time in 132 years, with 81 points from 38 matches, 10 points clear of Arsenal and only losing three times, twice to Arsenal! Before Leicester, the Premiership had been won by just four clubs, Arsenal, Chelsea, Manchester United and Manchester City. Duane Eddy was still touring and recording, and Garratts were still performing in the UK, on the WHR. I had more than 50 books published and I was still enjoying my photographic outings. Even though the number of locos was fewer, new types kept appearing, keeping the interest well and truly alive.

Some sad times, with loved ones lost, but also the delight of seeing Leicester City at the top of the league. A truly roller-coaster of a year, but one that proved I had very loving and supportive family and friends and I looked forward to many more outings and celebrations with them.

Little Stretton times two, 6 May 2006!